W I N

T H E

Y E A R

365 DAILY DEVOTIONALS

SEAN PAYNE

ISBN 979-8-9893267-0-9 (paperback)
ISBN 979-8-9893267-1-6 (ebook)

This book is dedicated to my wife, Mollie.

No single person has had a greater impact upon my life than you. God used you to play a major role in my salvation and call to ministry. You inspire me every day and exemplify what it means to be a virtuous woman.

"Many women have done excellently, but you surpass them all." (Proverbs 31:29)

Love,
Sean

JANUARY 1

The steadfast love of the Lord never ceases; his mercies never come to an end; they are new every morning; great is your faithfulness.

Lamentations 3:22-23

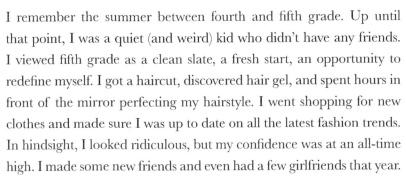

I remember the summer between fourth and fifth grade. Up until that point, I was a quiet (and weird) kid who didn't have any friends. I viewed fifth grade as a clean slate, a fresh start, an opportunity to redefine myself. I got a haircut, discovered hair gel, and spent hours in front of the mirror perfecting my hairstyle. I went shopping for new clothes and made sure I was up to date on all the latest fashion trends. In hindsight, I looked ridiculous, but my confidence was at an all-time high. I made some new friends and even had a few girlfriends that year.

Every day, I mess up. I say something I shouldn't say, think something I shouldn't think, or do something I shouldn't do. I begin every day with prayer. I spend my short commute to the office (and usually a few minutes in the parking lot) praying and asking God for forgiveness. There's not much better than a fresh start. And by God's grace, a fresh start is always only one prayer away.

Maybe this previous year didn't go as well as planned. Perhaps you made some mistakes and wish you could go back and do things differently. Good news! His mercies are new every morning! It is a new year. Today is a new day. Praise the Lord for a fresh start.

Lord, thank you for your mercy. Thank you for forgiving me and giving me a fresh start. This year, help me fully surrender to you and use me to further your kingdom. Amen.

JANUARY 2

Brothers, I do not consider that I have made it my own. But one thing I do: forgetting what lies behind and straining forward to what lies ahead.

Philippians 3:13

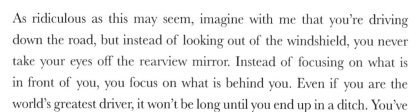

As ridiculous as this may seem, imagine with me that you're driving down the road, but instead of looking out of the windshield, you never take your eyes off the rearview mirror. Instead of focusing on what is in front of you, you focus on what is behind you. Even if you are the world's greatest driver, it won't be long until you end up in a ditch. You've probably heard some version of that illustration before. Here's the point: you will never fully live in the present until you let go of the past.

My past is full of mistakes, regret, and sin. Unfortunately, I've done things that I'm ashamed to admit. If some of the things I've done became publicly known, I would be embarrassed and humiliated. But fortunately, God met me right where I was, in the middle of a mess, and he transformed me into someone I never thought I would be. I'm still far from perfect, and I make mistakes daily, but I'm no longer defined by what I've done. I'm defined by what Jesus did on the cross.

What you did yesterday doesn't define you. Your past doesn't define you. I don't know what you've been through, what mistakes you've made, or what's been done to you. But I do know that you will never fully live in the present until you let go of the past. Don't live your life looking in the rearview mirror.

Lord, thank you for the future that you have planned for me. Help me stop looking in the rearview mirror and start looking out the windshield. Amen.

JANUARY 3

If we confess our sins, he is faithful and just to forgive us our sins and to cleanse us from all unrighteousness.

1 John 1:9

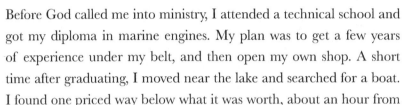

Before God called me into ministry, I attended a technical school and got my diploma in marine engines. My plan was to get a few years of experience under my belt, and then open my own shop. A short time after graduating, I moved near the lake and searched for a boat. I found one priced way below what it was worth, about an hour from where I lived. I went and looked it over and ended up buying it.

I brought it home and went straight to the lake. I made it about 50 yards away from the boat ramp, and it shut down on me. I had to swim it back to shore. I quickly realized why it was so cheap: the engine block was cracked. How humiliating! I'm a certified boat mechanic, and I let somebody sell me a boat with a bad engine. I was also out a good bit of cash.

Have you ever done something humiliating? Have you ever messed up? Said something you wish you could take back? Done something you said you would never do again? Made the same mistake for the millionth time? If you confess your sins, he is faithful and just to forgive you of your sins and to cleanse you of all unrighteousness. Is there any unconfessed sin in your life?

Lord, thank you for being faithful. Show me if there is any unconfessed sin in my life. Forgive me for all the mistakes I've made. Amen.

JANUARY 4

I, I am he who blots out your transgressions for my own sake, and I will not remember your sins.

Isaiah 43:25

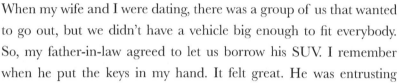

When my wife and I were dating, there was a group of us that wanted to go out, but we didn't have a vehicle big enough to fit everybody. So, my father-in-law agreed to let us borrow his SUV. I remember when he put the keys in my hand. It felt great. He was entrusting me with something valuable. I had worked hard to earn his trust and respect, and I felt like I had finally accomplished just that. I drove the speed limit, made sure everybody wore seatbelts, and was as cautious as possible.

On the way home, we were running low on fuel, and there was no way I was going to return it with an empty tank. So, I pulled into a gas station and filled it up. We got a few miles from the gas station when the entire vehicle shut down, and I had to pull over. Long story short, I filled the vehicle slap full of diesel, not gasoline. Fortunately, he forgave me, although he still hasn't offered to let me borrow his car again.

Some of you right now are struggling to believe that God can forgive you. You're thinking like this, "After what I did, there's no way God can forgive me." The truth is that Jesus's sacrifice on the cross is more than enough to cover your sin. When you repent, not only does God forgive your sins, but he also forgets your sins.

Lord, thank you for your sacrifice on the cross. Thank you for no longer holding my sin against me. Help me move on from my past. Amen.

JANUARY 5

Because he inclined his ear to me, therefore I will call on him as long as I live.

Psalm 116:2

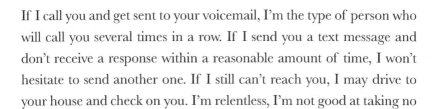

If I call you and get sent to your voicemail, I'm the type of person who will call you several times in a row. If I send you a text message and don't receive a response within a reasonable amount of time, I won't hesitate to send another one. If I still can't reach you, I may drive to your house and check on you. I'm relentless, I'm not good at taking no for an answer, and I can't stand being unable to reach someone when I need them.

Can you relate? Maybe there have been times when you needed someone, but you couldn't get a hold of them for whatever reason. The good news is that there will never be a time that you can't get a hold of God. His line is always open. Twenty-four hours a day and seven days a week, God is always available. He's never too busy to take your call.

Maybe you are in a place where you feel alone. Perhaps you feel like you have no one to talk to, or maybe you're not quite ready to talk to someone else. You can always talk to your Father in Heaven. Not only is he available to listen, but he also longs to hear from you.

Lord, thank you for always being available. Thank you for always hearing my prayers. Help me run to you when I need someone to talk to. Amen.

JANUARY 6

Then he summoned Moses and Aaron by night and said, "Up, go out from among my people, both you and the people of Israel; and go, serve the Lord, as you have said. Take your flocks and your herds, as you have said, and be gone, and bless me also!"

Exodus 12:31-32

God promised to give the Israelites a land flowing with milk and honey. So, he sent Moses to Egypt to lead the Israelites out of slavery, but it didn't turn out to be an easy job. When Moses got there, Pharaoh, the leader of Egypt, refused to let the Israelites go. God sent a total of ten plagues to get Pharaoh's attention. He turned their water into blood. He sent frogs, gnats, and flies. He attacked their livestock. He caused them to break out in boils. He sent hail, locusts, and darkness. Pharaoh still refused to let the Israelites go.

Finally, God instructed the Israelites to kill a lamb and to put blood on the door frames of their houses. In the middle of the night, God killed every firstborn of the Egyptians, but he passed over the houses that had blood on their door frames. The next morning, there was great sorrow in Egypt, and Pharaoh finally agreed to let the Israelites go.

Nothing can stop God's plan. The Israelites spent hundreds of years living in slavery and being treated harshly, but God was true to his word. He went to great lengths to set them free. This story proves that if God says it, you can take it to the bank. He's a promise maker and a promise keeper.

Lord, thank you for always keeping your promises. Help me trust your sovereign plan and align my desires with your will. Amen.

JANUARY 7

Thus the Lord saved Israel that day from the hand of the Egyptians, and Israel saw the Egyptians dead on the seashore.

Exodus 14:30

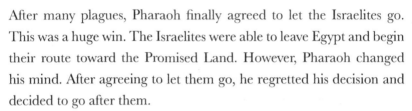

After many plagues, Pharaoh finally agreed to let the Israelites go. This was a huge win. The Israelites were able to leave Egypt and begin their route toward the Promised Land. However, Pharaoh changed his mind. After agreeing to let them go, he regretted his decision and decided to go after them.

He took an army and caught up to the Israelites as they were encamped by the Red Sea. The Israelites were trapped. They had nowhere to go, the Egyptians were on one side of them, and the Red Sea was on the other. God told Moses to stretch out his hand over the sea, and when he did, the waters split in half so that they could cross on dry ground. When they got to the other side, God told Moses to stretch out his hand over the sea, and when he did, the waters closed in on the Egyptians.

When the Israelites saw the Egyptians, they began to question and doubt God's plan for them, but he made a way. This story proves that if God calls you to it, in his time and in his way, he will bring you through it. Regardless of what you're facing today, you can trust him.

Lord, thank you for always making a way. Help me trust you, even when things get difficult. Show me if there's any area of my life where I'm not fully trusting you. Amen.

JANUARY 8

I have chosen the way of faithfulness; I set your rules before me.

Psalm 119:30

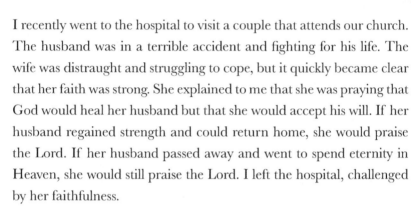

I recently went to the hospital to visit a couple that attends our church. The husband was in a terrible accident and fighting for his life. The wife was distraught and struggling to cope, but it quickly became clear that her faith was strong. She explained to me that she was praying that God would heal her husband but that she would accept his will. If her husband regained strength and could return home, she would praise the Lord. If her husband passed away and went to spend eternity in Heaven, she would still praise the Lord. I left the hospital, challenged by her faithfulness.

I'd like to think that I would respond similarly, but I'm not sure that I would. It's easy to talk about having strong faith. It's another thing to live with strong faith. This woman wasn't just talking the talk. She was walking the walk.

What about you? How's your faith? Does it depend on your circumstances? Is your faith strong when things are good and weak when things are bad? Or is your faith unwavering, regardless of what's going on around you? Today, choose the way of faithfulness.

Lord, forgive me for the times I've allowed my circumstances to determine my faithfulness. Help me have unwavering faith, regardless of what's happening around me. Amen.

JANUARY 9

Do not say, "I will repay evil"; wait for the Lord, and he will deliver you.

Proverbs 20:22

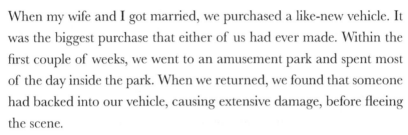

When my wife and I got married, we purchased a like-new vehicle. It was the biggest purchase that either of us had ever made. Within the first couple of weeks, we went to an amusement park and spent most of the day inside the park. When we returned, we found that someone had backed into our vehicle, causing extensive damage, before fleeing the scene.

Fortunately, there was an eyewitness who was able to write down the company name that was on the side of the truck. I ended up getting in contact with the owner of the company, and I wasn't very nice. I was angry. I wanted the person to pay for what they did. The owner of the company was very apologetic and told me that he was going to fire the employee. After I calmed down, I convinced him to let the employee keep his job and simply asked him to fix my vehicle, which he was more than happy to do.

When others do us wrong, our first instinct is usually to seek retaliation. We want them to feel the pain that they've caused us. We want them to pay for what they've done. We want to teach them a lesson. However, it's best to forgive, move on, and leave the judgment up to God.

Lord, thank you for being the perfect judge. Help me forgive others when they wrong me instead of seeking retaliation. Amen.

JANUARY 10

Whoever goes about slandering reveals secrets, but he who is trustworthy in spirit keeps a thing covered.

Proverbs 11:13

Have you ever failed to keep a secret? I remember when I unintentionally ruined my friend's surprise birthday party. In the days leading up to the party, I conversed with him and before leaving, I mentioned that I would see him that weekend. As soon as the words left my mouth, I knew I messed up. Although skeptical, fortunately, he didn't ask any questions. It's one thing to ruin a secret unintentionally. It's another thing to do it intentionally.

The Bible has a lot to say about being trustworthy. Are you the type of person that others can trust? Do you keep confidential information confidential? What about your friends? Are they trustworthy? Can you trust them to keep confidential information confidential? It's important to be a trustworthy friend, and it's important to have trustworthy friends.

If someone comes to you with someone else's confidential information, it's best to walk away. It usually sounds something like this, "I promised I wouldn't tell anyone, so please keep this to yourself." Instead of leaning in and anxiously awaiting what they are going to share, it's best to say, "If you promised you wouldn't tell, then you probably shouldn't." Be trustworthy and refuse to take part in any slander.

Lord, thank you for the trustworthy friends you have placed in my life. Help me recognize when I am taking part in slander and give me the courage to walk away. Amen.

JANUARY 11

With all humility and gentleness, with patience, bearing with one another in love.

Ephesians 4:2

A few years back, my truck was about to run out of gas. I mean, I barely made it to the gas station. I paid at the pump, put the nozzle in my truck, and let it go until it clicked off. On the screen, it showed that I received 25 gallons of gas, but when I got in my truck to leave, I noticed that my gauge still showed I was on E. I immediately assumed that something was wrong with the pump. I went inside and spoke with the cashier, who ended up calling the owner of the store. After a long discussion, they were getting ready to refund my money but asked me to move my truck so they could look at the pump. When I got in my truck to move it, the gauge corrected itself and showed I had a full gas tank. Turns out, there was nothing wrong with the pump. There was something wrong with my gauge. I went back into the store to apologize and admit that I was wrong.

A little humility goes a long way. Before assuming someone else is wrong, make sure you're not the one who is wrong. Before accusing someone else of being at fault, make sure you're not the one who is at fault. Treat others with humility, gentleness, and patience.

Lord, forgive me for my pride. Help me treat others with humility, gentleness, and patience. Show me when I'm at fault. Amen.

JANUARY 12

The light of the eyes rejoices the heart, and good news refreshes the bones.

Proverbs 15:30

I remember receiving one of the worst phone calls I've ever received. It was on a weekend, and I was outside washing my truck when the phone rang. The person on the other line told me that someone in our church had tragically passed away. This man was a pillar in the community and an important part of our church. The news hit me like a ton of bricks.

As a pastor, I've gotten accustomed to receiving bad news and find it refreshing to receive good news. It's refreshing to pick up the phone and hear that God has answered a prayer. It's refreshing to open an email and see that God has opened a door. It's refreshing to bump into someone and hear about how God is working in their life.

Unfortunately, bad news is all around us. Every time we turn on the TV, open social media, or listen to the radio, we hear about something bad that has happened. Negativity seems to sell, but positivity makes a difference. It's more important now than ever before that you share your good news with others. Go out today and let someone know what the Lord is doing in your life.

Lord, thank you for what you're doing in my life. Help me spread positivity in a world full of negativity. Help me refresh those that I encounter today. Amen.

JANUARY 13

Fret not yourself because of evildoers; be not envious of wrongdoers! For they will soon fade like the grass and wither like the green herb.

Psalm 37:1-2

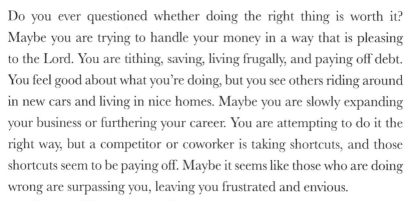

Do you ever questioned whether doing the right thing is worth it? Maybe you are trying to handle your money in a way that is pleasing to the Lord. You are tithing, saving, living frugally, and paying off debt. You feel good about what you're doing, but you see others riding around in new cars and living in nice homes. Maybe you are slowly expanding your business or furthering your career. You are attempting to do it the right way, but a competitor or coworker is taking shortcuts, and those shortcuts seem to be paying off. Maybe it seems like those who are doing wrong are surpassing you, leaving you frustrated and envious.

There will be times in life when there is a strong temptation to give in to immediate gratification. Those who give in to immediate gratification get what they want now but usually at the cost of what they want most. Satisfaction may come quickly, but just as quickly, it fades and withers.

In today's passage, you are encouraged not to worry about or be envious of those who do the wrong thing. Don't let the short-lived success of someone taking shortcuts keep you from doing what is God-honoring. Stay the course, trust the process, and continue doing the right thing.

Lord, forgive me for giving in to immediate gratification. Help me stay the course, trust the process, and continue doing what honors you. Amen.

JANUARY 14

In all toil there is profit, but mere talk tends only to poverty.

Proverbs 14:23

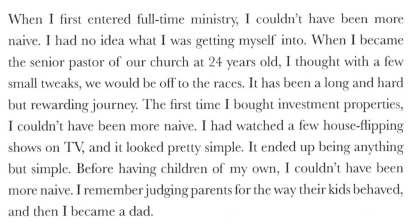

When I first entered full-time ministry, I couldn't have been more naive. I had no idea what I was getting myself into. When I became the senior pastor of our church at 24 years old, I thought with a few small tweaks, we would be off to the races. It has been a long and hard but rewarding journey. The first time I bought investment properties, I couldn't have been more naive. I had watched a few house-flipping shows on TV, and it looked pretty simple. It ended up being anything but simple. Before having children of my own, I couldn't have been more naive. I remember judging parents for the way their kids behaved, and then I became a dad.

We tend to think of naiveness as a bad thing, but I am thankful for my naiveness. The truth is that if I knew then what I know now, I probably would have never started. My naiveness is what pushed me toward action.

As you gain experience and wisdom, you tend to stop taking risks and trying new things. You know what challenges lie ahead, so instead of moving forward, you hold back in fear. Instead of doing, you fall into the trap of talking. Sometimes, it's best to stop overthinking and start taking action. Maybe one of those times is right now.

Lord, thank you for my naiveness. Show me what you want me to do and give me the courage to do it, regardless of what challenges may lie ahead. Amen.

JANUARY 15

Call to me and I will answer you, and will tell you great and hidden things that you have not known.

Jeremiah 33:3

In college, I worked a couple of minimum-wage jobs, but when I got engaged, I knew I needed to find a job that paid better. As I was searching online, I came across a supervisor position. It sounded important, so I applied. A few days later, to my surprise, they asked me to come in for an interview. I went out and bought a professional-looking outfit and researched potential interview questions to better prepare myself.

When I arrived for the interview, I was placed in a waiting room with three or four other candidates. They were all twice my age. I felt unqualified and like I didn't belong in the room. Finally, my turn arrived. They called me into the interview room and asked me a series of questions. I was so nervous I forgot every answer I had rehearsed and fumbled my words. By God's grace, I still got the job.

Many approach the throne room of God like a job interview. They pray rehearsed and well-thought-out prayers. There's nothing wrong with that approach as long as the prayers are heartfelt. However, you don't have to worry about having the right words. God already knows your heart. It doesn't matter if you fumble your words or if they don't come out how you intend. God just wants to hear from you.

Lord, thank you for wanting to hear from someone imperfect like me. Help me care more about sharing my heart with you than coming up with the right words. Amen.

JANUARY 16

Moses' father-in-law said to him, "What you are doing is not good. You and the people with you will certainly wear yourselves out, for the thing is too heavy for you. You are not able to do it alone."

Exodus 18:17-18

Several years back, I was overwhelmed and burnt out. I knew I couldn't walk away from what God called me to, but I did fantasize about leaving the ministry. I met with a close friend, and he suggested that I needed to do a better job asking for help. Instead of trusting staff and volunteers, I was trying to do everything myself. After that meeting, I realized that I had to get better at delegating tasks if I wanted the church to continue to grow.

In today's passage, Moses found himself in a similar predicament. Moses was exhausting himself, trying to lead the people without help. When Jethro, Moses's father-in-law, saw what was taking place, he pulled Moses off to the side and gave him some advice. He warned Moses that he was going to wear himself out and do the people an injustice if he attempted to do it alone. Moses listened to Jethro's advice and delegated some of the work to other men.

What are you attempting to do alone? Maybe your independence is wearing you out and preventing your organization from growing. If so, it's time to loosen the reins, trust others, and delegate some tasks. With the help of others, you can accomplish far more than you could ever accomplish by yourself.

Lord, thank you for the responsibility that you have given me. Help me trust others and delegate tasks when necessary. Amen.

JANUARY 17

For lack of wood the fire goes out, and where there is no whisperer, quarreling ceases.

Proverbs 26:20

There was a key family that left our church because they were displeased with the way I handled a situation. A couple years later, I bumped into the couple, and I was glad to hear that they had gotten plugged into another local church where they seemed to be happy and growing. For the first time, they told me what they didn't like about the way I handled the situation. Turns out, what they believed to have taken place wasn't even close to what had actually taken place. Someone gave them bad information; they believed it without seeking clarification, and as a result, they left the church. Fortunately, God used a bad situation to bring about good, but I can't help but wonder how much trouble could have been avoided had they sought out factual information.

In today's verse, gossip and arguments are compared to wood and fire. Without wood, a fire will go out and without gossip, arguments will cease. In every church and organization, there are people who thrive on drama and look for opportunities to stir the pot. They repeat what they hear with little care as to whether it is true or false.

Gossip builds wedges between people, destroys relationships, and causes disunity. Whether you realize it or not, you can help squash gossip in whatever organizations you're a part of. When you participate in gossip, you feed the fire. When you refuse to participate, you extinguish the fire.

Lord, forgive me for participating in gossip. Help me squash gossip and promote unity in the organizations I am a part of. Amen.

JANUARY 18

Do not be deceived: "Bad company ruins good morals."

1 Corinthians 15:33

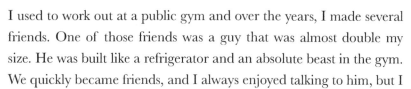

I used to work out at a public gym and over the years, I made several friends. One of those friends was a guy that was almost double my size. He was built like a refrigerator and an absolute beast in the gym. We quickly became friends, and I always enjoyed talking to him, but I hated working out with him.

When we worked out together, I would kill myself trying to keep up and attempt to lift more than I should. Every time I worked out with him, I couldn't walk for at least three days. It was difficult to get out of bed because I was so sore. The truth is that I didn't like to work out with him, but he did push me to be the best version of myself physically.

You need people like that in your life. People that will push you to be the best version of yourself spiritually. People who will challenge you to step out of your comfort zone and become all that God created you to be. It might be easy to hang around people who lack motivation, but they won't help you get where you need to be. Remember, bad company ruins good morals.

Lord, thank you for placing people in my life that challenge me to be the best version of myself spiritually. Help me choose my friends wisely. Amen.

JANUARY 19

Woe to those who call evil good and good evil, who put darkness for light and light for darkness, who put bitter for sweet and sweet for bitter!

Isaiah 5:20

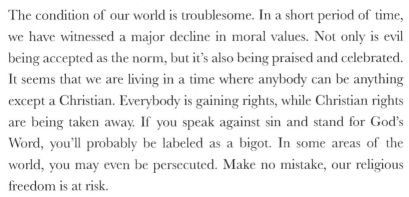

The condition of our world is troublesome. In a short period of time, we have witnessed a major decline in moral values. Not only is evil being accepted as the norm, but it's also being praised and celebrated. It seems that we are living in a time where anybody can be anything except a Christian. Everybody is gaining rights, while Christian rights are being taken away. If you speak against sin and stand for God's Word, you'll probably be labeled as a bigot. In some areas of the world, you may even be persecuted. Make no mistake, our religious freedom is at risk.

In today's verse, Isaiah confronts the people of Judah for their wickedness. They were calling evil things good and good things evil. Corruption was prevalent, and it was blinding them from the truth. What was happening in Judah sounds similar to what is happening in our world today. Corruption is blinding many from the truth. Many are living lifestyles contrary to God's Word without realizing it. Their disobedience is not the result of rebellion but of ignorance.

The sad reality is that if you are doing what everybody else is doing, you're probably not doing what is right. Spend some time praying, reading your Bible, and talking with other Christians to ensure that you haven't fallen into the trap of calling evil things good and good things evil.

Lord, thank you for your patience with me. Show me if I am doing anything that is contrary to your Word. Help me live a life that is pleasing to you. Amen.

JANUARY 20

I appeal to you therefore, brothers, by the mercies of God, to present your bodies as a living sacrifice, holy and acceptable to God, which is your spiritual worship.

Romans 12:1

In today's verse, Paul instructs us to present our bodies as living sacrifices, holy and acceptable to God. What does that mean? That means we should surrender every area of our lives to the Lord. It means we should lay everything down at the altar. Our finances, our families, our careers, our time, nothing should be off limits to God. We should evaluate every area and ask ourselves, "Is this holy and acceptable to God?"

You might evaluate your life and conclude that you aren't doing anything too bad. Maybe there's no habitual sin in your life. Maybe you're not regularly doing anything that is directly prohibited by scripture. That's good, but you're called to a higher standard. The question is not, "Are the things I'm doing wicked and offensive to God?" The question is, "Are the things I'm doing holy and acceptable to God?"

The way you handle your finances might not be wicked and offensive to God, but is it holy and acceptable to God? The conversations you have might not be wicked and offensive to God, but are they holy and acceptable to God? The way you spend your time might not be wicked and offensive to God, but is it holy and acceptable to God? Take some time today and ask yourself, "Am I presenting my body as a living sacrifice, holy and acceptable to God?"

Lord, show me if there is anything in my life that is not holy and acceptable to you. Help me present my body as a living sacrifice. Amen.

JANUARY 21

You shall have no other gods before me.

Exodus 20:3

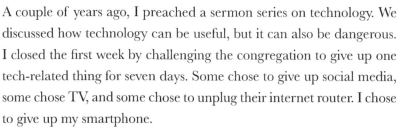

A couple of years ago, I preached a sermon series on technology. We discussed how technology can be useful, but it can also be dangerous. I closed the first week by challenging the congregation to give up one tech-related thing for seven days. Some chose to give up social media, some chose TV, and some chose to unplug their internet router. I chose to give up my smartphone.

I caught myself looking at my phone in the middle of family meals, important meetings, and church functions. I recognized that my phone had become a crutch. So, I took the SIM card out of my smartphone and put it in a flip phone. The only thing the flip phone could do was make and receive phone calls. I couldn't text, check email, browse social media, or do anything at all. I knew my phone had become a problem, but I didn't realize the depth of the problem until I went without it for a week.

An idol is anything you put before God, anything that becomes the focus and priority of your life. My phone had become an idol. Your career can become an idol. Your spouse can become an idol. Your kids can become an idol. Your hobby can become an idol. It's important to regularly evaluate your life to ensure that no idols have crept in.

Lord, show me if anything in my life has become an idol. Help me keep you first and make furthering your kingdom my focus and priority. Amen.

JANUARY 22

Whoever believes in him is not condemned, but whoever does not believe is condemned already, because he has not believed in the name of the only Son of God.

John 3:18

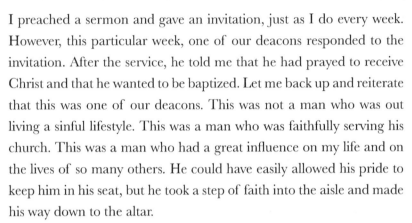

I preached a sermon and gave an invitation, just as I do every week. However, this particular week, one of our deacons responded to the invitation. After the service, he told me that he had prayed to receive Christ and that he wanted to be baptized. Let me back up and reiterate that this was one of our deacons. This was not a man who was out living a sinful lifestyle. This was a man who was faithfully serving his church. This was a man who had a great influence on my life and on the lives of so many others. He could have easily allowed his pride to keep him in his seat, but he took a step of faith into the aisle and made his way down to the altar.

Several weeks later, he got up in front of the church and shared his testimony. He shared how he had been in church, but he had a nagging feeling that something wasn't quite right. He concluded that he knew all about Jesus but that he didn't have a personal relationship with him. His vulnerability challenged and continues to challenge many people to this day.

The harsh reality is that Jesus is your only hope. Without him, you are condemned. You will spend an eternity in Hell. Are you sure that you have a relationship with him? If so, thank him for that relationship. If not, you can begin a relationship with him right now.

Lord, thank you for your saving grace. Thank you for taking my place on that cross. If my relationship with you is genuine, give me assurance. If it's not genuine, convict and bring me to repentance. Amen.

JANUARY 23

Listen, my beloved brothers, has not God chosen those who are poor in the world to be rich in faith and heirs of the kingdom, which he has promised to those who love him?

James 2:5

When I became a pastor, I went shopping. I bought a suit, several ties, dress shirts, pants, and shoes. I figured I needed to look the part. I needed nice clothes to wear on Sunday morning and a nice suit to officiate weddings and funerals. At the time, most people in our church dressed up, and it was unusual to see someone wearing a T-shirt and jeans.

One day, I invited a person to church, and they wanted to come, but one thing was holding them back. They explained to me that they didn't feel comfortable attending any of the churches in our area because they didn't have nice enough clothes. I lost sleep that night thinking about how we have failed as a church if people think they can't attend because they don't have nice clothes.

I decided to change. I knew it would be difficult. I knew that some people wouldn't like it. But I knew it would be worth it. It's been several years since I made that decision. I now regularly preach in jeans and a T-shirt. And it's unusual to see someone who is wearing anything dressier than a collared shirt and a nice pair of jeans.

We tell people to come as they are, but do we really mean it? What about you? Do you care more about outward appearances or inward transformations?

Lord, thank you for caring more about what is on the inside than the outside. Give me eyes to see people the way that you see people. Help me extend grace to others. Amen.

JANUARY 24

For the time is coming when people will not endure sound teaching, but having itching ears they will accumulate for themselves teachers to suit their own passions.

2 Timothy 4:3

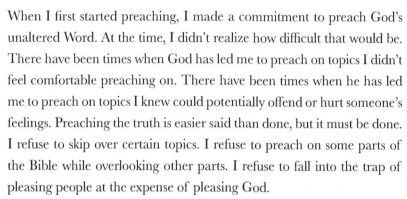

When I first started preaching, I made a commitment to preach God's unaltered Word. At the time, I didn't realize how difficult that would be. There have been times when God has led me to preach on topics I didn't feel comfortable preaching on. There have been times when he has led me to preach on topics I knew could potentially offend or hurt someone's feelings. Preaching the truth is easier said than done, but it must be done. I refuse to skip over certain topics. I refuse to preach on some parts of the Bible while overlooking other parts. I refuse to fall into the trap of pleasing people at the expense of pleasing God.

Contrary to popular belief, I think many are hungry for the truth. Many are sick and tired of the perversion and corruption, and they're desperately searching for more. But there are also many who want to hear what they want to hear. They don't want to be challenged and convicted. They want to be uplifted and encouraged, regardless of the lifestyle they're living. They don't want to hear sound teaching; they want their ears to be tickled.

As you listen to messages, read books, and watch videos, be warned that not everything is sound. Make sure the content you are consuming aligns with the unaltered Word of God.

Lord, thank you for your unaltered Word. Help me seek out the whole truth of your Word. Show me if there is anything I'm consuming that is not pleasing to you. Amen.

JANUARY 25

Delight yourself in the Lord, and he will give you the desires of your heart.

Psalm 37:4

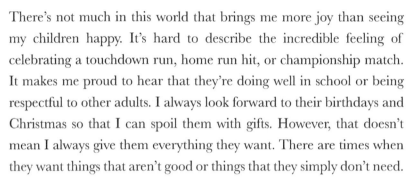

There's not much in this world that brings me more joy than seeing my children happy. It's hard to describe the incredible feeling of celebrating a touchdown run, home run hit, or championship match. It makes me proud to hear that they're doing well in school or being respectful to other adults. I always look forward to their birthdays and Christmas so that I can spoil them with gifts. However, that doesn't mean I always give them everything they want. There are times when they want things that aren't good or things that they simply don't need.

In that same way, God finds joy in blessing his children. This doesn't mean that he always gives his children whatever they want. It simply means that he knows what's best for his children and it brings him joy to give it to them.

Today's verse instructs you to "Delight yourself in the Lord." That means you should look for joy and satisfaction in the Lord. It means you should pursue him with your whole heart. The verse goes on to say, "and he will give you the desires of your heart." That is not a promise for wealth or materialistic things. That doesn't mean that God will give you whatever you want. It means that as you delight in him, your desires will align with his desires and never go unfulfilled.

Lord, thank you for always knowing what I need. Thank you for blessing me with so much more than I deserve. Help me delight in you and align my desires with your desires. Amen.

JANUARY 26

Gray hair is a crown of glory; it is gained in a righteous life.

Proverbs 16:31

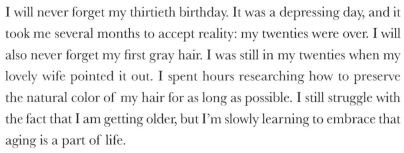

I will never forget my thirtieth birthday. It was a depressing day, and it took me several months to accept reality: my twenties were over. I will also never forget my first gray hair. I was still in my twenties when my lovely wife pointed it out. I spent hours researching how to preserve the natural color of my hair for as long as possible. I still struggle with the fact that I am getting older, but I'm slowly learning to embrace that aging is a part of life.

Not only is aging a part of life, but it is also a beneficial part of life. The Bible tells us that gray hair is a crown of glory. As you age, you may not physically be able to do what you were once able to do. You may not look the way that you once looked. However, with age often comes wisdom and sound judgment. The longer you walk with God, the more your life should align with his will.

Don't think of aging as a burden, think of it as a blessing. Every day is a gift from God and an opportunity to leave this world better than you found it. And if you are in Christ, you have an eternity in Heaven to look forward to.

Lord, thank you for the gift of life. Help me cherish the time that you've given me on this Earth. As I grow older, give me wisdom and sound judgment. Amen.

JANUARY 27

Let everything that has breath praise the Lord! Praise the Lord!

Psalm 150:6

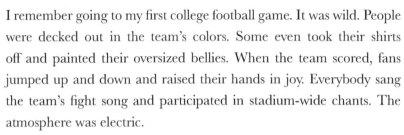

I remember going to my first college football game. It was wild. People were decked out in the team's colors. Some even took their shirts off and painted their oversized bellies. When the team scored, fans jumped up and down and raised their hands in joy. Everybody sang the team's fight song and participated in stadium-wide chants. The atmosphere was electric.

The next morning, I woke up and went to church. As I looked around, I saw people standing around with their hands in their pockets; some sat down during the music, and some fell asleep during the sermon. I couldn't help but think, "What would it be like if we came to church with the same enthusiasm that we go to football games with?" After all, we have something much greater to celebrate than our favorite team winning the big game. Our Savior has defeated the grave!

It's okay to get excited about the things of God. When songs glorifying God are being sung, it's okay to sing along and raise your hands. When someone makes a public profession of faith, it's okay to shout and cheer. When the Word is preached, it's okay to let out an amen. As a matter of fact, if you don't get excited about the things of God, it's probably time to take a good look within.

Lord, thank you for who you are and for what you have done. Forgive me for not giving you the praise that you deserve. Amen.

JANUARY 28

Give your servant therefore an understanding mind to govern your people, that I may discern between good and evil, for who is able to govern this your great people?

1 Kings 3:9

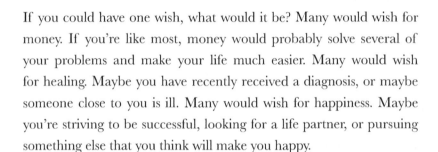

If you could have one wish, what would it be? Many would wish for money. If you're like most, money would probably solve several of your problems and make your life much easier. Many would wish for healing. Maybe you have recently received a diagnosis, or maybe someone close to you is ill. Many would wish for happiness. Maybe you're striving to be successful, looking for a life partner, or pursuing something else that you think will make you happy.

In today's passage, God appeared to Solomon in a dream and told him that he would give him anything he asked for. Solomon got his one wish but didn't wish for what you would probably expect. He asked for wisdom to lead God's people. God was pleased to grant Solomon's request, and because of his humility, he also blessed him with riches and honor.

Solomon asked for what we all need: wisdom. Wisdom is one of the most undervalued qualities. There will be times in life when wisdom will take you further than money, health, and success combined. And the good thing about wisdom is that God gives it to all who ask (James 1:5). So, if you find yourself in a situation where you don't know what to do, ask God for wisdom.

Lord, thank you for giving me direction when I don't know what to do. Give me wisdom. Help me make decisions that will bring glory and honor to your name. Amen.

JANUARY 29

Then the king answered and said, "Give the living child to the first woman, and by no means put him to death; she is his mother."

1 Kings 3:27

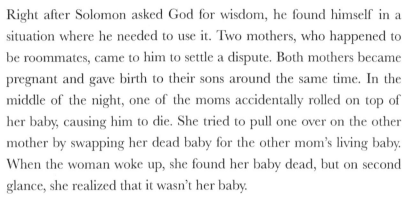

Right after Solomon asked God for wisdom, he found himself in a situation where he needed to use it. Two mothers, who happened to be roommates, came to him to settle a dispute. Both mothers became pregnant and gave birth to their sons around the same time. In the middle of the night, one of the moms accidentally rolled on top of her baby, causing him to die. She tried to pull one over on the other mother by swapping her dead baby for the other mom's living baby. When the woman woke up, she found her baby dead, but on second glance, she realized that it wasn't her baby.

The women were arguing over whose baby was whose. Solomon asked for a sword and said he was going to cut the baby in half and give half to one mom and half to the other mom. The real mom spoke up and begged Solomon not to harm the baby but to give it to the other woman. The other woman insisted that he cut the baby in half. It quickly became obvious who the real mom was.

Solomon's intention was never to harm the baby but simply to identify who the real mom was. After handling this situation, it became clear to all that Solomon had wisdom from God. Like Solomon, you can navigate some of the most difficult situations if you rely on God for understanding and wisdom.

Lord, give me wisdom like Solomon. Help me look to you for direction when I am in the midst of difficult circumstances. Help me discern your voice. Amen.

JANUARY 30

His master said to him, 'Well done, good and faithful servant. You have been faithful over a little; I will set you over much. Enter into the joy of your master.'

Matthew 25:23

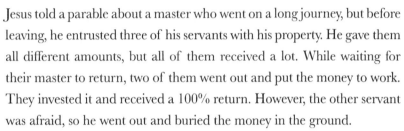

Jesus told a parable about a master who went on a long journey, but before leaving, he entrusted three of his servants with his property. He gave them all different amounts, but all of them received a lot. While waiting for their master to return, two of them went out and put the money to work. They invested it and received a 100% return. However, the other servant was afraid, so he went out and buried the money in the ground.

After a long time, the master returned to settle accounts with his servants. The first two servants proudly went forward with double what their master entrusted them with. The master said, "'Well done, good and faithful servant. You have been faithful over a little; I will set you over much." And then the third servant went forward with nothing more than what his master entrusted him with. The master responded by calling him a "wicked and slothful servant" (Matthew 25:26) and then cast him into a place of outer darkness.

You probably want more. You want to make a difference and leave your mark on this world. Here's the question: Are you being trustworthy right now, where you are, and with what you have? If you want God to bless you with more, are you being a good steward of what he's already given you? If you want him to trust you with a lot, are you proving yourself trustworthy with a little?

Lord, thank you for entrusting me with your property. Help me be a good steward and prove myself trustworthy with a little. Amen.

JANUARY 31

And he said to them, "Take care, and be on your guard against all covetousness, for one's life does not consist in the abundance of his possessions."

Luke 12:15

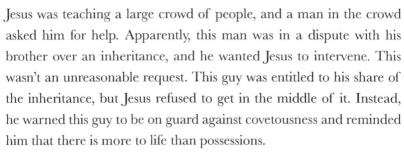

Jesus was teaching a large crowd of people, and a man in the crowd asked him for help. Apparently, this man was in a dispute with his brother over an inheritance, and he wanted Jesus to intervene. This wasn't an unreasonable request. This guy was entitled to his share of the inheritance, but Jesus refused to get in the middle of it. Instead, he warned this guy to be on guard against covetousness and reminded him that there is more to life than possessions.

Jesus wasn't condemning wealth or even the desire to have wealth. Jesus was condemning an unbalanced, wrongly focused life. Regardless of how much or little you have, covetousness is something you must be on guard against.

Greed is not the desire for more. It's the excessive desire for more. So, that begs the question, when does a person's desire for more become excessive? And here's the answer: when a person's preoccupation with stuff, possessions, and money distracts them from fully doing what they're called by God to do.

It's okay to desire more, but has your desire for more become excessive? Is a preoccupation with stuff, possessions, and money distracting you from fully doing what God has called you to do? Remember, one's life does not consist in the abundance of his possessions.

Lord, thank you for blessing me in so many ways. Help me be content. Show me when greed becomes a problem in my life. Amen.

FEBRUARY 1

For God so loved the world, that he gave his only Son, that whoever believes in him should not perish but have eternal life.

John 3:16

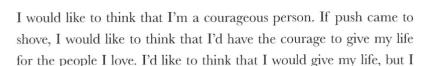

I would like to think that I'm a courageous person. If push came to shove, I would like to think that I'd have the courage to give my life for the people I love. I'd like to think that I would give my life, but I wouldn't give any of my kids' lives.

I am blessed to have three kids, two sons and a daughter. At the time of writing, they are seven, five, and two. The past seven years have been the best seven years of my life. I love being a dad, and I would do just about anything for my kids. I can promise you that I wouldn't give any of my three kids for anyone in this world. Nobody means that much to me. I don't love anyone that much, not even close. But that's exactly how much God loves you. That's exactly how much you mean to him.

You were dead in your sin, so he sent his one and only son, Jesus. He came to Earth and lived a sinless life. He healed the sick, gave sight to the blind, and brought hope to the hopeless. Despite the good that he did, he was betrayed, arrested, and crucified. He paid the penalty for your sin. He took your place on the cross. Take a few minutes to reflect on the sacrifice he made for you. Remember, there is no love like his love.

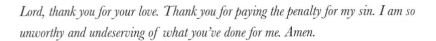

Lord, thank you for your love. Thank you for paying the penalty for my sin. I am so unworthy and undeserving of what you've done for me. Amen.

FEBRUARY 2

Come now, let us reason together, says the Lord: though your sins are like scarlet, they shall be as white as snow; though they are red like crimson, they shall become like wool.

Isaiah 1:18

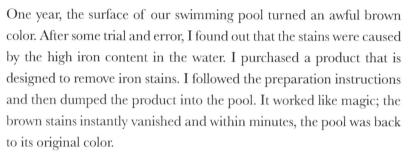

One year, the surface of our swimming pool turned an awful brown color. After some trial and error, I found out that the stains were caused by the high iron content in the water. I purchased a product that is designed to remove iron stains. I followed the preparation instructions and then dumped the product into the pool. It worked like magic; the brown stains instantly vanished and within minutes, the pool was back to its original color.

I have a past. Before Christ, my life was a total mess. I was mixed up in drugs, alcohol, lust, and the list goes on. I'm hesitant to admit that, but I know my story brings glory and honor to God. He specializes in using broken people like me to do big things. I was a total mess, but then he intervened. He washed away my sin. Though my sins were like scarlet, they became white as snow. Though they were red like crimson, they became like wool. Now, that doesn't mean that I no longer struggle with sin, but it does mean that I'm no longer defined by my sin. In Christ, I am a brand-new creation. Because of him, I am in a right standing with God.

If you're a Christian, the same is true for you. Take some time today and thank him for his sacrifice. Praise him for saving a wretch like you.

Lord, thank you for saving a wretch like me. Thank you for washing away my sin. Forgive me for the times I take your sacrifice for granted. Amen.

FEBRUARY 3

Peter said to him, "Even if I must die with you, I will not deny you!" And all the disciples said the same.

Matthew 26:35

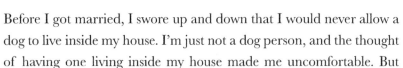

Before I got married, I swore up and down that I would never allow a dog to live inside my house. I'm just not a dog person, and the thought of having one living inside my house made me uncomfortable. But then I got married. Within twelve months, we had a dog living inside our house. I learned a valuable lesson: never say never.

After Jesus was arrested and taken away, Peter did what he said he'd never do. He denied Jesus, not once, but three times. He blew it big time but recovered. He went on to preach on the day of Pentecost and 3,000 people came to know Jesus as Savior and Lord. He went on to heal a lame beggar. He boldly preached before the Sanhedrin. He was arrested, beaten, and threatened for proclaiming the gospel of Jesus Christ. Tradition has it that he was martyred and crucified upside down in Rome. Peter messed up, but he went on to make a tremendous impact for the kingdom of God.

Maybe you have done something you never thought you'd do. Maybe you're in a place you never thought you'd be in. Maybe you've blown it. Maybe you've messed up. Maybe you're starting over and unsure of what the future holds. You have no control over what has already been done, but by God's grace, you can recover and go on to make a tremendous impact for the kingdom of God.

Lord, thank you for not giving up on me. Thank you for second chances. Forgive me for doing what I said I'd never do. Help me recover and adjust going forward. Amen.

FEBRUARY 4

He said to him the third time, "Simon, son of John, do you love me?" Peter was grieved because he said to him the third time, "Do you love me?" and he said to him, "Lord, you know everything; you know that I love you." Jesus said to him, "Feed my sheep."

John 21:17

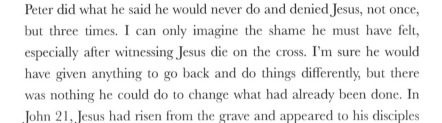

Peter did what he said he would never do and denied Jesus, not once, but three times. I can only imagine the shame he must have felt, especially after witnessing Jesus die on the cross. I'm sure he would have given anything to go back and do things differently, but there was nothing he could do to change what had already been done. In John 21, Jesus had risen from the grave and appeared to his disciples at the Sea of Galilee. Peter came face to face with Jesus and had a conversation with him.

Jesus asked Peter if he loved him three times. Peter replied by saying that he did, and each time, Jesus instructed him to feed his sheep. Jesus was restoring Peter to ministry and preparing him for the future. Peter would go on to play a major role in leading the church and shepherding God's people.

God is a God of second chances. No matter what you've done, he still loves you. He can restore you to ministry and use you in ways you cannot imagine. When you mess up, instead of running from God in shame, run to God in repentance.

Lord, thank you for second chances. I have made many mistakes, yet you've continued to love and forgive me. I am nothing without your grace. Amen.

FEBRUARY 5

Therefore, we are ambassadors for Christ, God making his appeal through us. We implore you on behalf of Christ, be reconciled to God.

2 Corinthians 5:20

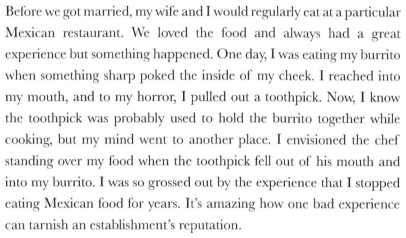

Before we got married, my wife and I would regularly eat at a particular Mexican restaurant. We loved the food and always had a great experience but something happened. One day, I was eating my burrito when something sharp poked the inside of my cheek. I reached into my mouth, and to my horror, I pulled out a toothpick. Now, I know the toothpick was probably used to hold the burrito together while cooking, but my mind went to another place. I envisioned the chef standing over my food when the toothpick fell out of his mouth and into my burrito. I was so grossed out by the experience that I stopped eating Mexican food for years. It's amazing how one bad experience can tarnish an establishment's reputation.

We are called to be ambassadors for Christ. In other words, we are called to represent Christ in everything we do and say. This is not something that should be taken lightly. Unfortunately, many want nothing to do with Christ because they had a bad experience with someone who claimed to follow him.

When others see you, they should see Christ. You will make many mistakes along the way, but this truth should challenge you to live up to a higher standard. Somebody is always watching. What you do and say can point them to Christ or turn them away.

Lord, thank you for allowing me to be an ambassador for you. Help me represent you well in all that I do and say. Amen.

FEBRUARY 6

Little children, let us not love in word or talk but in deed and in truth.

1 John 3:18

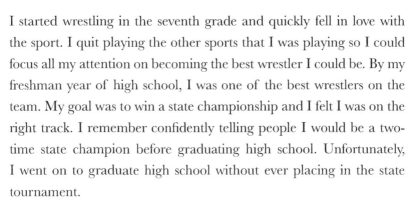

I started wrestling in the seventh grade and quickly fell in love with the sport. I quit playing the other sports that I was playing so I could focus all my attention on becoming the best wrestler I could be. By my freshman year of high school, I was one of the best wrestlers on the team. My goal was to win a state championship and I felt I was on the right track. I remember confidently telling people I would be a two-time state champion before graduating high school. Unfortunately, I went on to graduate high school without ever placing in the state tournament.

Have you ever said you were going to do something and then failed to follow through? It's one thing to talk about something. It's another thing to do something. As we've all grown accustomed to saying, talk is cheap. In today's verse, John writes, "Let us not love in word or talk but in deed and in truth." It's not enough to say that we love others with our mouths. We must show that we love others through our actions.

True love calls for more than words. It demands action. When it comes to loving others, are you saying something and then failing to follow through? Are you loving in word and talk or in deed and in truth?

Lord, thank you for loving me. Help me extend your love to others and show that love through my actions. Amen.

FEBRUARY 7

Whoever says he is in the light and hates his brother is still in darkness.

1 John 2:9

In middle school, I remember going with my mom to a shoe sale. The shoe sale was set up in a parking lot under a big white tent, and they advertised low prices. To my surprise, the prices were as advertised, and I was able to get a popular pair of Nikes at a fraction of the cost. I was extremely proud of those shoes and eager to show them off. The following day at school, I didn't make it through the first period, and someone pointed out that they were fakes. Sure enough, I looked down, and for the first time, I noticed that the Nike check was backwards. That was the last time I wore those shoes.

In today's verse, John tells us the quickest way to spot a fake Christian is to observe how they treat others. It is impossible for a person to hate others and to be in fellowship with God. So, if a person says that they are a Christian and hates another person, they are fake.

Is there any hate in your heart? Are you holding on to any bitterness or resentment? If so, repent for being fake and ask God to help you love everyone, regardless of what they've done to you.

Lord, forgive me for being fake. Help me love others the way that you have loved me. Show me if there is any hate in my heart. Amen.

FEBRUARY 8

And if it is evil in your eyes to serve the Lord, choose this day whom you will serve, whether the gods your fathers served in the region beyond the River, or the gods of the Amorites in whose land you dwell. But as for me and my house, we will serve the Lord.

Joshua 24:15

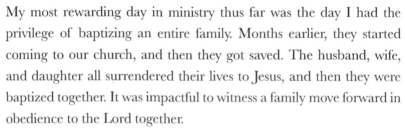

My most rewarding day in ministry thus far was the day I had the privilege of baptizing an entire family. Months earlier, they started coming to our church, and then they got saved. The husband, wife, and daughter all surrendered their lives to Jesus, and then they were baptized together. It was impactful to witness a family move forward in obedience to the Lord together.

In Joshua 24, Joshua's life was quickly coming to an end. As the leader of the Israelites, he gathered the people up to give them some final words of advice. He urged them to be on guard against idolatry, put away the gods their fathers served, and fear and serve the Lord alone. He told them that they had a choice to make for themselves. Joshua made it clear that he had already made his choice. His house would be a house that served the Lord.

Like the Israelites, you have a choice to make. You can serve whatever or whomever you want to serve. You can become obsessed with money, success, or fame. You can lead your family to believe the most important things are the things of this world. Or you can make a firm decision that your house will be a house that serves the Lord. So, what's it going to be?

Lord, thank you for my family. Help me lead them in a way that is pleasing to you. My house will be a house that serves you. Amen.

FEBRUARY 9

Besides that, they learn to be idlers, going about from house to house, and not only idlers, but also gossips and busybodies, saying what they should not.

1 Timothy 5:13

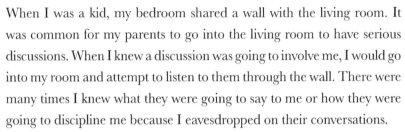

When I was a kid, my bedroom shared a wall with the living room. It was common for my parents to go into the living room to have serious discussions. When I knew a discussion was going to involve me, I would go into my room and attempt to listen to them through the wall. There were many times I knew what they were going to say to me or how they were going to discipline me because I eavesdropped on their conversations.

In Timothy 5, Paul wrote to Timothy and gave him instructions concerning ministry to widows. Paul explained that younger widows tended to get caught up in gossip. Some spent their time spreading rumors and poking their noses into things that were none of their business.

Of course, it's not only young widows who can fall into the trap of being nosey. We all tend to poke our noses into things that are none of our business. We can find ourselves seeking a thrill by always looking to get the inside scoop. This usually only leads to problems. And when you're so focused on everybody else's business, you usually do a poor job caring for your own business. It's one thing to be genuinely concerned. It's another thing to be nosey. It's important to know the difference.

Lord, forgive me for the times I have fallen into the trap of being nosey. Help me keep my nose out of things that are none of my business. Amen.

FEBRUARY 10

Let no one despise you for your youth, but set the believers an example in speech, in conduct, in love, in faith, in purity.

1 Timothy 4:12

I became a youth pastor when I was 22 years old. At the time, my wife and I were the youngest people in the congregation by close to 20 years. It was intimidating to lead people who were twice my age. I felt like I needed to prove myself and held back in many ways because I lacked confidence. Today's verse was one I kept returning to in those early days of ministry. It reminded me that age is only a number. It reminded me that even as the youngest person in the room, I could lead, set an example, and make a difference for the kingdom.

God has a history of using people of all ages to further his kingdom. David was just a teenager when he fought Goliath. Joseph was just a teenager when he was sold into slavery by his brothers. Mary was just a teenager when she gave birth to Jesus. These are just a few examples of young people in the Bible who made a big difference for the kingdom.

No matter what your age is, God can use you. He has a plan for you right now. Even as the youngest person in the room, you can lead, set an example, and make a difference.

Lord, thank you for using people of all ages. Help me lead, set an example, and make a difference. Forgive me for the times I've let my insecurities hold me back. Amen.

FEBRUARY 11

A good name is to be chosen rather than great riches, and favor is better than silver or gold.

Proverbs 22:1

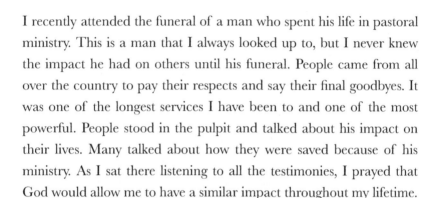

I recently attended the funeral of a man who spent his life in pastoral ministry. This is a man that I always looked up to, but I never knew the impact he had on others until his funeral. People came from all over the country to pay their respects and say their final goodbyes. It was one of the longest services I have been to and one of the most powerful. People stood in the pulpit and talked about his impact on their lives. Many talked about how they were saved because of his ministry. As I sat there listening to all the testimonies, I prayed that God would allow me to have a similar impact throughout my lifetime.

What will matter 100 years from now? It won't matter how big your house was, how nice your car was, or how green your grass was. It won't matter how much money you had in the bank, what job title you held, or how successful your business was. The only things that will matter 100 years from now are the things you do to further the kingdom of God.

Your reputation is far more important than riches. What are you known for? What testimonies will people share at your funeral? Are you making a temporary difference or an eternal one?

Lord, forgive me for the times I've cared more about obtaining riches than building a godly reputation. Help me make an eternal difference in this world. Amen.

FEBRUARY 12

Take no part in the unfruitful works of darkness, but instead expose them.

Ephesians 5:11

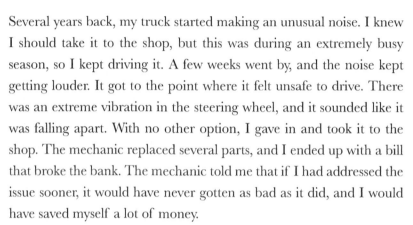

Several years back, my truck started making an unusual noise. I knew I should take it to the shop, but this was during an extremely busy season, so I kept driving it. A few weeks went by, and the noise kept getting louder. It got to the point where it felt unsafe to drive. There was an extreme vibration in the steering wheel, and it sounded like it was falling apart. With no other option, I gave in and took it to the shop. The mechanic replaced several parts, and I ended up with a bill that broke the bank. The mechanic told me that if I had addressed the issue sooner, it would have never gotten as bad as it did, and I would have saved myself a lot of money.

Small oversights can result in big compromises. Marriages usually don't fail overnight. It starts with small oversights. Addictions usually don't happen overnight. They start with small oversights. Financial trouble usually doesn't start overnight. It starts with small oversights. You get the idea: small problems that are ignored usually only lead to bigger problems down the road.

Maybe there's an issue in your life that you're trying to ignore and sweep under the rug. Maybe there's a problem, but you're telling yourself you don't have the time to address it. Be warned, the longer you delay, the worse it will get.

Lord, forgive me for overlooking sin in my life. Show me where I am falling short. Help me align my life with your Word. Amen.

FEBRUARY 13

"When therefore the owner of the vineyard comes, what will he do to those tenants?"
They said to him, "He will put those wretches to a miserable death and let out the
vineyard to other tenants who will give him the fruits in their seasons."

Matthew 21:40-41

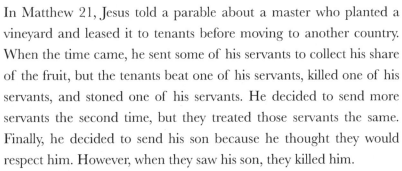

In Matthew 21, Jesus told a parable about a master who planted a
vineyard and leased it to tenants before moving to another country.
When the time came, he sent some of his servants to collect his share
of the fruit, but the tenants beat one of his servants, killed one of his
servants, and stoned one of his servants. He decided to send more
servants the second time, but they treated those servants the same.
Finally, he decided to send his son because he thought they would
respect him. However, when they saw his son, they killed him.

This parable was directed at the religious authorities. They were
claiming to be obedient to God, but like the tenants of the vineyard,
they were rejecting those who were sent by him. They rejected several
that preached the message of repentance, and now they were rejecting
his son, who they would eventually kill. The message of repentance
was being preached, but they remained unrepentant.

The religious authorities aren't alone. Self-righteousness is a trap
that we can all fall into from time to time. We can begin to think more
highly of ourselves than we ought to. We can begin to look down on
others and believe that we are more deserving of God's love than the
next person. We must remember that the only thing that separates a
Christian from a non-Christian is God's amazing grace.

Lord, thank you for your amazing grace. Forgive me for the times I've had a self-
righteous attitude. It's only by your grace that I am saved. Amen.

FEBRUARY 14

Love bears all things, believes all things, hopes all things, endures all things.

1 Corinthians 13:7

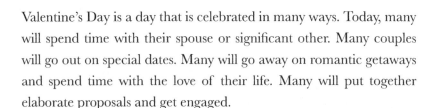

Valentine's Day is a day that is celebrated in many ways. Today, many will spend time with their spouse or significant other. Many couples will go out on special dates. Many will go away on romantic getaways and spend time with the love of their life. Many will put together elaborate proposals and get engaged.

On the flipside, many will spend today alone. Some have lost their spouse or significant other; all they have are memories from previous holidays. Many have been dumped or are going through a divorce, and today brings painful memories to the surface. Some are still searching for someone special to spend their life with, and today just reminds them that they're still alone.

For many, today is a happy, exciting day they look forward to. For others, today is a depressing, painful day they dread. Whether you spend today with the love of your life or all alone, your Father in Heaven loves you unconditionally. He loves you so much that he sent his one and only son to take your place on the cross. He sent his son to die so that you can have life. Take some time today to celebrate God's perfect love.

Lord, thank you for your perfect love. Thank you for loving me unconditionally. Help me extend your love to those around me. Amen.

FEBRUARY 15

Iron sharpens iron, and one man sharpens another.

Proverbs 27:17

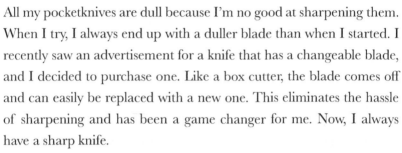

All my pocketknives are dull because I'm no good at sharpening them. When I try, I always end up with a duller blade than when I started. I recently saw an advertisement for a knife that has a changeable blade, and I decided to purchase one. Like a box cutter, the blade comes off and can easily be replaced with a new one. This eliminates the hassle of sharpening and has been a game changer for me. Now, I always have a sharp knife.

I wouldn't know from experience, but I'm told that when iron blades are rubbed together, they become sharper. In that same way, when like-minded people come together, they push each other to learn and grow. Today's verse of scripture is a call to fellowship. Your friends can either help you or hurt you. Your friends can sharpen you and help you become more effective, or they can dull you and make you less effective.

Are your friends pushing you to be the best Christian you can be, or are they leading you to compromise? Are your friends challenging you to make godly choices or pressuring you to make worldly choices? Remember, you are the sharpest and strongest when you're surrounded by the right people.

Lord, thank you for fellowship. Help me surround myself with the people that will sharpen me, and help me sharpen others. Amen.

FEBRUARY 16

Even a fool who keeps silent is considered wise; when he closes his lips, he is deemed intelligent.

Proverbs 17:28

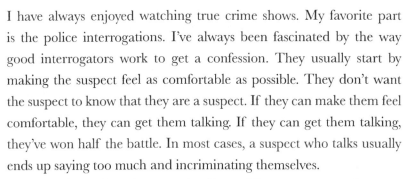

I have always enjoyed watching true crime shows. My favorite part is the police interrogations. I've always been fascinated by the way good interrogators work to get a confession. They usually start by making the suspect feel as comfortable as possible. They don't want the suspect to know that they are a suspect. If they can make them feel comfortable, they can get them talking. If they can get them talking, they've won half the battle. In most cases, a suspect who talks usually ends up saying too much and incriminating themselves.

Sometimes, there is power in silence. There are times when you need to speak up and voice your opinion, but there are also times when it's best to remain silent. President Abraham Lincoln once said, "It is better to remain silent and be thought a fool than to speak out and remove all doubt."

You learn by listening, not by talking. It's always wise to think and carefully analyze your words before speaking. If you have something profitable and beneficial to say, say it. If not, keep your mouth closed. Even if you aren't the sharpest tool in the shed, you can appear wise simply by reducing your words. Today, think before you speak.

Lord, forgive me for the careless words that I have spoken. Help me spend less time talking and more time listening. Amen.

FEBRUARY 17

For the simple are killed by their turning away, and the complacency of fools destroys them.

Proverbs 1:32

One thing that has caused a lot of tension in our marriage is restaurant selection. I frequently ask my wife, "Where do you want to eat?" She replies, "I don't care; where do you want to eat?" I then proceed to name a few restaurants that she rejects and continue until I finally land on the one she wanted to eat at in the first place. When this discussion is happening, we're usually driving around in circles, and the tension is growing by the minute. By the time we get to a restaurant and sit down, we're so irritated with one another that we eat in silence.

Today's verse tells us that complacency is destructive. Complacency keeps you from becoming who you were created to be and from doing what you were created to do. Often, complacency is rooted in indecisiveness. You're complacent in your career because you haven't decided to give it your all. You're complacent in your marriage because you haven't decided to fully commit yourself to becoming the best spouse you can be. You're complacent in your walk with the Lord because you haven't made the decision to fully surrender to him.

Take some time today to identify areas where you've become complacent. Ask God to forgive you and make a firm decision to change.

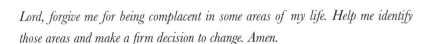

Lord, forgive me for being complacent in some areas of my life. Help me identify those areas and make a firm decision to change. Amen.

FEBRUARY 18

"Be still, and know that I am God. I will be exalted among the nations, I will be exalted in the earth!"

Psalm 46:10

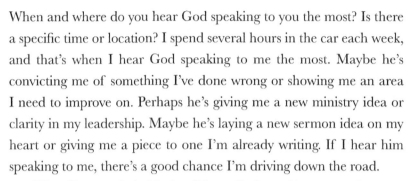

When and where do you hear God speaking to you the most? Is there a specific time or location? I spend several hours in the car each week, and that's when I hear God speaking to me the most. Maybe he's convicting me of something I've done wrong or showing me an area I need to improve on. Perhaps he's giving me a new ministry idea or clarity in my leadership. Maybe he's laying a new sermon idea on my heart or giving me a piece to one I'm already writing. If I hear him speaking to me, there's a good chance I'm driving down the road.

What I've concluded is that I hear God speaking to me the most when I'm driving because that's when I slow down enough to listen. It's not that he's not speaking at other times. It's just that I am too preoccupied with other things to hear his voice.

Maybe you can relate. Maybe you have a busy schedule. Maybe you have to carefully plan your day to make sure you accomplish everything that you need to accomplish. Maybe you're too preoccupied with other things to hear God's voice. Slowing down is not easy, but it is necessary. Take some time today to spend in stillness.

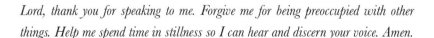

Lord, thank you for speaking to me. Forgive me for being preoccupied with other things. Help me spend time in stillness so I can hear and discern your voice. Amen.

FEBRUARY 19

Rejoice always, pray without ceasing, give thanks in all circumstances; for this is the will of God in Christ Jesus for you.

1 Thessalonians 5:16-18

It's so easy to get caught up in the never-ending pursuit of more and to become obsessed with stuff. There's nothing wrong with wanting to better yourself professionally, financially, or materialistically. God has given you the drive to better yourself, but you must be careful not to fall into the trap of greed. It's difficult to rejoice and be thankful when you are focused on and consumed by obtaining what you don't have.

Prayer will change your perspective. When you pray, you begin to realize how blessed you already are. Instead of being envious of the person who owns that beautiful home down the road, you realize how blessed you are to have the one you live in. Instead of complaining about how your spouse isn't living up to your expectations, you realize how blessed you are to have them in your life. Instead of griping about how busy your kids keep you, you realize how blessed you are to have healthy children who can do the things they love to do. Prayer will change your perspective.

It's important to slow down and take time to thank God for what you do have. The truth is that you probably take so much for granted. Prayer will take your greed and turn it into gratefulness.

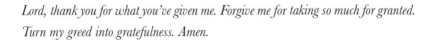

Lord, thank you for what you've given me. Forgive me for taking so much for granted. Turn my greed into gratefulness. Amen.

FEBRUARY 20

And the ravens brought him bread and meat in the morning, and bread and meat in the evening, and he drank from the brook.

1 Kings 17:6

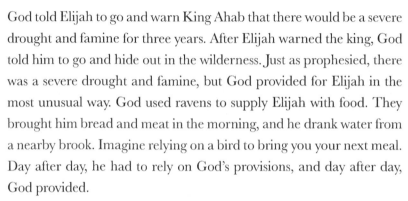

God told Elijah to go and warn King Ahab that there would be a severe drought and famine for three years. After Elijah warned the king, God told him to go and hide out in the wilderness. Just as prophesied, there was a severe drought and famine, but God provided for Elijah in the most unusual way. God used ravens to supply Elijah with food. They brought him bread and meat in the morning, and he drank water from a nearby brook. Imagine relying on a bird to bring you your next meal. Day after day, he had to rely on God's provisions, and day after day, God provided.

As I read this passage, I wonder how difficult it must have been for Elijah to hide out for three years. He was a prophet. I'm sure he wanted to be used by God and do big things, but God called him to remain in isolation. God used this season of silence and solitude to prepare Elijah for the next season of breakthrough and victory.

It can be frustrating when you find yourself on the sidelines and you feel like you should be doing more. Maybe God has you in the wilderness and you feel like you should be on the frontlines. If so, remember, God often uses seasons of silence and solitude to prepare for seasons of breakthrough and victory.

Lord, thank you for your perfect plan. Help me be obedient to you no matter where you call me. Give me the strength to be faithful in the wilderness and on the frontlines. Amen.

FEBRUARY 21

And Elijah came near to all the people and said, "How long will you go limping between two different opinions? If the Lord is God, follow him; but if Baal, then follow him." And the people did not answer him a word.

1 Kings 18:21

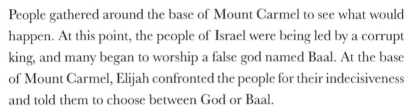

People gathered around the base of Mount Carmel to see what would happen. At this point, the people of Israel were being led by a corrupt king, and many began to worship a false god named Baal. At the base of Mount Carmel, Elijah confronted the people for their indecisiveness and told them to choose between God or Baal.

He then challenged the prophets of Baal to a showdown. The prophets of Baal would take a bull, build an altar, and then call on Baal to send fire. And then Elijah would do the same, but he would call on God to send the fire. There were 450 prophets of Baal and they tried from morning until noon, but despite their effort, nothing happened. Elijah took a bull, built an altar, and even drenched the altar in water so there wouldn't be any doubt. He called on God, and in the presence of all the people, God sent fire. The people fell on their faces before God and repented.

You may not worship a false god, but you can probably identify things in your life that are keeping you from wholeheartedly serving the Lord. Like the Israelites, maybe you're sitting on the fence. Maybe you're stuck somewhere between God and the things of this world. Now is the time to make a firm decision.

Lord, forgive me for my indecisiveness. Help me get off the fence and make a firm decision to follow you at all costs. Amen.

FEBRUARY 22

But he himself went a day's journey into the wilderness and came and sat down under a broom tree. And he asked that he might die, saying, "It is enough; now, O Lord, take away my life, for I am no better than my fathers."

1 Kings 19:4

At this point, Elijah was at the top of his game. His ministry was on fire. He had just defeated the prophets of Baal. The king and his wife, both worshipers of Baal, weren't too happy with Elijah. They wanted him dead, so Elijah went on the run. He went into the wilderness, where he found himself exhausted and depleted. Despite the recent victory, he felt defeated to the point that he no longer wanted to live. He pleaded with God and asked him to take his life. God sent an angel to instruct Elijah to eat and drink. In the wilderness, God provided Elijah with a cake to eat and water to drink. When he finished eating, he took a nap. The food and rest gave him the strength to press on.

Often, we run ourselves ragged, trying to keep up with the everyday demands of life. We must meet deadlines. We must get the kids to practices and after-school activities. We must attend meetings. We must further our careers and grow our businesses. Sometimes, in the process of pursuing our goals, we find ourselves exhausted and depleted.

Just because things are good doesn't mean you are good. Make sure you take care of yourself in the process. It's amazing what a little food and rest can do.

Lord, thank you for always providing. Help me take care of myself. Show me when I am doing too much and remind me to slow down and rest. Amen.

FEBRUARY 23

He said, "I have been very jealous for the Lord, the God of hosts. For the people of Israel have forsaken your covenant, thrown down your altars, and killed your prophets with the sword, and I, even I only, am left, and they seek my life, to take it away."

1 Kings 19:10

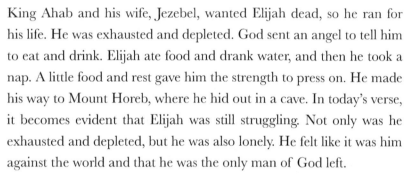

King Ahab and his wife, Jezebel, wanted Elijah dead, so he ran for his life. He was exhausted and depleted. God sent an angel to tell him to eat and drink. Elijah ate food and drank water, and then he took a nap. A little food and rest gave him the strength to press on. He made his way to Mount Horeb, where he hid out in a cave. In today's verse, it becomes evident that Elijah was still struggling. Not only was he exhausted and depleted, but he was also lonely. He felt like it was him against the world and that he was the only man of God left.

Elijah was so focused on the little picture that he was missing the bigger picture. He was so consumed by his immediate circumstance that it was taking an extreme toll on him. God appeared to Elijah and reminded him that he had a plan for his life and a plan for the Israelites.

Have you ever been so focused on the little picture that you missed the bigger picture? Have you ever been so consumed by your immediate circumstance that it took an extreme toll on you? Maybe that describes where you're at right now. If so, let me remind you that there is a bigger picture, and God still has a plan for your life.

Lord, thank you for always working behind the scenes. Give me strength when my circumstances take a toll on me. Help me stay focused on the bigger picture. Amen.

FEBRUARY 24

For everything there is a season, and a time for every matter under heaven.

Ecclesiastes 3:1

I am a bit of a neat freak. I like for things to be in order, and clutter gives me anxiety. When we started having kids, we started collecting a lot of items, and the house started getting cluttered beyond what I was comfortable with. In the common areas, there were baby swings, play mats, rolling toys, and the list goes on. Not only was the house a cluttered mess, but it became a full-time job trying to keep everything maintained. I still find fingerprints on the walls, crayon marks on the floors, and toys stuffed down the drains.

The messes drive me crazy, and it has been a major adjustment, but I'm slowly learning to be more patient. The reality is, one day, there won't be toys scattered all over the house, marks on the walls, and messes everywhere because one day, my kids will no longer be living under my roof. When that day comes, I know I will miss what I have now, so I will continue doing my best to embrace the chaos.

There is a season for everything. Some of those seasons may seem good, while others may seem bad, but seasons come and go. Try to embrace whatever season of life that you're in right now.

Lord, thank you for the good seasons and for the bad seasons. Instead of rushing through life, help me embrace whatever season I find myself in. Amen.

FEBRUARY 25

Now Sarai, Abram's wife, had borne him no children. She had a female Egyptian servant whose name was Hagar. And Sarai said to Abram, "Behold now, the Lord has prevented me from bearing children. Go in to my servant; it may be that I shall obtain children by her." And Abram listened to the voice of Sarai.

Genesis 16:1-2

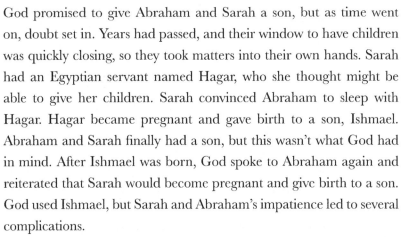

God promised to give Abraham and Sarah a son, but as time went on, doubt set in. Years had passed, and their window to have children was quickly closing, so they took matters into their own hands. Sarah had an Egyptian servant named Hagar, who she thought might be able to give her children. Sarah convinced Abraham to sleep with Hagar. Hagar became pregnant and gave birth to a son, Ishmael. Abraham and Sarah finally had a son, but this wasn't what God had in mind. After Ishmael was born, God spoke to Abraham again and reiterated that Sarah would become pregnant and give birth to a son. God used Ishmael, but Sarah and Abraham's impatience led to several complications.

Often, like Abraham and Sarah, we get impatient. When we can't see God visibly doing something, we assume he's doing nothing. We take matters into our own hands and try to speed God's plan along. This only leads to complications.

If God says it, you can trust it. It may not happen when or how you expect it, but rest assured, it will happen. Instead of taking matters into your own hands, be patient and wait on him.

Lord, thank you for always being true to your word. Forgive me for being impatient and taking matters into my own hands. Help me trust you and your timing. Amen.

FEBRUARY 26

He who dwells in the shelter of the Most High will abide in the shadow of the Almighty. I will say to the Lord, "My refuge and my fortress, my God, in whom I trust."

Psalm 91:1-2

In the area that we live in, we rarely get severe weather. Sure, we get thunderstorms and high winds, but we typically don't get much beyond that. Most people don't have a storm shelter or a safe room. So, on the rare occasion that we do get a tornado, everyone goes into panic mode. There is one family in our neighborhood that happens to have a well-built basement that has unintentionally become the neighborhood storm shelter. When there's a tornado warning, people usually run to this family's basement to take cover.

When the storms of life roll in, where do you run to take shelter? In today's passage, God invites you to take shelter in him. When tragedy strikes, you can take shelter in him. When you're scared and afraid, you can take shelter in him. When you're not sure how you're going to face tomorrow, you can take shelter in him. When your circumstances shake and stress you, you can take shelter in him. When everyone else goes into panic mode, you can take shelter in him.

The Lord is your refuge and strength, and you can always take shelter in him. When the storms of life roll in, you can find protection in his presence.

Lord, thank you for being my refuge and strength. When the storms of life come rolling in, help me remember to take shelter in you. Amen.

FEBRUARY 27

Do not lay up for yourselves treasures on earth, where moth and rust destroy and where thieves break in and steal, but lay up for yourselves treasures in heaven, where neither moth nor rust destroys and where thieves do not break in and steal.

Matthew 6:19-20

When I graduated college, I decided to reward myself with a new truck. It was everything I ever wanted. At least that's what I thought. I loved the truck, but I couldn't enjoy it. I was too concerned that I was going to mess it up. I didn't allow food or drink inside. I didn't haul anything in the bed. I washed it every week. I constantly checked it for scratches and imperfections. Long story short, I ended up selling that truck after owning it for less than two years. I took the money and bought a much older truck that I was able to use and enjoy without constantly worrying about scratches and imperfections. Here's the point: stuff rarely brings the satisfaction we expect.

In today's passage, Jesus is telling us not to waste our lives storing up treasure here on Earth. The cars, the houses, the clothes, they're all temporary. You can't take them with you, and they can all be taken away instantly. Earthly treasure can be lost in a fire or some kind of disaster. Someone could break into your house and steal your most valuable possessions. God forbid something could happen to you that could prevent you from enjoying the things you worked so hard to acquire.

Don't waste your life storing up treasure here on Earth. Instead, store up treasure in Heaven where it can't be destroyed or taken away. Remember, heavenly treasure is eternal.

Lord, thank you for the treasure that is awaiting me in Heaven. Help me stay focused on furthering your kingdom and keep me from being distracted by worldly things. Amen.

FEBRUARY 28

And he answered them, "Whoever has two tunics is to share with him who has none, and whoever has food is to do likewise."

Luke 3:11

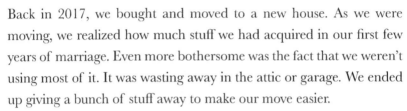

Back in 2017, we bought and moved to a new house. As we were moving, we realized how much stuff we had acquired in our first few years of marriage. Even more bothersome was the fact that we weren't using most of it. It was wasting away in the attic or garage. We ended up giving a bunch of stuff away to make our move easier.

Sadly, it didn't take long for us to re-acquire a bunch of stuff that we don't need. Our kids have hundreds of toys but only play with a handful. You can barely access our attic or park in our garage because they're so full of stuff. We have more than a few closets that can't be opened without an avalanche taking place. I'm convicted by the fact that I have stuff I'm not using that others could benefit from.

What about you? Do you have stuff wasting away that others could benefit from? If so, are you willing to do something about it? Maybe you clean out your closet and give some clothes to a local shelter, clothes closet, or family in need. Maybe you go through your kids' toys and give the unused ones to kids that aren't as blessed as yours. Maybe you have an extra vehicle that you could donate or loan to someone without transportation. Things that you don't use could be a blessing to someone else.

Lord, thank you for everything that you've given me. Help me use my possessions in ways that are pleasing to you. Show me what I need to give away. Amen.

MARCH 1

Therefore, if anyone is in Christ, he is a new creation. The old has passed away; behold, the new has come.

2 Corinthians 5:17

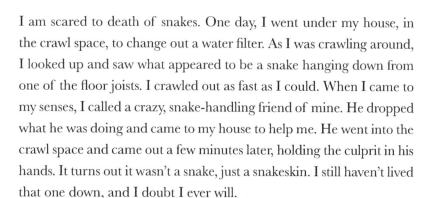

I am scared to death of snakes. One day, I went under my house, in the crawl space, to change out a water filter. As I was crawling around, I looked up and saw what appeared to be a snake hanging down from one of the floor joists. I crawled out as fast as I could. When I came to my senses, I called a crazy, snake-handling friend of mine. He dropped what he was doing and came to my house to help me. He went into the crawl space and came out a few minutes later, holding the culprit in his hands. It turns out it wasn't a snake, just a snakeskin. I still haven't lived that one down, and I doubt I ever will.

Snakes periodically shed their skin to allow for further growth and to remove any parasites that may have attached to their old skin. In that same way, as a believer, you must periodically shed your skin to become more like Christ.

Maybe there is something that needs to be removed from your life to allow for further growth. Maybe it's a secret sin that needs to be confessed and repented of. Maybe it's a relationship that is not pleasing to the Lord. Maybe it's a calendar that is so full that it's preventing you from fully doing what God wants you to do. Maybe it's something else. Is there any shedding you need to do?

Lord, thank you for making me a brand-new creation. Show me if there is any shedding that I need to do. Help me get rid of things that keep me from giving you my all. Amen.

MARCH 2

Then Jacob gave Esau bread and lentil stew, and he ate and drank and rose and went his way. Thus Esau despised his birthright.

Genesis 25:34

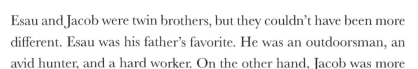

Esau and Jacob were twin brothers, but they couldn't have been more different. Esau was his father's favorite. He was an outdoorsman, an avid hunter, and a hard worker. On the other hand, Jacob was more of a mama's boy. He hung around the house and spent his time in the kitchen.

One day, Esau came in from the field and was hungry. Coincidentally, Jacob was cooking up a pot of lentil stew. Esau asked for some of the stew, and Jacob agreed to give him some on the condition that Esau sold him his birthright. The birthright entitled Esau to a double portion of his father's inheritance. Esau foolishly agreed and sold his birthright to his brother for a bowl of lentil stew.

It's easy to read this story and judge Esau harshly, but how often do you do the same thing? How often do you sacrifice what you want most for what you want now? You delay retirement a few years so you can drive that new car. You turn your back on God for just a moment of pleasure. You damage a significant relationship just to make a point. One of the most difficult parts of following Jesus is learning to say NO to instant gratification so that you can say YES to him. Don't make the foolish mistake of sacrificing what you want most for what you want now.

Lord, thank you for everything you have blessed me with. Help me be wise and choose what I want most over what I want now. Amen.

MARCH 3

Now as he went on his way, he approached Damascus, and suddenly a light from heaven shone around him. And falling to the ground, he heard a voice saying to him, "Saul, Saul, why are you persecuting me?"

Acts 9:3-4

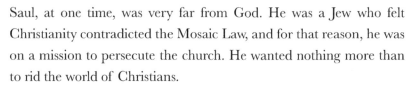

Saul, at one time, was very far from God. He was a Jew who felt Christianity contradicted the Mosaic Law, and for that reason, he was on a mission to persecute the church. He wanted nothing more than to rid the world of Christians.

In Acts 9, Saul went to the high priest and got permission to arrest and extradite back to Jerusalem any followers of Jesus that he found in Damascus. However, on his way to Damascus, a great light came down from Heaven. Saul fell to the ground and heard a voice saying, "Saul, Saul, why are you persecuting me?" Long story short, this encounter with the Lord forever changed his life. Saul, whose name was changed to Paul, made a complete 180. He went from persecuting the church to proclaiming Christ. He went on to preach the gospel, build the church, and write the majority of the New Testament. He goes down in history as one of the most influential Christians of all time.

Paul's story is proof: it's not the way you start that is most important. It's the way you finish. You may be ashamed of your past, but there's good news: if you're not dead, God's not done. He has a plan for your life, and in him, the best is always yet to come.

Lord, thank you for having a plan for my life. Forgive me for the mistakes that I've made. Help me get past my shame and finish strong. Amen.

MARCH 4

Strive for peace with everyone, and for the holiness without which no one will see the Lord. See to it that no one fails to obtain the grace of God; that no "root of bitterness" springs up and causes trouble, and by it many become defiled.

Hebrews 12:14-15

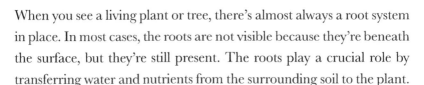

When you see a living plant or tree, there's almost always a root system in place. In most cases, the roots are not visible because they're beneath the surface, but they're still present. The roots play a crucial role by transferring water and nutrients from the surrounding soil to the plant. The reality is that without roots, a plant cannot have life.

Paul describes bitterness as a root. Often, we fail to recognize bitterness in our own lives and the lives of others because the roots of bitterness lie beneath the surface. The roots of bitterness absorb life from you and give life to things like anger and resentment.

If you're a Christian, bitterness affects your relationship with God. If you're married, bitterness affects your relationship with your spouse. If you're a parent, bitterness affects your relationship with your children. Bitterness not only affects you but every person you encounter.

You can't control what other people do, but you can control how you respond. You can allow bitterness to take root. You can harbor anger and resentment. You can allow it to affect every relationship in your life, or as difficult as it may be, you can choose to forgive.

Lord, thank you for the way you have forgiven me. Help me extend that same mercy to others. Show me if bitterness has taken root in my life. Amen.

MARCH 5

My brothers, show no partiality as you hold the faith in our Lord Jesus Christ, the Lord of glory.

James 2:1

We almost always have wrestling (not the fake stuff) on the TV at our house. My oldest son and I enjoy taking turns picking who we think will win the match before it gets started. Keep in mind, we have never seen most of these kids wrestle, so our picks are based solely on appearance. I usually pick the one with the better physique, the one that appears to be more confident, or the one with the sleeker-looking uniform. After witnessing a lot of my picks lose, I've come to realize that what they say is true, "You can't judge a book by the cover."

In today's verse, James instructs us to show no partiality. If you encounter a wealthy person, you should welcome them. If you encounter a homeless person, you should welcome them. People shouldn't be treated differently because of their appearance, race, standing, or status. Regardless of what a person looks like, they were created in the image of God. Regardless of what a person has or has not accomplished, they deserve to be respected and valued.

Are you treating all people with respect, or are you showing partiality? Are you viewing people through a biblical lens or a worldly lens? Remember, you can't judge a book by its cover.

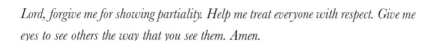

Lord, forgive me for showing partiality. Help me treat everyone with respect. Give me eyes to see others the way that you see them. Amen.

MARCH 6

And the Spirit said to Philip, "Go over and join this chariot."

Acts 8:29

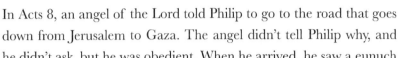

In Acts 8, an angel of the Lord told Philip to go to the road that goes down from Jerusalem to Gaza. The angel didn't tell Philip why, and he didn't ask, but he was obedient. When he arrived, he saw a eunuch sitting in his chariot, reading from the prophet Isaiah. The Holy Spirit told Philip to go over and join the man in his chariot, so he went.

Philip asked the man if he understood what he was reading. The man said no, and Philip took the time to explain it. Philip shared the gospel with him. The man surrendered his life to Jesus and was immediately baptized. Philip was open to the leading of the Holy Spirit. As a result, God used him to make a significant difference in someone's life.

Are you open to the leading of the Holy Spirit? If the Holy Spirit leads you to do something, are you willing to do it, even if it means going out of your way? Are you willing to drop everything, no questions asked, to move forward in obedience? If you obey and follow the directions of the Holy Spirit, like Philip, God will use you to make a significant difference.

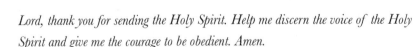

Lord, thank you for sending the Holy Spirit. Help me discern the voice of the Holy Spirit and give me the courage to be obedient. Amen.

MARCH 7

And he said to him, "You shall love the Lord your God with all your heart and with all your soul and with all your mind. This is the great and first commandment. And a second is like it: You shall love your neighbor as yourself."

Matthew 22:37-39

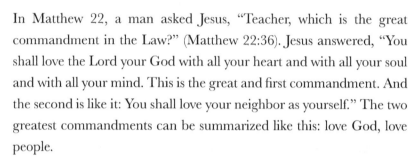

In Matthew 22, a man asked Jesus, "Teacher, which is the great commandment in the Law?" (Matthew 22:36). Jesus answered, "You shall love the Lord your God with all your heart and with all your soul and with all your mind. This is the great and first commandment. And the second is like it: You shall love your neighbor as yourself." The two greatest commandments can be summarized like this: love God, love people.

If I were to conduct a survey and ask Christians the following question: what is the best way to reach people with the gospel? I'm sure I would receive a variety of answers. Some would probably say the best way to reach people with the gospel is to invite them to church. Some would probably say the best way to reach people with the gospel is by handing out gospel tracts. Some would probably say the best way to reach people with the gospel is through the power of the internet. All of those might be effective, but the Bible tells us the best way to reach people with the gospel is by loving God and loving people.

It doesn't matter who you are, how educated you are, or what you do for a living. Today, you can make a difference. You can reach people with the gospel by simply loving God and loving people.

Lord, thank you for loving me. Help me love you and people. Give me an opportunity today to serve someone in need. Amen.

MARCH 8

The simple believes everything, but the prudent gives thought to his steps.

Proverbs 14:15

When I was in college, my roommate and I were workout partners. We were both on the skinnier side, and our goal was to put on size. I read on the internet about an unconventional way to put on muscle mass, and I was intrigued. What I stumbled across was the GOMAD diet. GOMAD is an acronym that stands for "gallon of milk a day."

We went out and bought as many gallons of milk as we could fit in our fridge. We made it through the first couple of days, but it was challenging. We pressed on and made it through the first week before abandoning the plan all together. Unfortunately, we didn't put on any noticeable muscle mass. Instead, we felt bloated and had little appetite, and without going into detail, we spent a lot of time in the restroom.

Unfortunately, you can't believe everything that you hear or read. There are so many teachings, beliefs, rumors, and crazy ideas out there that will lead you astray. If there was ever a time when God's people needed discernment, that time is now. Fortunately, he has given you his Word as a measuring stick. As the world changes and conforms, his Word remains the same. If it doesn't align with his Word, don't believe it.

Lord, thank you for your Word. Help me use your Word as a measuring stick. Give me discernment as I seek to know what to believe. Amen.

MARCH 9

Set a guard, O Lord, over my mouth; keep watch over the door of my lips!

Psalm 141:3

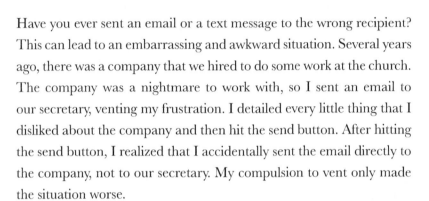

Have you ever sent an email or a text message to the wrong recipient? This can lead to an embarrassing and awkward situation. Several years ago, there was a company that we hired to do some work at the church. The company was a nightmare to work with, so I sent an email to our secretary, venting my frustration. I detailed every little thing that I disliked about the company and then hit the send button. After hitting the send button, I realized that I accidentally sent the email directly to the company, not to our secretary. My compulsion to vent only made the situation worse.

In the age of technology, not only do you need to be careful about what you say but also about what you type. The messages you send and the posts you make are impactful. They can lift others up, or they can tear others down.

Regardless of the intended recipient, God sees and hears it all. If sending something to the wrong recipient would lead to an embarrassing and awkward situation, it's probably best not to send it to any recipient. Before saying or typing anything, ask yourself, "Is this pleasing and honoring to God?"

Lord, forgive me for saying and typing things that I shouldn't. Help me understand the impact of my words and honor you with the things that I say and type. Amen.

MARCH 10

If I then, your Lord and Teacher, have washed your feet, you also ought to wash one another's feet.

John 13:14

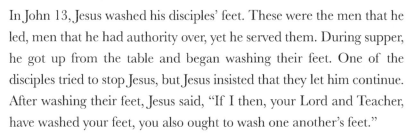

In John 13, Jesus washed his disciples' feet. These were the men that he led, men that he had authority over, yet he served them. During supper, he got up from the table and began washing their feet. One of the disciples tried to stop Jesus, but Jesus insisted that they let him continue. After washing their feet, Jesus said, "If I then, your Lord and Teacher, have washed your feet, you also ought to wash one another's feet."

Jesus, the perfect Savior of the world, humbled himself and washed feet. He gave all his followers an example to follow. The way that Jesus lived is quite different from how most live today. Many don't want to serve, they want to be served, but Jesus lived a life of servanthood. The world tells us that we're blessed by how much we have, but Jesus shows us that we're blessed by how well we serve.

Regardless of what position you hold on this Earth, if you are a follower of Jesus, you are called to humble yourself and serve others. You're called to wash feet. So, here's the big question: Are you living a life of servanthood?

Lord, thank you for giving me an example to follow. Help me follow your example, humble myself, and serve others. Amen.

MARCH 11

Now there was in Joppa a disciple named Tabitha, which, translated, means Dorcas. She was full of good works and acts of charity.

Acts 9:36

Tabitha, also known as Dorcas, is often overlooked in the scriptures, but her story comes with many valuable lessons. When we're introduced to her, we immediately learn what kind of person she was, "She was full of good works and acts of charity." She was a seamstress who used her talent to help others and make a difference within her community. In Acts 9, she passed away and everyone was gathered around, mourning her loss and remembering the difference that she made. Peter showed up and prayed for her, and miraculously, she rose from the dead. As a result of her resurrection, many believed in Jesus.

What I love about Dorcas is how she used something small to make a big difference. She found a way to use what she had to serve others and further God's kingdom. She simply made clothing for the widows and the poor.

You don't need to do something extravagant to serve others and further God's kingdom. You just need to find a way to leverage what you're already doing. Instead of looking to acquire something you don't have, ask how you can be faithful with what you do have. Remember, God often uses small things to make a big difference.

Lord, thank you for all that you have given me. Show me how I can leverage the gifts that you've given me to serve others and further your kingdom. Amen.

MARCH 12

So he went down and dipped himself seven times in the Jordan, according to the word of the man of God, and his flesh was restored like the flesh of a little child, and he was clean.

2 *Kings* 5:14

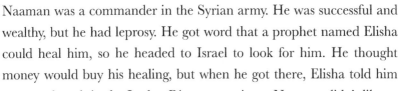

Naaman was a commander in the Syrian army. He was successful and wealthy, but he had leprosy. He got word that a prophet named Elisha could heal him, so he headed to Israel to look for him. He thought money would buy his healing, but when he got there, Elisha told him to go and wash in the Jordan River seven times. Naaman didn't like or understand Elisha's proposal. He was furious and stormed off in a rage.

Eventually, those with Naaman convinced him to go and do what Elisha instructed him to do. He went and washed in the Jordan River, and he was healed. Naaman went back to Elisha and tried to pay him for the healing, but Elisha refused to take payment for what God did.

God's blessings cost nothing, but sometimes they do require obedience. There will be times when you expect things to play out a certain way, but God has something different in mind. Naaman expected Elisha to come out, wave his hand, and heal his leprosy for a fee. God, through Elisha, told him to go and wash in the Jordan River seven times. Here's the takeaway: you should obey God's Word, even when you don't understand it.

Lord, thank you for your Word. Help me obey your Word, even when I don't understand it. Help me trust your plan, even when it seems irrational. Amen.

MARCH 13

"Therefore the leprosy of Naaman shall cling to you and to your descendants forever." So he went out from his presence a leper, like snow.

2 *Kings* 5:27

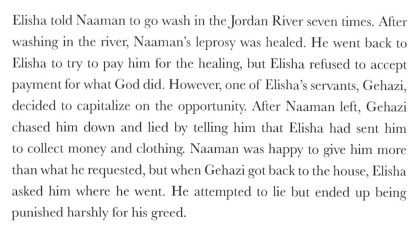

Elisha told Naaman to go wash in the Jordan River seven times. After washing in the river, Naaman's leprosy was healed. He went back to Elisha to try to pay him for the healing, but Elisha refused to accept payment for what God did. However, one of Elisha's servants, Gehazi, decided to capitalize on the opportunity. After Naaman left, Gehazi chased him down and lied by telling him that Elisha had sent him to collect money and clothing. Naaman was happy to give him more than what he requested, but when Gehazi got back to the house, Elisha asked him where he went. He attempted to lie but ended up being punished harshly for his greed.

Gehazi witnessed God perform a miracle right before his eyes. He witnessed God instantaneously heal a man from a terrible disease, but all he could think about was money. He took what should have been an opportunity to glorify God and used it to pad his own pockets.

Scripture makes it clear that greed is one of the most common things that separates people from God. Take some time today to evaluate the intentions of your heart, and ask God to forgive you for any greed you may find.

Lord, thank you for your mercy. Forgive me for my greed. Help me place less emphasis on stuff and more emphasis on you. Amen.

MARCH 14

Immediately the father of the child cried out and said, "I believe; help my unbelief!"

Mark 9:24

In Mark 9, there's a story about a man who had a demon-possessed son. He took his son to the disciples, but they were unable to cast the demon out. In a last-ditch effort to get his son help, he went directly to Jesus. He told Jesus that the disciples were unable to cast the demon out and asked Jesus to do what he could.

Jesus explained to the man that nothing is impossible for those who believe, and that's when the man cried out, "I believe; help my unbelief." This man wanted to believe, and there was a part of him that clearly did, but there was another part of him that was struggling with doubt. Jesus went on to help this man's unbelief by doing what no one else could do and healing his son.

There will be times in life when you find yourself in a similar situation. Times when there's a part of you that believes, but there's another part of you that is struggling with doubt. When those times come, it's best to be honest with God. If you are lacking faith, ask him to give you more faith. Like the man in Mark 9, don't hesitate to ask him to help your unbelief.

Lord, thank you for giving me everything I need. Forgive me for my imperfect faith. Help my unbelief and give me the faith to trust you. Amen.

MARCH 15

And my God will supply every need of yours according to his riches in glory in Christ Jesus.

Philippians 4:19

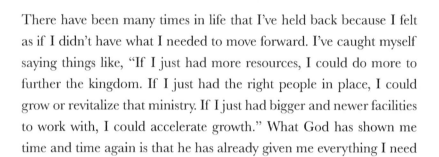

There have been many times in life that I've held back because I felt as if I didn't have what I needed to move forward. I've caught myself saying things like, "If I just had more resources, I could do more to further the kingdom. If I just had the right people in place, I could grow or revitalize that ministry. If I just had bigger and newer facilities to work with, I could accelerate growth." What God has shown me time and time again is that he has already given me everything I need to do everything I am supposed to do.

Maybe you can relate. Maybe there is something you feel you need to do, something you feel God wants you to do, but you also feel like you're missing something. You feel as if you don't have the talent, resources, time, or finances. Maybe you've been putting it off and telling yourself that you'll proceed whenever you have the missing piece to the puzzle.

The truth is, right now, you have everything you need to do everything you're supposed to do. Maybe it's time to stop focusing on what you're missing and start focusing on what he has already provided.

Lord, thank you for supplying my needs. Help me use what you have given me to do what you've called me to do. Show me when I am making excuses. Amen.

MARCH 16

Let both grow together until the harvest, and at harvest time I will tell the reapers, "Gather the weeds first and bind them in bundles to be burned, but gather the wheat into my barn."

Matthew 13:30

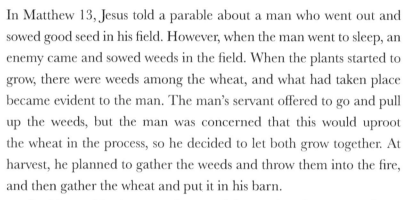

In Matthew 13, Jesus told a parable about a man who went out and sowed good seed in his field. However, when the man went to sleep, an enemy came and sowed weeds in the field. When the plants started to grow, there were weeds among the wheat, and what had taken place became evident to the man. The man's servant offered to go and pull up the weeds, but the man was concerned that this would uproot the wheat in the process, so he decided to let both grow together. At harvest, he planned to gather the weeds and throw them into the fire, and then gather the wheat and put it in his barn.

In this parable, the man who sowed the good seed represents Jesus, the enemy who sowed the weeds represents the devil, and the field represents the world. In this world, there is both good and bad. The gospel is being preached and people are coming to know Jesus, but the enemy is also at work. His mission is to sabotage the work of Christ.

There will come a day, harvest time, when Jesus will separate the weeds from the wheat. Unbelievers will be thrown into Hell, while believers will go to Heaven. This parable should challenge those that don't have a relationship with Jesus and encourage those that do.

Lord, thank you for your saving grace. Thank you for sowing good seed. I look forward to spending an eternity in Heaven with you. Amen.

MARCH 17

Even though I walk through the valley of the shadow of death, I will fear no evil,
for you are with me; your rod and your staff, they comfort me.

Psalm 23:4

In Psalm 23, the Lord is compared to a shepherd. A good shepherd provides for and protects his sheep at all costs. In that same way, the Lord provides for and protects his children at all costs. He provides his children with everything that they need. He provides them with contentment, peace, restoration, and guidance. He knows their needs before they know their needs. Also, like a good shepherd, he is willing to lay down his life to protect his children. He proved this on the cross when he took the punishment we deserved. He took our place on the cross to protect us from the consequences of our sin.

This is an encouraging chapter of scripture that should give God's children assurance as they navigate through life. However, it's important to note that God doesn't promise to always keep us from sorrow, but he does promise to be with us in the middle of it.

Maybe you find yourself facing a circumstance that seems impossible. Maybe you feel as if the world is crashing down on you. Maybe you are walking through the valley of the shadow of death. If so, let me remind you that he is with you. His rod and staff are there to comfort you.

Lord, thank you for being the Good Shepherd. Thank you for providing for me
and protecting me at all costs. Help me trust you in the valley of the shadow of
death. Amen.

MARCH 18

But his delight is in the law of the Lord, and on his law he meditates day and night. He is like a tree planted by streams of water that yields its fruit in its season, and its leaf does not wither. In all that he does, he prospers.

Psalm 1:2-3

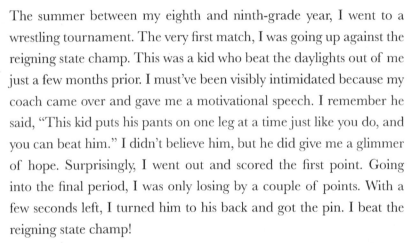

The summer between my eighth and ninth-grade year, I went to a wrestling tournament. The very first match, I was going up against the reigning state champ. This was a kid who beat the daylights out of me just a few months prior. I must've been visibly intimidated because my coach came over and gave me a motivational speech. I remember he said, "This kid puts his pants on one leg at a time just like you do, and you can beat him." I didn't believe him, but he did give me a glimmer of hope. Surprisingly, I went out and scored the first point. Going into the final period, I was only losing by a couple of points. With a few seconds left, I turned him to his back and got the pin. I beat the reigning state champ!

An inspired person is a dangerous person, in a good way. When I am inspired to write a message, to work on a project, or to get in shape, I see results. Inspiration enables and equips me to operate at a level I otherwise wouldn't be able to operate at.

Where can you find inspiration to live out your faith and live your life to the fullest? The Bible. Devotions, like this one, are a great tool but no substitute for God's Word. Are you reading his Word on a daily basis? If not, will you make a commitment to get started today?

Lord, thank you for your Word. Help me be more intentional about reading my Bible on a daily basis. Amen.

MARCH 19

Jesus said to him, "Have you believed because you have seen me? Blessed are those who have not seen and yet have believed."

John 20:29

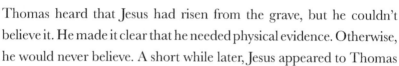

Thomas heard that Jesus had risen from the grave, but he couldn't believe it. He made it clear that he needed physical evidence. Otherwise, he would never believe. A short while later, Jesus appeared to Thomas and gave him the physical evidence he requested. Thomas believed, and Jesus said, "Have you believed because you have seen me? Blessed are those who have not seen and yet have believed."

As I read through the Gospels, I can't help but imagine what it must've been like living during those days. Truthfully, I wish I could have experienced what Jesus's disciples experienced. I can only imagine what it must've been like to witness him heal the sick, give sight to the blind, and bring people back to life. It must've been incredible to witness Jesus in the flesh, but he tells us that there will be a greater blessing waiting for those who have not seen him and yet have believed.

When life gets difficult, choose to believe. When tragedy strikes, choose to believe. When God seems distant, choose to believe. When you don't understand, choose to believe. When it's easier said than done, choose to believe. Even when you can't see it, choose to believe and you will be blessed.

Lord, thank you for being present, even when I can't see you. Help me believe, regardless of what's going on around me. Amen.

MARCH 20

And the peace of God, which surpasses all understanding, will guard your hearts and your minds in Christ Jesus.

Philippians 4:7

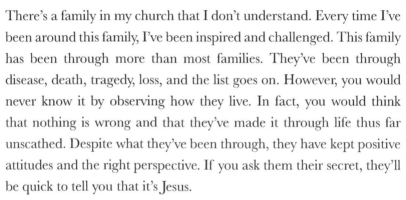

There's a family in my church that I don't understand. Every time I've been around this family, I've been inspired and challenged. This family has been through more than most families. They've been through disease, death, tragedy, loss, and the list goes on. However, you would never know it by observing how they live. In fact, you would think that nothing is wrong and that they've made it through life thus far unscathed. Despite what they've been through, they have kept positive attitudes and the right perspective. If you ask them their secret, they'll be quick to tell you that it's Jesus.

The peace of God is unexplainable. It doesn't make any sense. When a person should panic, instead, they worship. When a person should give up, instead, they persevere. When a person should grow angry and bitter, instead, they get better. God's peace surpasses all understanding, and it is promised to those who give their concerns and worries to him.

Maybe you're in the midst of a challenging season. Maybe you're facing disease, death, tragedy, or loss. Maybe you feel like everything is falling apart and you don't know where to turn. If so, let me encourage you to turn to God and allow his peace to guard your heart and mind.

Lord, thank you for your peace. I trust you with my concerns and worries. Fill me with your peace that surpasses all understanding. Amen.

MARCH 21

Faithful are the wounds of a friend; profuse are the kisses of an enemy.

Proverbs 27:6

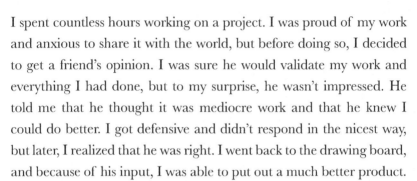

I spent countless hours working on a project. I was proud of my work and anxious to share it with the world, but before doing so, I decided to get a friend's opinion. I was sure he would validate my work and everything I had done, but to my surprise, he wasn't impressed. He told me that he thought it was mediocre work and that he knew I could do better. I got defensive and didn't respond in the nicest way, but later, I realized that he was right. I went back to the drawing board, and because of his input, I was able to put out a much better product.

We are called to love others, but what exactly does that mean? True love is not avoiding the truth. True love is not supporting others as they make bad decisions. True love is not condoning behavior when it's contrary to the Bible. True love is embracing the uncomfortable. True love is speaking the truth. True love is telling others what they need to hear, even when it's not what they want to hear.

Today's verse has a couple points of application. First, surround yourself with people who will tell you the truth in a loving way. Second, make sure you extend that same love to others.

Lord, thank you for my friends. Place people in my life who will tell me what I need to hear and give me the courage to do the same for others. Amen.

MARCH 22

The thief comes only to steal and kill and destroy. I came that they may have life and have it abundantly.

John 10:10

Over the years, I've been on many trips with different groups of people from our church. I'm convinced there are two types of people: under-packers and over-packers. Under-packers show up with the clothes on their back and a few necessities. Over-packers have a bag for every day of the week. Under-packers always forget things like their toothbrush, phone charger, or bathing suit. Over-packers bring three of everything, just in case of an apocalypse.

Throughout life, we all tend to pick up baggage, not physical baggage, but emotional and spiritual baggage. Baggage that weighs us down, holds us captive, and prevents us from living the abundant life Jesus died for us to live.

What kind of baggage are you carrying? Maybe a traumatic event from your past has left deep scars. Maybe something was done to you and you're holding on to bitterness. Maybe you made a mistake and you're struggling to forgive yourself. Maybe you failed and you can't seem to move forward. Maybe there's a sin or addiction in your life that you can't seem to beat. Regardless of what baggage you're carrying, God can lighten your load. Trust in him and begin to live the abundant life he died for you to live.

Lord, thank you for abundant life. Show me what's preventing me from living the life you died for me to live. Help me get rid of any baggage I may be carrying. Amen.

MARCH 23

Submit yourselves therefore to God. Resist the devil, and he will flee from you.

James 4:7

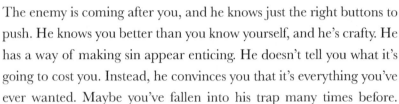

The enemy is coming after you, and he knows just the right buttons to push. He knows you better than you know yourself, and he's crafty. He has a way of making sin appear enticing. He doesn't tell you what it's going to cost you. Instead, he convinces you that it's everything you've ever wanted. Maybe you've fallen into his trap many times before. Perhaps it seems as if you'll never overcome whatever you may be struggling with. The devil is persistent, but the Bible says that if you resist him, he will flee from you.

James starts by instructing us, "Submit yourselves therefore to God." Before we can even begin to resist the devil, we must submit ourselves to God. As we submit to God, we will naturally become more resistant to the attacks of the enemy. Jesus gave us the perfect example in the wilderness. At the beginning of his public ministry, Jesus was tempted three times by the devil. Each time Jesus submitted to God and resisted temptation, and eventually, the devil fled from him.

As difficult as it may seem, because of Christ, you have the power to be victorious over the sin in your life. So, don't give up. Keep fighting, resist the devil, and eventually, he will flee from you.

Lord, thank you for giving me the power to be victorious over sin. Help me fight and resist the devil. Show me when I'm not submitting to you. Amen.

MARCH 24

I tell you, this man went down to his house justified, rather than the other. For everyone who exalts himself will be humbled, but the one who humbles himself will be exalted.

Luke 18:14

In Luke 18, Jesus tells a parable about a Pharisee and a tax collector. Pharisees were educated and religious. They were well-liked and respected. Tax collectors were considered scum. They were despised and hated by most.

A Pharisee and a tax collector both went to the temple to pray. The Pharisee prayed, "God, I thank you that I am not like other men, extortioners, unjust, adulterers, or even like this tax collector" (Luke 18:11). On the other hand, the tax collector would not even look up toward Heaven. He was clearly ashamed and simply prayed, "God, be merciful to me, a sinner!" (Luke 18:13). Jesus went on to say the tax collector, and not the Pharisee, is the one that went home justified. It wasn't the one that studied the law and did the right things. It was the one who was humble enough to see his need for God.

Spiritual pride is an easy trap to fall into. It's easy to pat yourself on the back for how much you give, how many hours you serve, or how many people you lead to Christ. This is what the enemy wants and something all Christians should be on guard against. Remember, those who exalt themselves will be humbled, but those who humble themselves will be exalted.

Lord, thank you for being merciful to me, a sinner. Forgive me for the times I have fallen into the trap of spiritual pride. Help me walk in humility going forward. Amen.

MARCH 25

Let another praise you, and not your own mouth; a stranger, and not your own lips.

Proverbs 27:2

I've conducted a few interviews over the years. I always ask the most common interview question: "What's your greatest strength, and what's your greatest weakness?" With few exceptions, the candidate almost always gives an elaborate answer about their greatest strength, but then beats around the bush when it comes to their greatest weakness. The bottom line is that we all like to talk about our strengths, and we like to avoid talking about our weaknesses.

We want to promote ourselves. We want others to be aware of what we've accomplished. We want others to be impressed by our achievements. We want others to envy our success. Often, we look for opportunities to talk about ourselves and interject our self-praise where we see fit. Some may even stretch the truth to make themselves sound better than they really are. This desire to promote ourselves is rooted in arrogance and insecurity, neither of which are pleasing to God.

In today's verse, the psalmist tells us, "Let another praise you, and not your own mouth." In other words, stop tooting your own horn. If you are doing something worthwhile, others will take notice. Let them be the ones to praise you, and resist the urge to praise yourself.

Lord, forgive me for praising myself. I am nothing without you and everything I've accomplished is because of you. Help me stop tooting my own horn. Amen.

MARCH 26

Good sense makes one slow to anger, and it is his glory to overlook an offense.

Proverbs 19:11

During football season, there is always a lot of chatter from the sidelines. People who were third string on their high school team criticize how the D1 coach leads the team. Fans are upset because the team they cheer for isn't winning. They may voice that someone on the bench should be starting, or that one of the coaches should be fired, or they complain about the calls the referee makes. It's easy to talk from the bleachers. It's another thing to be on the field.

In life, there will be a lot of chatter from the sidelines. No matter what you do, there will be someone that doesn't like it. It's funny because the ones that talk the most are usually those who know the least. The ones that want to tell you how to do your job are usually the ones that have never done your job. The ones that want to tell you how to navigate that challenge are usually the ones that have never faced that challenge. If you're going to go far, you must learn to ignore the noise.

It's important to take advice and be open to feedback from others but know who's for you and who's against you. Rather than taking offense at every little thing, let some things go in one ear and out the other.

Lord, thank you for putting me where I am. Give me wisdom as I strive to do what you have created me to do. Help me ignore the noise and seek your voice. Amen.

MARCH 27

And a young man named Eutychus, sitting at the window, sank into a deep sleep as Paul talked still longer. And being overcome by sleep, he fell down from the third story and was taken up dead.

Acts 20:9

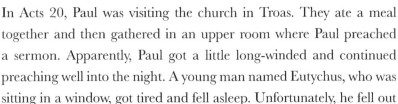

In Acts 20, Paul was visiting the church in Troas. They ate a meal together and then gathered in an upper room where Paul preached a sermon. Apparently, Paul got a little long-winded and continued preaching well into the night. A young man named Eutychus, who was sitting in a window, got tired and fell asleep. Unfortunately, he fell out of the window and to his death. Paul went downstairs and took him by the hand, and miraculously, he came back to life.

While it's probably not a good idea to sit in a second-story window or to fall asleep during a sermon, that's not what's at the root of this passage. This story is less about Eutychus's poor judgment and more about God's incredible power. God reversed what should have been a tragedy and used it to bring about a miracle. He took what should have shaken a church and used it to grow a church. He took what should have taken a man's life and used it to shape a man's life.

God is all-powerful. He can use anything to bring about good. He can even use your poor judgment for your good and his glory.

Lord, thank you for your incredible power. Thank you for shaping me into the person that I am. I give you all the praise, glory, and honor. Amen.

MARCH 28

Cain spoke to Abel his brother. And when they were in the field, Cain rose up against his brother Abel and killed him.

Genesis 4:8

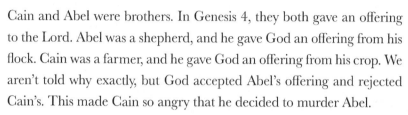

Cain and Abel were brothers. In Genesis 4, they both gave an offering to the Lord. Abel was a shepherd, and he gave God an offering from his flock. Cain was a farmer, and he gave God an offering from his crop. We aren't told why exactly, but God accepted Abel's offering and rejected Cain's. This made Cain so angry that he decided to murder Abel.

Why did God accept Abel's offering but reject Cain's? Perhaps it was because Abel gave the best of his flock, and Cain only gave some of his crops. Since the Bible doesn't tell us, we can only speculate. However, the Bible does tell us that God cares more about what's going on internally than externally. With that in mind, the issue seems to be less about what they offered and more about how they offered it. God was more concerned with how they gave than with what they gave. Abel gave with the right heart and attitude, while Cain gave with the wrong heart and attitude.

This story proves that it's not just your actions but also your attitude that matters to God. You can do the right things with the wrong attitude. You can serve your church and community with the wrong attitude. You can give to the poor with the wrong attitude. You can read your Bible with the wrong attitude. Take some time today to check your attitude.

Lord, forgive me for the times that I've had the wrong attitude. From this point forward, help me serve you with the right heart and attitude. Amen.

MARCH 29

And I will put my Spirit within you, and you shall live, and I will place you in your own land. Then you shall know that I am the Lord; I have spoken, and I will do it, declares the Lord.

Ezekiel 37:14

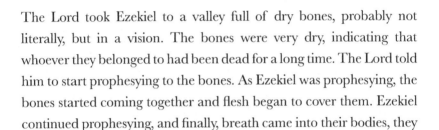

The Lord took Ezekiel to a valley full of dry bones, probably not literally, but in a vision. The bones were very dry, indicating that whoever they belonged to had been dead for a long time. The Lord told him to start prophesying to the bones. As Ezekiel was prophesying, the bones started coming together and flesh began to cover them. Ezekiel continued prophesying, and finally, breath came into their bodies, they came alive, and they stood up to their feet.

God told Ezekiel that the bones represented the whole house of Israel. At this time, Israel was a defeated nation; they had been crushed, and from an earthly perspective, they were as good as dead. It appeared as if there was no hope, but God promised to give them new life. Just as God gave life to the dried-up bones in the valley, God would give life to the Israelites.

We serve a God that can give life to bones. There's always hope in him. There's no person he can't save. There's no circumstance he can't change. There's no obstacle he can't overcome. No matter how hopeless your situation might seem, remember, there's hope in Jesus Christ.

Lord, thank you for hope. Help me trust you and keep the faith, even when I find myself in situations where it seems there is no hope. Amen.

MARCH 30

For we brought nothing into the world, and we cannot take anything out of the world. But if we have food and clothing, with these we will be content.

1 Timothy 6:7-8

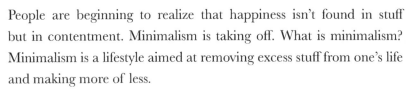

People are beginning to realize that happiness isn't found in stuff but in contentment. Minimalism is taking off. What is minimalism? Minimalism is a lifestyle aimed at removing excess stuff from one's life and making more of less.

Often, we believe the lie that contentment will come with the next big purchase or life-altering event. Have you ever thought, "I will be content when _____." Fill in the blank. I will be content when I get that promotion. I will be content when I buy that land or property. I will be content when I get that degree. I will be content when I save a certain amount of money. I will be content when I reach that goal or milestone. We believe that lie, but the truth is that contentment is not something you chase but a choice that you make.

What if I told you that you can be content right now, where you are, with what you have? Well, you can be, but you must make a choice. You can continue acquiring more stuff and looking for contentment in possessions. You can continue believing that contentment will come when you reach a certain place in life. Or you can recognize that contentment will come as soon as you make the choice to be content.

Lord, forgive me for always chasing the next thing. Help me choose contentment and acknowledge how blessed I already am. Amen.

MARCH 31

Behold, to the Lord your God belong heaven and the heaven of heavens, the earth with all that is in it.

Deuteronomy 10:14

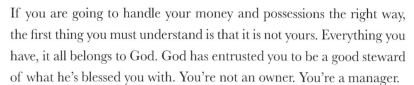

If you are going to handle your money and possessions the right way, the first thing you must understand is that it is not yours. Everything you have, it all belongs to God. God has entrusted you to be a good steward of what he's blessed you with. You're not an owner. You're a manager.

It's not your house. It's his house. It's not your property. It's his property. It's not your car. It's his car. It's not your money. It's his money. When you begin to understand this, there is a mental shift that will take place. You'll stop seeing what you have as simply things for you to enjoy, and you'll start seeing what you have as tools to further the kingdom.

I know a couple that has a goal of meeting with a certain number of ministry leaders around their dining room table each year. They use the home God has entrusted them with as a tool to further the kingdom. I know people who regularly loan out a spare vehicle to people who need transportation. They recognize that it's not theirs, it's his, and they use it to bless others. I know people who give generously to so many worthy causes. They use the money God has entrusted them with to bless others financially. What can you start doing today to be a better steward of what he's entrusted you with?

Lord, thank you for entrusting me with so many good things. Help me be a better steward and use what I have to further your kingdom. Amen.

APRIL 1

And Zacchaeus stood and said to the Lord, "Behold, Lord, the half of my goods I give to the poor. And if I have defrauded anyone of anything, I restore it fourfold."

Luke 19:8

If you grew up in the church, you probably remember the story of Zacchaeus. Maybe you remember the song, "Zacchaeus was a wee little man and a wee little man was he." If not, Zacchaeus was a chief tax collector, which meant he was one of the most hated men around. Tax collectors cheated people. They would collect more money than required and keep the difference for themselves. This was a lucrative profession, and Zacchaeus was rich, but he knew something was missing from his life.

He heard that Jesus was coming to town, and he figured he would see what all the chatter was about. He went to see Jesus, but there was a crowd, and he was too short to see. So, he climbed to the top of a sycamore tree. He caught a glimpse of Jesus, and Jesus caught a glimpse of him. Long story short, Jesus went to his house. We don't know exactly what took place at his house, but we do know that Zacchaeus was saved. Not only was he saved, but he also agreed to do everything he could to right his wrongs.

No matter what you've done or how disliked you are, you can find forgiveness in Jesus. You might feel like damaged goods, but you are valuable and loved by God. Change starts right now.

Lord, thank you for loving me. Thank you for giving me many chances. Help me change my life for the better and serve you with all my heart. Amen.

APRIL 2

Whoever conceals his transgressions will not prosper, but he who confesses and forsakes them will obtain mercy.

Proverbs 28:13

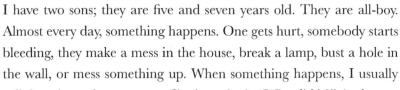

I have two sons; they are five and seven years old. They are all-boy. Almost every day, something happens. One gets hurt, somebody starts bleeding, they make a mess in the house, break a lamp, bust a hole in the wall, or mess something up. When something happens, I usually call them into whatever room I'm in and ask, "Who did it?" And every single time, they always point to and blame each other. It never fails. I'm waiting for the day when one of them comes in with no excuses and admits it was their fault, but I'm not holding my breath.

This is one of those human tendencies that starts when we're kids, but it's not one we naturally outgrow. Even as adults, we don't like admitting we're wrong. We make excuses, point the finger, shift the blame, and do everything possible to conceal our wrongdoings. This might occasionally save face, but it ultimately holds us back and prevents us from growth.

Are there any skeletons in your closet? Any secret and unconfessed sin? A fault that you haven't admitted? A wrongdoing that needs to be brought to light? You might worry about how someone will react or what it will cost you if it becomes known. The consequences might seem severe, but those who confess and forsake their transgressions will obtain mercy.

Lord, thank you for your mercy. Help me own my mistakes, regardless of the consequences. Amen.

APRIL 3

So also my heavenly Father will do to every one of you, if you do not forgive your brother from your heart.

Matthew 18:35

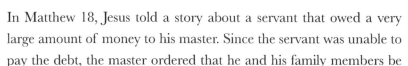

In Matthew 18, Jesus told a story about a servant that owed a very large amount of money to his master. Since the servant was unable to pay the debt, the master ordered that he and his family members be sold. The servant begged his master to have mercy, and not only did the master have mercy, but he decided to forgive the debt in full.

This servant who had just been forgiven an enormous debt went into the streets and found a fellow servant who owed him a very insignificant amount of money. He beat him, choked him, and demanded immediate payment. The guy begged for mercy, but he refused and punished him harshly. When the master heard what had taken place, he threw the servant into jail. After telling that story, Jesus said, "So also my heavenly Father will do to every one of you if you do not forgive your brother from your heart."

All of us have been forgiven an enormous debt. We could never pay for our sin, so Jesus stepped in on our behalf and took our place on the cross. We have been forgiven, but sometimes we struggle to forgive others. Maybe someone cheated, abused, or betrayed you. Maybe you're struggling with unforgiveness. If so, take some time today to remember the enormous debt that you've been forgiven.

Lord, thank you for not only forgiving my debt but paying for it in full. Forgive me for any bitterness that I am holding on to. Help me forgive others. Amen.

APRIL 4

By this all people will know that you are my disciples, if you have love for one another.

John 13:35

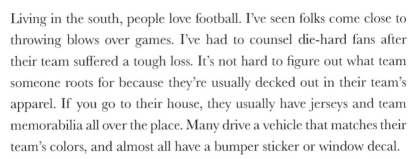

Living in the south, people love football. I've seen folks come close to throwing blows over games. I've had to counsel die-hard fans after their team suffered a tough loss. It's not hard to figure out what team someone roots for because they're usually decked out in their team's apparel. If you go to their house, they usually have jerseys and team memorabilia all over the place. Many drive a vehicle that matches their team's colors, and almost all have a bumper sticker or window decal.

Jesus says others will know we are his disciples if we have love for one another. People claim to love God and to have a relationship with him, but actions speak louder than words. It becomes evident how close a person is to God by how well they love others. And there are no contingencies here. Jesus doesn't say love people unless they hurt you. Or love people unless they have different beliefs than you. He simply commands us to love people.

How well are you loving others? Do you hurt when others are hurting? Do you celebrate when others are celebrating? Does the thought of people going to Hell keep you up at night? Are you loving like Jesus? Are you going out of your way to meet people where they are? Is it evident that you follow Jesus by the way that you love?

Lord, thank you for your love. Help me love others the way that you have loved me. Show me how I can love those around me today. Amen.

APRIL 5

He said, "The one who showed him mercy." And Jesus said to him, "You go, and do likewise."

Luke 10:37

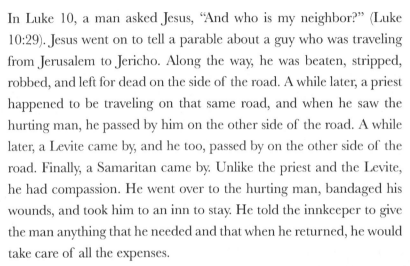

In Luke 10, a man asked Jesus, "And who is my neighbor?" (Luke 10:29). Jesus went on to tell a parable about a guy who was traveling from Jerusalem to Jericho. Along the way, he was beaten, stripped, robbed, and left for dead on the side of the road. A while later, a priest happened to be traveling on that same road, and when he saw the hurting man, he passed by him on the other side of the road. A while later, a Levite came by, and he too, passed by on the other side of the road. Finally, a Samaritan came by. Unlike the priest and the Levite, he had compassion. He went over to the hurting man, bandaged his wounds, and took him to an inn to stay. He told the innkeeper to give the man anything that he needed and that when he returned, he would take care of all the expenses.

After telling this parable, Jesus asked the man, "Which of these three, do you think, proved to be a neighbor to the man who fell among the robbers?" (Luke 10:36). The man answered, "The one who showed him mercy." And then Jesus said, "You go, and do likewise."

Are you too busy to be the hands and feet of Jesus? Are you missing opportunities to minister because you are preoccupied? Are you passing by those who need help because you're distracted? Today, choose to be a good neighbor.

Lord, forgive me for allowing busyness to keep me from helping others. Help me slow down and be a good neighbor. Amen.

APRIL 6

And he said, "Jesus, remember me when you come into your kingdom." And he said to him, "Truly, I say to you, today you will be with me in paradise."

Luke 23:42-43

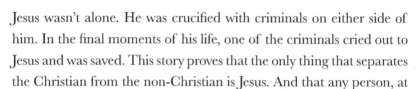

Jesus wasn't alone. He was crucified with criminals on either side of him. In the final moments of his life, one of the criminals cried out to Jesus and was saved. This story proves that the only thing that separates the Christian from the non-Christian is Jesus. And that any person, at any time prior to death, can surrender to him.

I recently read a news article that detailed one of the most horrific cases I've ever heard of. It was disturbing, to say the least. My first emotion was anger. I thought, "How could someone do what this person did to another person? They deserve to rot! There is a special place in Hell for people like that." As I was having those thoughts, the Holy Spirit reminded me that Jesus is the only thing that separates me from that person. And If I believe that Jesus can save me, I have to believe that he can save that person as well.

It's not uncommon for church people to write others off. They assume that a person is too far gone, but no one is too far gone for Jesus. He can save who he wants when he wants. Today, I encourage you to pray for someone you may have written off. Pray that God will get a hold of their heart and save their soul, and don't stop until he does.

Lord, help me understand that it is only by your grace that I am saved. I pray that you will save every person I know who doesn't know you. Amen.

APRIL 7

And as you wish that others would do to you, do so to them.

Luke 6:31

My second day of high school, I got into a fight. A kid was running his mouth, I asked him to stop, and he kept going. Eventually, I stood up, he knocked some papers out of my hand, I pushed him, and the rest is history. Before I knew it, we were in the principal's office waiting for our parents to pick us up because we were both suspended from school.

Our instinct is to treat others the way that they treat us, but the Bible calls us higher. If you grew up in Sunday school, at some point, you were taught the Golden Rule, "Do unto others as you would have them do unto you." In other words, treat others how you want to be treated, regardless of how they treat you. If you want others to be nice to you, be nice to others. If you want others to help you, help others. If you want others to forgive you, forgive others. If you want others to encourage you, encourage others. If you want others to be generous to you, be generous to others. Are you getting the idea?

Don't wait for others to treat you the way you want to be treated. Instead, take the initiative and treat them the way you want to be treated.

Lord, forgive me for the times I've sought retaliation and treated others poorly because that's the way they treated me. Help me treat others the way I want to be treated. Amen.

APRIL 8

And when Jesus was baptized, immediately he went up from the water, and behold, the heavens were opened to him, and he saw the Spirit of God descending like a dove and coming to rest on him; and behold, a voice from heaven said, "This is my beloved Son, with whom I am well pleased."

Matthew 3:16-17

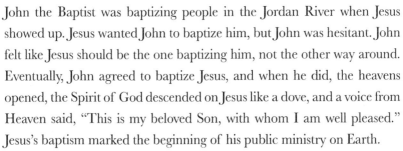

John the Baptist was baptizing people in the Jordan River when Jesus showed up. Jesus wanted John to baptize him, but John was hesitant. John felt like Jesus should be the one baptizing him, not the other way around. Eventually, John agreed to baptize Jesus, and when he did, the heavens opened, the Spirit of God descended on Jesus like a dove, and a voice from Heaven said, "This is my beloved Son, with whom I am well pleased." Jesus's baptism marked the beginning of his public ministry on Earth.

Jesus was not a sinner, but he chose to identify with sinners. He came to Earth to pay the penalty for our sins on the cross. Baptism is not just something he commands his followers to participate in but also something he participated in. One of the main things we can learn from Jesus's baptism is that baptism is central to the Christian faith.

The Bible makes it clear that baptism should follow salvation. No, baptism is not necessary to get into Heaven, but it is necessary to be obedient. If you are a Christian who hasn't been baptized, what are you waiting for? If you're a Christian who has, thank God for the gift of baptism.

Lord, thank you for the gift of baptism. Thank you for not only instructing me to participate in baptism but also for participating in baptism yourself. Amen.

APRIL 9

God said to Balaam, "You shall not go with them. You shall not curse the people, for they are blessed."

Numbers 22:12

Balak, the king of the Moabites, sent a group of people to ask Balaam to curse the Israelites so that he could defeat them and drive them out of their land. God told Balaam not to curse the Israelites but to bless them, so he sent word back to the king that God would not allow him to do what he asked. The king sent a second group of people and promised Balaam money and materialistic things. This time, Balaam saddled his donkey and went.

God was upset that Balaam went and sent an angel to divert his direction, but Balaam couldn't see the angel. When the donkey saw the angel, she veered off the road. Balaam got angry and beat the donkey. This happened a few times. The donkey ended up speaking (yes, you read that correctly) to Balaam, and eventually, God opened his eyes, and he could see what his donkey saw all along. God will use whatever means necessary to get the attention of his children. In Balaam's case, he used a talking donkey.

Is God trying to get your attention? Maybe you're ignoring the signs or too preoccupied with other things to notice. Take some time today to slow down, and ask God to open your eyes to the direction he wants you to go.

Lord, forgive me for the times I am too blind to notice you. Open my eyes to the direction you want me to go. Amen.

APRIL 10

Now to him who is able to do far more abundantly than all that we ask or think, according to the power at work within us.

Ephesians 3:20

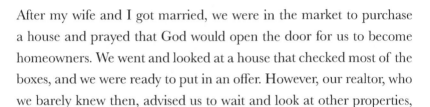

After my wife and I got married, we were in the market to purchase a house and prayed that God would open the door for us to become homeowners. We went and looked at a house that checked most of the boxes, and we were ready to put in an offer. However, our realtor, who we barely knew then, advised us to wait and look at other properties, so we decided to take his advice.

A few weeks later, a house came on the market that was far nicer than anything we thought we could afford, and we were able to purchase it. That's just one of many examples in my life of God doing far more abundantly than I can ask or think. In hindsight, I recognize many times that God didn't answer my prayer because he had something bigger in store.

It's impossible to ask God for more than he can deliver. Not only can he deliver, but as he often does, he can deliver far more than you ask or think. He has unlimited power. As you spend time in prayer, don't be afraid to ask big. God is still in the miracle-working business, and he is able.

Lord, thank you for being able to do far more abundantly than I can ask or think. Help me pray big and expectantly. Amen.

APRIL 11

"And he answered him, 'Sir, let it alone this year also, until I dig around it and put on manure. Then if it should bear fruit next year, well and good; but if not, you can cut it down.'"

Luke 13:8-9

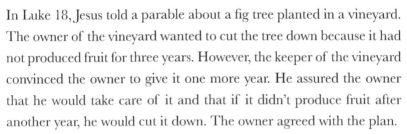

In Luke 18, Jesus told a parable about a fig tree planted in a vineyard. The owner of the vineyard wanted to cut the tree down because it had not produced fruit for three years. However, the keeper of the vineyard convinced the owner to give it one more year. He assured the owner that he would take care of it and that if it didn't produce fruit after another year, he would cut it down. The owner agreed with the plan.

The owner of the vineyard represents God. The keeper of the vineyard represents Jesus. And the fig tree itself represents the nation of Israel. At this time, John the Baptist, along with Jesus, had been preaching the message of repentance for three years, but many still were not producing the fruit of repentance. This parable served as a warning of God's imminent judgment. Those trees that did not bear fruit would be cut down.

God is patient, but his patience does have limits. He is a God of mercy, but he is also a God of judgment. Every day, every breath, every minute that you have on this Earth is a gift from him. In his mercy, he has given you the time that you have, but eventually, that time will come to an end. Judgment is imminent. One day, you will stand before God and give an account of your life. Are you producing fruit?

Lord, thank you for your patience. Thank you for giving me another day. Forgive me for the mistakes that I've made and help me bear fruit. Amen.

APRIL 12

For John came to you in the way of righteousness, and you did not believe him, but the tax collectors and the prostitutes believed him. And even when you saw it, you did not afterward change your minds and believe him.

Matthew 21:32

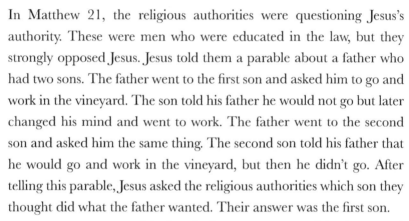

In Matthew 21, the religious authorities were questioning Jesus's authority. These were men who were educated in the law, but they strongly opposed Jesus. Jesus told them a parable about a father who had two sons. The father went to the first son and asked him to go and work in the vineyard. The son told his father he would not go but later changed his mind and went to work. The father went to the second son and asked him the same thing. The second son told his father that he would go and work in the vineyard, but then he didn't go. After telling this parable, Jesus asked the religious authorities which son they thought did what the father wanted. Their answer was the first son.

Jesus went on to explain that the first son represented the sinners and the tax collectors. They initially rejected the law, but they accepted him. The second son represented the religious authorities. They believed the law but did not accept him. In other words, they claimed to be obedient to the Father but failed to follow through with their actions.

There's a big difference between saying and doing. Don't make the same mistake as the religious leaders. Don't just express your allegiance to the Father with words. Show it with your actions.

Lord, thank you for being my Father. Help me obey you with my words and actions. Show me when I'm failing to follow through. Amen.

APRIL 13

He sent and had John beheaded in the prison, and his head was brought on a platter and given to the girl, and she brought it to her mother.

Matthew 14:10-11

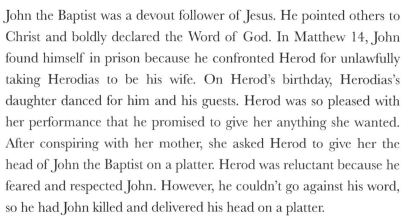

John the Baptist was a devout follower of Jesus. He pointed others to Christ and boldly declared the Word of God. In Matthew 14, John found himself in prison because he confronted Herod for unlawfully taking Herodias to be his wife. On Herod's birthday, Herodias's daughter danced for him and his guests. Herod was so pleased with her performance that he promised to give her anything she wanted. After conspiring with her mother, she asked Herod to give her the head of John the Baptist on a platter. Herod was reluctant because he feared and respected John. However, he couldn't go against his word, so he had John killed and delivered his head on a platter.

John was martyred for speaking the truth and refusing to back down. John's example teaches us to boldly speak the truth and to rebuke evil, regardless of the potential consequences.

We live in a time where the truth is being watered down and overlooked all together. People are opposed and accused of being close-minded for speaking the truth of God's Word. If there was ever a time Christians needed to stand up for what they believe, that time is right now. Like John, boldly speak the truth and rebuke evil, regardless of the potential consequences.

Lord, thank you for your Word. Help me be bold, speak the truth, and rebuke evil, regardless of the potential consequences. Amen.

APRIL 14

Mary therefore took a pound of expensive ointment made from pure nard, and anointed the feet of Jesus and wiped his feet with her hair. The house was filled with the fragrance of the perfume.

John 12:3

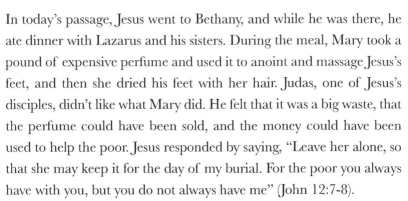

In today's passage, Jesus went to Bethany, and while he was there, he ate dinner with Lazarus and his sisters. During the meal, Mary took a pound of expensive perfume and used it to anoint and massage Jesus's feet, and then she dried his feet with her hair. Judas, one of Jesus's disciples, didn't like what Mary did. He felt that it was a big waste, that the perfume could have been sold, and the money could have been used to help the poor. Jesus responded by saying, "Leave her alone, so that she may keep it for the day of my burial. For the poor you always have with you, but you do not always have me" (John 12:7-8).

Mary gave Jesus something of extreme value to express her love for him. This was an act of worship and a way to show Jesus that her wholehearted devotion belonged to him. A short time after this, Jesus died on the cross. What Mary gave Jesus was valuable, but it was nothing in comparison to what Jesus gave her.

Jesus didn't hold anything back from you, and you shouldn't hold anything back from him. Like Mary, give your wholehearted devotion to him.

Lord, thank you for not holding anything back from me. Thank you for taking my place on the cross. Show me if I'm holding anything back from you. Amen.

APRIL 15

Other seeds fell on good soil and produced grain, some a hundredfold, some sixty, some thirty. He who has ears, let him hear.

Matthew 13:8-9

In today's passage, Jesus told a parable about a sower who went out to sow seeds. Some of the seeds fell on a path, and the birds came and quickly devoured them. This type of soil represents the person whose heart is hardened. They hear God's Word but refuse to let it penetrate their heart. Some seeds fell on rocky ground and immediately sprouted but died since roots couldn't be established in the rocks. This type of soil represents the person who desires to have a relationship with the Lord, but there's no follow-through. Some seeds fell among the thorns and were quickly choked out. This type of soil represents the lukewarm Christian. The Christian that has surrendered some but not all. And lastly, some seeds fell on good soil and produced grain, "some a hundredfold, some sixty, some thirty." This type of soil represents the person who is living at the center of and fully surrendered to God's will.

Which type of soil represents you? Is your heart hardened toward God's Word? Do you have a desire to have a relationship with the Lord but no follow-through? Have you surrendered some but not all? Or are you living at the center of and fully surrender to God's will?

Lord, help me produce a harvest for your kingdom and live at the center of your will. Show me when I fall short. Amen.

APRIL 16

Now the eleven disciples went to Galilee, to the mountain to which Jesus had directed them. And when they saw him they worshiped him, but some doubted.

Matthew 28:16-17

After rising from the grave, Jesus instructed the disciples to meet him at a mountain in Galilee for the very first time. When they saw Jesus, "They worshiped him, but some doubted." These are the men who were closest to Jesus. They spent three years by his side. They witnessed him give sight to the blind, heal the sick, and bring the dead back to life. Jesus was standing in front of them. He was living, breathing, and talking, yet some of them doubted.

What was there to doubt? Maybe they thought that Jesus had a clone. Maybe they thought the man standing in front of them was an imposter. Maybe they thought it was all a big hoax and that it wasn't really Jesus who died on the cross. We don't know exactly what they doubted, but we know that they doubted. These same men went on to face persecution and death for proclaiming the gospel.

The truth is that even the most devoted followers of Jesus struggle with doubt. If you're not struggling with doubt now, odds are you will at some point in the future, but doubt is not always bad. Just as it did for the disciples, doubt can actually strengthen your faith. If you are struggling with doubt, confess it to God, and ask him to give you the faith to move forward.

Lord, forgive me for doubting you. Give me the faith to move forward, even when I don't have the answers. Help me choose faith in the midst of doubt. Amen.

APRIL 17

For you have need of endurance, so that when you have done the will of God you may receive what is promised.

Hebrews 10:36

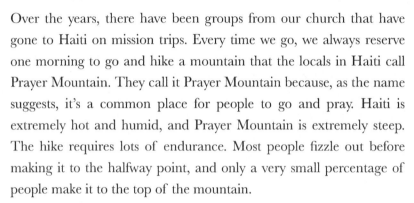

Over the years, there have been groups from our church that have gone to Haiti on mission trips. Every time we go, we always reserve one morning to go and hike a mountain that the locals in Haiti call Prayer Mountain. They call it Prayer Mountain because, as the name suggests, it's a common place for people to go and pray. Haiti is extremely hot and humid, and Prayer Mountain is extremely steep. The hike requires lots of endurance. Most people fizzle out before making it to the halfway point, and only a very small percentage of people make it to the top of the mountain.

The Bible makes it clear that endurance is necessary to finish the race of life. As believers, we will face difficulties and trials. There will be times when we are excluded or persecuted for our faith. There will be seasons of exhaustion, but by God's grace, the best is always yet to come.

Maybe you find yourself running low on endurance. Maybe you're on the verge of stopping short, giving up, and throwing in the towel. If so, let this be your sign to keep going. Remember why you're doing what you're doing, and ask God to reignite your passion. Continue doing the will of God so that you may receive what is promised.

Lord, forgive me for stopping short. Reignite my passion and give me the endurance to keep going. Help me remember why I'm doing what I'm doing. Amen.

APRIL 18

He put another parable before them, saying, "The kingdom of heaven is like a grain of mustard seed that a man took and sowed in his field. It is the smallest of all seeds, but when it has grown it is larger than all the garden plants and becomes a tree, so that the birds of the air come and make nests in its branches."

Matthew 13:31-32

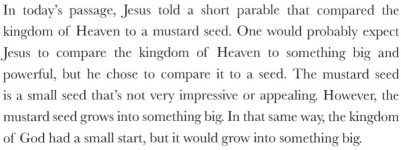

In today's passage, Jesus told a short parable that compared the kingdom of Heaven to a mustard seed. One would probably expect Jesus to compare the kingdom of Heaven to something big and powerful, but he chose to compare it to a seed. The mustard seed is a small seed that's not very impressive or appealing. However, the mustard seed grows into something big. In that same way, the kingdom of God had a small start, but it would grow into something big.

At the time this parable was spoken, nobody could even begin to imagine the impact Jesus's ministry would have. Jesus came to Earth in the humblest of ways, but he would forever change the world. He had only a handful of devoted followers, but countless lives would be changed by his sacrifice. His ministry took place in a small area, but it would go on to have an impact worldwide.

It's easy to get discouraged when you're failing to see the results you want to see, but it's important to remember that even the kingdom of God had humble beginnings. Instead of focusing on the results, focus on planting seeds, and trust God to bring the growth.

Lord, thank you for growing big things from small seeds. Help me stop focusing so much on the results and start focusing on planting seeds. Amen.

APRIL 19

The next morning, about the time of offering the sacrifice, behold, water came from the direction of Edom, till the country was filled with water.

2 Kings 3:20

Three kings, the king of Israel, Judah, and Edom, made an agreement to team up to go into battle against the Moabites. This was an enemy that should have been easily defeated, but after marching for seven days, they ran out of water. They became very weak and started to panic.

Eventually, they decided to look for a prophet who could inquire of the Lord on their behalf, and they found Elisha. Through Elisha, God told them to start digging ditches. They did what God told them to do, and without rain, God miraculously filled the ditches full of water. They also went on to do what they set out to do and defeated the Moabites.

What ditch is God calling you to dig? There will be times in life when things don't go according to the plan. There will be times in life when it feels like your back is up against the wall and you start to panic. When those times come, inquire of the Lord and do what he tells you to do. Before he provided the water, the people had to dig ditches. If you find yourself in a similar situation, maybe it's time to pick up a shovel.

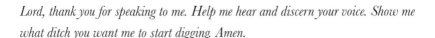

Lord, thank you for speaking to me. Help me hear and discern your voice. Show me what ditch you want me to start digging. Amen.

APRIL 20

Therefore encourage one another and build one another up, just as you are doing.

1 Thessalonians 5:11

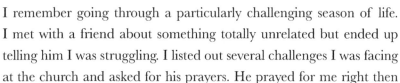

I remember going through a particularly challenging season of life. I met with a friend about something totally unrelated but ended up telling him I was struggling. I listed out several challenges I was facing at the church and asked for his prayers. He prayed for me right then and there, and he encouraged me. He told me I was doing a good job and assured me that there were better days ahead, and I knew he meant it. He helped me see the big picture, and I left that meeting feeling better than I had in several weeks.

You can probably recall a time in your life when someone encouraged you at just the right time. Maybe you were depressed, struggling, or feeling inadequate, and somebody came along and encouraged you. A few simple words changed your perspective and motivated you to get back up, dust yourself off, and keep going. Encouragement is powerful. People keep going when they're encouraged. People work harder when they're encouraged. People put forth more effort when they're encouraged.

The Bible commands us to encourage and build one another up. There is so much negativity in the world. Now more than ever, people need to be encouraged. Who can you encourage today? Your spouse, child, friend, neighbor, coworker, or employee? One word of encouragement might just be what someone in your life needs to keep going.

Lord, help me become a better encourager. Show me someone who needs to be encouraged today and give me the words to encourage them. Amen.

APRIL 21

But Moses' hands grew weary, so they took a stone and put it under him, and he sat on it, while Aaron and Hur held up his hands, one on one side, and the other on the other side. So his hands were steady until the going down of the sun.

Exodus 17:12

In Exodus 17, the Israelites were en route to the Promised Land, but there was an enemy that stood in their way, Amalek, so they went to battle. During the battle, Moses, the leader of the Israelites, went and stood on top of a hill with the staff of God in his hands. When he held up his hands, Israel prevailed and defeated Amalek. Whenever he lowered his hands, Amalek prevailed and defeated Israel. Eventually, his arms grew weary. He could no longer hold his hands up. Fortunately, he didn't go to the top of that hill alone. Two of his buddies, Aaron and Hur, went with him, and they came to his rescue. They got a stone for him to sit on, and they got on either side of him and literally held his hands up until the battle was won.

Moses was no pushover. He killed a man with his bare hands. He stood face to face with Pharaoh. He led the Israelites into battle on multiple occasions. He audibly spoke with God. Moses was as hardcore as they come, yet he still needed help from others.

It's so important that you surround yourself with the right people. We all need an Aaron and a Hur in our life. We all need people who will come alongside us and help us when we don't have the strength to do it alone.

Lord, thank you for placing people in my life that I can rely on. Help me be humble enough to recognize when I'm in a situation that is bigger than me. Amen.

APRIL 22

Let us test and examine our ways, and return to the Lord!

Lamentations 3:40

One day, I was driving home from class. I didn't sleep the night before because I was up studying for a final exam. I got on the highway, set cruise control, and started to doze off. In an effort to stay awake, I turned up the music, rolled down the windows, and blasted the A/C, but nothing seemed to work. I convinced myself I was fine and kept driving, but then it happened. I woke up in the median, driving at highway speed. Cruise control kept my truck from decelerating. I panicked, slammed the brakes, and frantically swerved back onto the highway. I ended up doing a 360 in the middle of the highway and crashing into a guardrail. Fortunately, no other cars were coming, and I wasn't injured.

I didn't recognize the danger I was putting myself in until the damage was done. I knew I was tired, but never in a million years did I think I would fall asleep and crash my truck.

The Bible instructs us to examine our ways. Take some time today to examine yourself. Is there any sin that you've become okay with? Is there any compromising situation that you are putting yourself in? Is there any relationship that is leading you astray? Don't make the same mistake I did. Recognize the danger before the damage is done.

Lord, show me where I'm falling short. Help me examine myself and recognize the danger I'm putting myself in before the damage is done. Amen.

APRIL 23

It happened, late one afternoon, when David arose from his couch and was walking on the roof of the king's house, that he saw from the roof a woman bathing; and the woman was very beautiful.

2 Samuel 11:2

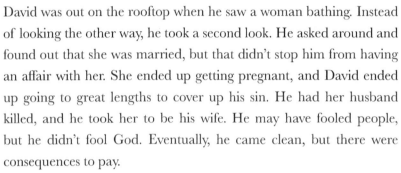

David was out on the rooftop when he saw a woman bathing. Instead of looking the other way, he took a second look. He asked around and found out that she was married, but that didn't stop him from having an affair with her. She ended up getting pregnant, and David ended up going to great lengths to cover up his sin. He had her husband killed, and he took her to be his wife. He may have fooled people, but he didn't fool God. Eventually, he came clean, but there were consequences to pay.

David's story proves a couple of things. First, it proves that all of us are only one bad decision away from wrecking our lives. David is described as a man after God's own heart, yet he made a mistake that hurt his future and his family's future. If David blew it, don't be foolish enough to think that you can't. Second, it proves that there are earthly consequences for our actions. There's not a sin that God can't forgive, but that doesn't mean there won't be permanent damage. Your decisions will affect not only you but also the people that you love the most.

The enemy wants nothing more than for you to give in to sin. So, stay alert and don't let your guard down.

Lord, forgive me for the times I've failed and given in to sin. Help me be strong, stay alert, and always keep my guard up. Amen.

APRIL 24

And those who know your name put their trust in you, for you, O Lord, have not forsaken those who seek you.

Psalm 9:10

When you think about it, there is very little that you have control of. You don't have control over your health. Sure, you can exercise and diet, but that doesn't guarantee a long, healthy life. You don't have control over your finances. Sure, you can work hard, save and invest, but don't be mistaken. All of it can be taken away in an instant. You don't have control over your relationships. Sure, you can do your part, and invest in your marriage, and be a good friend, but you can't control what others do. You don't have control over your kids. Sure, you can raise them right and bring them up in the ways of the Lord, but eventually, they're going to go out and make their own decisions. When you think about it, there is really very little that you have control of.

How much weight would be lifted off your shoulders if you stopped worrying about the many things that are outside of your control and just focused on the few things that are inside of your control? How much weight would be lifted off your shoulders if you just did your very best with the little bit that is inside of your control, and then trusted God with the rest?

Lord, forgive me for not trusting you with things that are outside of my control. Help me do my best and trust you with the rest. Amen.

APRIL 25

When I am afraid, I put my trust in you.

Psalm 56:3

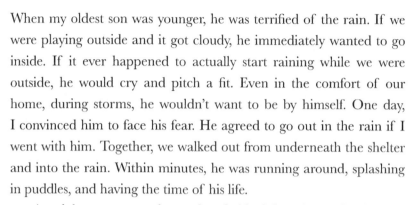

When my oldest son was younger, he was terrified of the rain. If we were playing outside and it got cloudy, he immediately wanted to go inside. If it ever happened to actually start raining while we were outside, he would cry and pitch a fit. Even in the comfort of our home, during storms, he wouldn't want to be by himself. One day, I convinced him to face his fear. He agreed to go out in the rain if I went with him. Together, we walked out from underneath the shelter and into the rain. Within minutes, he was running around, splashing in puddles, and having the time of his life.

As adults, we may no longer be afraid of the rain, or the dark, or the monster under our bed, but make no mistake, we all have fears. Those fears often hold us back and keep us from reaching our potential.

The good news is that you don't have to face your fears alone. You have a heavenly Father who loves and cares for you in a way you cannot even begin to fathom. When you are afraid, you can put your trust in him.

Lord, thank you for the way you love and care for me. Help me face my fears, knowing that you are with me every step of the way. Amen.

APRIL 26

What then shall we say to these things? If God is for us, who can be against us?

Romans 8:31

A couple of years into my tenure as a pastor, I faced a difficult challenge. There was something going on in the church that I felt I needed to address. However, I knew that if I chose to address the situation, I would be met with major opposition. Several families would likely leave the church, and at that time, we couldn't afford to lose anyone.

I had a choice to make. I could do what I knew was right, or I could do what was easy. I chose to do what I knew was right, and the aftermath turned out to be even more difficult than I anticipated. Several families did end up leaving the church, but God ended up using it for good.

Always strive to do what is right, not what is easy. At the end of the day, it's much more important to be in a right standing with God than in a right standing with people. If you make God-honoring decisions, the whole world can be against you, but with God by your side, you can face any challenge that may come your way. If God is for you, who can be against you?

Lord, thank you for always being by my side. Help me make decisions that honor you, even if that means being opposed by people. Amen.

APRIL 27

The grass withers, the flower fades, but the word of our God will stand forever.

Isaiah 40:8

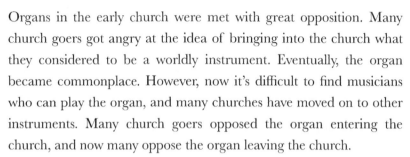

Organs in the early church were met with great opposition. Many church goers got angry at the idea of bringing into the church what they considered to be a worldly instrument. Eventually, the organ became commonplace. However, now it's difficult to find musicians who can play the organ, and many churches have moved on to other instruments. Many church goers opposed the organ entering the church, and now many oppose the organ leaving the church.

The bottom line is, over time, things change. The music we play and the songs we sing have changed. At one time, Sunday school was a revolutionary new ministry. Now, many churches are having more success with small groups throughout the week. At one time, door-to-door evangelism and bulk mailings were some of the best ways to spread the gospel and invite people to church. These methods can still be effective, but the internet has changed the game. We can now reach people across the world instantaneously. Change is an inevitable part of life, but there is one thing that will never change: the Word of God.

Don't be afraid of change, be afraid of compromise. In other words, don't be afraid to change your methods and try new things, but always ensure that you are living in a way that is pleasing to God. Times change, but his Word never changes.

Lord, thank you for your unchanging Word. Thank you for the fact that in a rapidly changing world, I can rest assured that you will never change. Amen.

APRIL 28

So the people shouted, and the trumpets were blown. As soon as the people heard the sound of the trumpet, the people shouted a great shout, and the wall fell down flat, so that the people went up into the city, every man straight before him, and they captured the city.

Joshua 6:20

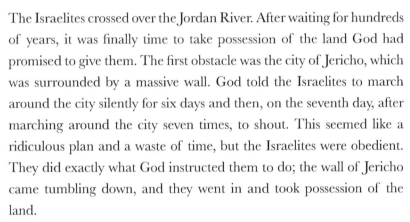

The Israelites crossed over the Jordan River. After waiting for hundreds of years, it was finally time to take possession of the land God had promised to give them. The first obstacle was the city of Jericho, which was surrounded by a massive wall. God told the Israelites to march around the city silently for six days and then, on the seventh day, after marching around the city seven times, to shout. This seemed like a ridiculous plan and a waste of time, but the Israelites were obedient. They did exactly what God instructed them to do; the wall of Jericho came tumbling down, and they went in and took possession of the land.

One key takeaway from this story is that obedience brings victory. If you are obedient to God, victory is sure to follow. In every situation, it's important to seek God's will. Often, his plan is much different than ours. The Israelites initial plan of attack probably wasn't to march around the city in hopes that the wall would just come tumbling down.

The same may be true for you. Maybe you are facing an obstacle, and you have a solution in mind, but maybe it's not God's solution. Seek his will, move forward in obedience, and victory is sure to follow.

Lord, thank you for always making a way. Show me your will in every situation and help me be obedient. Amen.

APRIL 29

For you are still of the flesh. For while there is jealousy and strife among you, are you not of the flesh and behaving only in a human way?

1 Corinthians 3:3

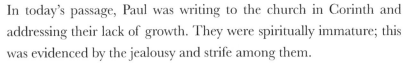

In today's passage, Paul was writing to the church in Corinth and addressing their lack of growth. They were spiritually immature; this was evidenced by the jealousy and strife among them.

With the internet's and social media's increasing popularity, comparison is at an all-time high. We see the vacations that our friends are going on, the houses they're building, and the cars they're driving. We see pictures of their children excelling in school or athletics. We see posts about the growth of their businesses or promotions in their careers. Often, we feel as if we don't measure up, and this leads to jealousy. We begin to covet what they have.

What we see on the internet usually doesn't portray reality, but there will always be someone who has something you don't have. You can buy the biggest house in the world; eventually, someone will build one bigger. You can go on the nicest vacation, and eventually, someone will top it. You can have tons of money, but someone will be better looking, more talented, or have something else you don't have.

Jealousy makes you blind to what God has blessed you with and distracts you from what truly matters in this life. Instead of coveting what someone else has, why not thank God for what you have?

Lord, thank you for everything that you have blessed me with. Forgive me for coveting what others have. Help me focus on what truly matters in this life. Amen.

APRIL 30

Not that I am speaking of being in need, for I have learned in whatever situation I am to be content.

Philippians 4:11

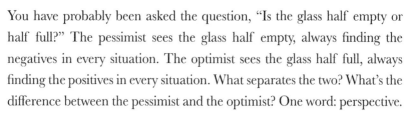

You have probably been asked the question, "Is the glass half empty or half full?" The pessimist sees the glass half empty, always finding the negatives in every situation. The optimist sees the glass half full, always finding the positives in every situation. What separates the two? What's the difference between the pessimist and the optimist? One word: perspective.

Regardless of how much you have or how great life is, if you have the wrong perspective, you will always be unhappy and miserable. On the flipside of that, regardless of how little you have or how bad life is, if you have the right perspective, you will always be grateful and happy. The right perspective changes everything.

In today's verse, Paul writes that he has learned to be content in every situation. This is a guy that has been through it. He's been beaten, stoned, shipwrecked, thrown into prison, and the list goes on. He faced things that many of us will never have to face, yet he found contentment. He chose to see the glass half full.

I don't want to downplay what you may be going through, but I do want to encourage you to have the right perspective. No matter what, you have a Savior who loves you unconditionally. That is reason enough to choose contentment. Today, will you see the glass half empty or half full?

Lord, thank you for loving me unconditionally. Like Paul, help me have the right perspective. Give me eyes to see the glass half full. Amen.

MAY 1

Many Samaritans from that town believed in him because of the woman's testimony, *"He told me all that I ever did."*

John 4:39

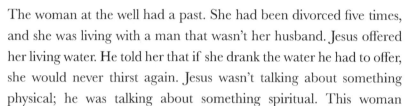

The woman at the well had a past. She had been divorced five times, and she was living with a man that wasn't her husband. Jesus offered her living water. He told her that if she drank the water he had to offer, she would never thirst again. Jesus wasn't talking about something physical; he was talking about something spiritual. This woman was looking for satisfaction, fulfillment, and lasting contentment in relationships with men, but she didn't find it.

The first marriage didn't bring her lasting contentment. The second marriage didn't bring her lasting contentment. Neither did the third, fourth, or fifth. The relationship that she was in wasn't bringing her lasting contentment. These failed relationships only left her confused, letdown, and disappointed. Jesus was telling her that he had something different. He was telling her that he could give her what she was searching for. He could satisfy and fulfill her soul and he did. This woman returned and told everybody about Jesus, and many others came to know him because of her testimony.

Maybe you've wasted time looking for lasting contentment in all the wrong places. No person, church, event, accomplishment, title, salary, net worth, or anything else will ever completely satisfy and fulfill your soul. Only Jesus can do that. If you drink from the water he has to offer, you will never thirst again.

Lord, thank you for your living water. Thank you for satisfying and fulfilling my soul. Like the woman at the well, help me celebrate what you've done for me. Amen.

MAY 2

And Jesus said to him, "Foxes have holes, and birds of the air have nests, but the Son of Man has nowhere to lay his head."

Matthew 8:20

In today's passage, there were people who said they wanted to follow Jesus, but they weren't ready to fully commit. Jesus's response to their excuses makes it clear that nothing is more urgent than responding to him.

When the call of God comes upon your life, it's easy to think of reasons why you can't respond at that moment. It's easy to put it off and to procrastinate. It's easy to come up with excuses. I'll do it tomorrow, next week, or at another time when it's more convenient. First, I need to do this, or first, I need to do that. The truth is: nothing is more urgent than responding to him.

Right now, what are you putting off? What is that one thing you know you need to do? That one thing that he is leading you to do? Maybe it's reading your Bible, getting involved in a church, spending time in prayer, making a commitment to tithe, giving up a bad habit, going to counseling, or something else. You probably know exactly what it is because God continues to place it at the forefront of your heart. Remember, there's no better time to respond to him than right now.

Lord, thank you for inviting me to follow you. Help me respond to you with urgency. Help me fully commit and follow you wholeheartedly. Amen.

MAY 3

And throwing down the pieces of silver into the temple, he departed, and he went and hanged himself.

Matthew 27:5

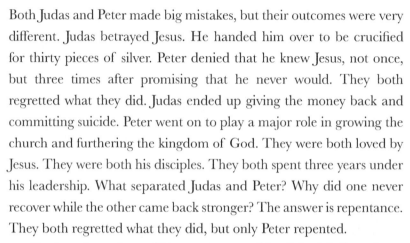

Both Judas and Peter made big mistakes, but their outcomes were very different. Judas betrayed Jesus. He handed him over to be crucified for thirty pieces of silver. Peter denied that he knew Jesus, not once, but three times after promising that he never would. They both regretted what they did. Judas ended up giving the money back and committing suicide. Peter went on to play a major role in growing the church and furthering the kingdom of God. They were both loved by Jesus. They were both his disciples. They both spent three years under his leadership. What separated Judas and Peter? Why did one never recover while the other came back stronger? The answer is repentance. They both regretted what they did, but only Peter repented.

I've heard people say, "I have no regrets," but I don't believe them. We all make mistakes, and all of us have regrets. What we do with that regret is what separates us. Like Judas, some become crippled and never recover, while others, like Peter, come back stronger.

It's one thing to regret what you've done. It's another thing to repent for what you've done. You can allow regret to cripple you, or you can allow Jesus to transform you through repentance. No matter what you've done, right now, you can find forgiveness and a fresh start in him.

Lord, forgive me for all the mistakes I've made. Like Peter, help me recover and come back stronger and better than ever. Amen.

MAY 4

You have heard that it was said, 'You shall love your neighbor and hate your enemy.'
But I say to you, Love your enemies and pray for those who persecute you.

Matthew 5:43-44

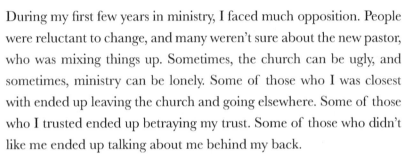

During my first few years in ministry, I faced much opposition. People were reluctant to change, and many weren't sure about the new pastor, who was mixing things up. Sometimes, the church can be ugly, and sometimes, ministry can be lonely. Some of those who I was closest with ended up leaving the church and going elsewhere. Some of those who I trusted ended up betraying my trust. Some of those who didn't like me ended up talking about me behind my back.

I quickly learned that to do what God called me to do, I would have to learn to love those who hurt me. I didn't want to. I wanted to seek revenge, hold a grudge, and cut them out of my life and ministry, but God called me higher. It is not easy, but it is necessary.

You love your family. You love your friends. You love those who are good to you, but what about your enemies? What about those who have hurt you? What about those who have betrayed you? Even those who don't know Christ, love those who love them; those who do know Christ are called higher. You're called to love those who hate and persecute you. You're called to love and pray for your enemies. Those people who despise you are probably the ones who need your love and prayer the most.

Lord, forgive me for not loving others the way that you have loved me. Help me love everybody, even those that despise me. Amen.

MAY 5

Do nothing from selfish ambition or conceit, but in humility count others more significant than yourselves. Let each of you look not only to his own interests, but also to the interests of others.

Philippians 2:3-4

We all naturally gravitate toward selfishness. Our instinct is to look out for ourselves and make sure our needs are met. I first realized this truth when I started having kids. Around age two, I noticed that my kids started pitching fits when they didn't get their way. They started fighting with other kids over their toys and refusing to share. They started getting jealous when another child got more attention than them. Selfishness is not something that has to be taught. It comes naturally.

The Bible teaches us to go against what is natural. The Bible teaches us to do nothing from selfish ambition. The Bible teaches us to humble ourselves and to count others more significant than ourselves. The Bible teaches us to put the needs of others before the needs of ourselves.

This is a tall order and an area in which all of us can probably improve. What about you? Are you selfish with your money, or do you see it as a tool to help and bless others? Are you selfish with your possessions, or do you see them as blessings that can be used to minister to others? Are you selfish with your time, or do you see your time as an opportunity to serve God and people? Are you out to further yourself or the kingdom of God?

Lord, forgive me for my selfishness. Help me count others more significant than myself. Help me put the needs of others before my own needs. Amen.

MAY 6

If I speak in the tongues of men and of angels, but have not love, I am a noisy gong or a clanging cymbal.

1 Corinthians 13:1

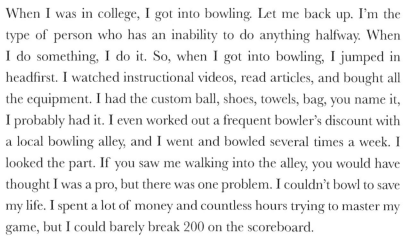

When I was in college, I got into bowling. Let me back up. I'm the type of person who has an inability to do anything halfway. When I do something, I do it. So, when I got into bowling, I jumped in headfirst. I watched instructional videos, read articles, and bought all the equipment. I had the custom ball, shoes, towels, bag, you name it, I probably had it. I even worked out a frequent bowler's discount with a local bowling alley, and I went and bowled several times a week. I looked the part. If you saw me walking into the alley, you would have thought I was a pro, but there was one problem. I couldn't bowl to save my life. I spent a lot of money and countless hours trying to master my game, but I could barely break 200 on the scoreboard.

Many go to church, tithe, and even hold leadership positions. They read their Bibles, pray, and do many of the right things. They want to be used by God; they want to become who he created them to be, but they're missing the point. They haven't realized that love is non-negotiable and absolutely necessary to make an eternal impact on this Earth.

Here's the bottom line: you can go to church. You can wear the Christian shirt or sport the bumper sticker. You can look the part, but without love, all of that means nothing.

Lord, thank you for loving me. Show me If there is any area of my life where I am missing the point. Help me extend your love to others. Amen.

MAY 7

Rejoice with those who rejoice, weep with those who weep.

Romans 12:15

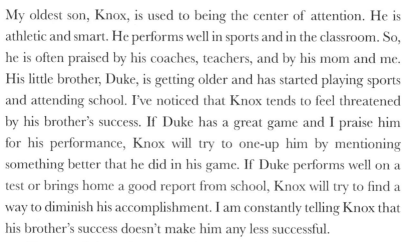

My oldest son, Knox, is used to being the center of attention. He is athletic and smart. He performs well in sports and in the classroom. So, he is often praised by his coaches, teachers, and by his mom and me. His little brother, Duke, is getting older and has started playing sports and attending school. I've noticed that Knox tends to feel threatened by his brother's success. If Duke has a great game and I praise him for his performance, Knox will try to one-up him by mentioning something better that he did in his game. If Duke performs well on a test or brings home a good report from school, Knox will try to find a way to diminish his accomplishment. I am constantly telling Knox that his brother's success doesn't make him any less successful.

Even as adults, we're not good at rejoicing when others rejoice and weeping when others weep. We may applaud and congratulate others outwardly, but inwardly, there can be bitterness and jealousy. We may sympathize with others outwardly, but inwardly, become inflated with pride.

Somebody else's success doesn't make you any less successful, nor does somebody's lack of success make you any more successful. God wants you to genuinely rejoice and weep with others. This begins with an internal change, not an external one.

Lord, help me rejoice and weep with others. Help me understand that someone else's success doesn't make me any less successful. Change me from the inside out. Amen.

MAY 8

Therefore, my beloved brothers, be steadfast, immovable, always abounding in the work of the Lord, knowing that in the Lord your labor is not in vain.

1 Corinthians 15:58

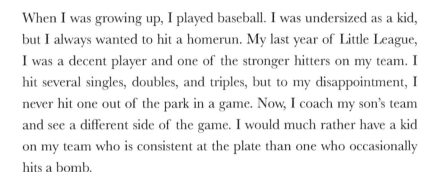

When I was growing up, I played baseball. I was undersized as a kid, but I always wanted to hit a homerun. My last year of Little League, I was a decent player and one of the stronger hitters on my team. I hit several singles, doubles, and triples, but to my disappointment, I never hit one out of the park in a game. Now, I coach my son's team and see a different side of the game. I would much rather have a kid on my team who is consistent at the plate than one who occasionally hits a bomb.

We live in a homerun society. It seems that everybody is looking for that one big break. We want to be noticed. We want to go viral. We want overnight success. Base hits aren't attractive; we want to hit the ball out of the park, but the truth is that being consistent will take you much farther in life.

In today's verse, Paul encourages us to be "steadfast, immovable, always abounding in the work of the Lord." This requires consistency. God's not looking for home-run hitters. He's looking for people who will be trustworthy. He's looking for people who will be consistent at the plate.

Lord, forgive me for the times I fail to be steadfast. Help me be trustworthy and consistent at the plate. Amen.

MAY 9

Then these men said, "We shall not find any ground for complaint against this Daniel unless we find it in connection with the law of his God."

Daniel 6:5

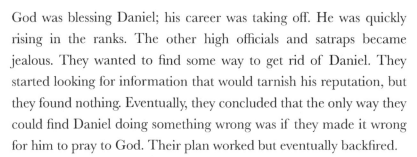

God was blessing Daniel; his career was taking off. He was quickly rising in the ranks. The other high officials and satraps became jealous. They wanted to find some way to get rid of Daniel. They started looking for information that would tarnish his reputation, but they found nothing. Eventually, they concluded that the only way they could find Daniel doing something wrong was if they made it wrong for him to pray to God. Their plan worked but eventually backfired.

When God raises you up, expect people to tear you down. As you step out and make a difference in this world, others will become envious. It is impossible to please both God and people. Take Jesus, for example. He came to Earth and lived a perfect life. He never did a single thing wrong. He healed the sick, gave sight to the blind, and brought hope to the hopeless. He did everything right, yet he was hated and rejected by a large group of people and eventually crucified on a cross.

We pride ourselves in being liked by everybody, but this should be a cause for concern. It's not fun being betrayed, excluded or talked about in a negative context. It's not fun being torn down by others, but that might just be a sign that you're doing something right.

Lord, thank you for always being with me. Help me understand that opposition from other people is not always a bad thing. Help me do what pleases you at all costs. Amen.

MAY 10

When Daniel knew that the document had been signed, he went to his house where he had windows in his upper chamber open toward Jerusalem. He got down on his knees three times a day and prayed and gave thanks before his God, as he had done previously.

Daniel 6:10

King Darius passed a decree making it illegal to pray to God, but that didn't stop Daniel. He knew his life was on the line, but he continued to pray. The Bible tells us that Daniel went home and prayed three times a day, as he had always done. Not only did he pray, he did it from the upper chamber of his house with the windows wide open. Daniel could have closed the windows. He could have tried to conceal what he was doing. He probably could have continued to pray without getting caught, but he wasn't willing to compromise, even in the slightest way.

Most of us are blessed with the freedom to be able to worship. We can read the Bible, spend time in prayer, attend church, and live out our faith without fear of punishment. Even with that freedom, many of us still lack consistency. If we lack consistency now, what will happen if our freedom to worship is taken away?

Daniel was consistent in prayer after the decree was passed only because he was consistent in prayer before the decree was passed. He didn't become a prayer warrior in the lion's den. He became a prayer warrior in his living room. Like Daniel, make a commitment to be consistent and refuse to compromise, even in the slightest way.

Lord, forgive me for falling short. Help me be consistent when it comes to living out my faith. Give me the strength to resist compromise, even in the slightest way. Amen.

MAY 11

Then the king commanded, and Daniel was brought and cast into the den of lions. The king declared to Daniel, "May your God, whom you serve continually, deliver you!"

Daniel 6:16

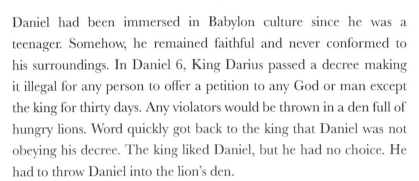

Daniel had been immersed in Babylon culture since he was a teenager. Somehow, he remained faithful and never conformed to his surroundings. In Daniel 6, King Darius passed a decree making it illegal for any person to offer a petition to any God or man except the king for thirty days. Any violators would be thrown in a den full of hungry lions. Word quickly got back to the king that Daniel was not obeying his decree. The king liked Daniel, but he had no choice. He had to throw Daniel into the lion's den.

Daniel never complained. He never begged the king for mercy. He never second-guessed himself. Daniel went into the lion's den, confident that he had made the right decision. He knew that God could save him, but even if God didn't, he was willing to die. In the end, God did save Daniel, and he came out of the lion's den unharmed. King Darius went on to make a new decree saying that all people are to tremble and fear before the God of Daniel.

Daniel's story is proof that if you honor God, you can trust him with the results. This doesn't mean that things will always work out the way you want or expect, but it does mean that God will work it out.

Lord, thank you for always having a plan. Like Daniel, help me honor you in all I do and trust you with the results. Amen.

MAY 12

Make yourself an ark of gopher wood. Make rooms in the ark, and cover it inside and out with pitch.

                                                        Genesis 6:14

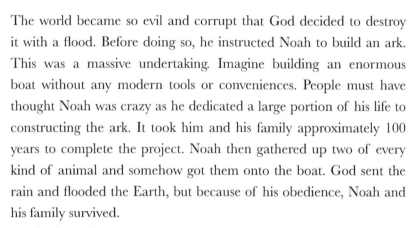

The world became so evil and corrupt that God decided to destroy it with a flood. Before doing so, he instructed Noah to build an ark. This was a massive undertaking. Imagine building an enormous boat without any modern tools or conveniences. People must have thought Noah was crazy as he dedicated a large portion of his life to constructing the ark. It took him and his family approximately 100 years to complete the project. Noah then gathered up two of every kind of animal and somehow got them onto the boat. God sent the rain and flooded the Earth, but because of his obedience, Noah and his family survived.

God may lead you to do things that you don't understand. He may give you the "what" without giving you the "why." In other words, he may tell you what he wants you to do without telling you why he wants you to do it.

I'm sure Noah had some questions and reservations. I'm sure Noah had some fears and doubts. I'm sure there were times throughout the process when he questioned whether he was doing the right thing, but he continued to trust God. Noah's story is proof that you don't have to understand God's plan to trust God's purpose.

Lord, thank you for your divine purpose. Help me trust your purpose, even when I don't understand your plan. Give me faith like Noah. Amen.

MAY 13

But Lot's wife, behind him, looked back, and she became a pillar of salt.

Genesis 19:26

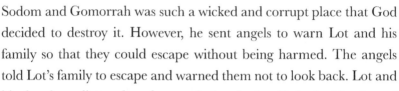

Sodom and Gomorrah was such a wicked and corrupt place that God decided to destroy it. However, he sent angels to warn Lot and his family so that they could escape without being harmed. The angels told Lot's family to escape and warned them not to look back. Lot and his daughters listened to the angels, but Lot's wife looked back, and when she did, she became a pillar of salt. God wanted to give Lot's wife something new, but she only wanted her old life back.

I remember when I was growing up, I thought God was a fun-sucker. Everything that I considered "fun" seemed to be prohibited in the Bible. Christianity seemed like a bunch of rules. I thought that God wanted to take something from me, but later, I came to realize that he only wanted something better for me.

Maybe, like Lot's wife, you're in between where you used to be and where God wants you to be. Maybe you're questioning God and wondering if you were better off before. Like Lot's wife, maybe you're tempted to look back and return to your old life. If so, remember God doesn't want to take something from you. He wants something better for you.

Lord, thank you for wanting something better for me. Help me surrender to the life you have for me without looking back. Amen.

MAY 14

Having said these things, he spit on the ground and made mud with the saliva. Then he anointed the man's eyes with the mud and said to him, "Go, wash in the pool of Siloam" (which means Sent). So he went and washed and came back seeing.

John 9:6-7

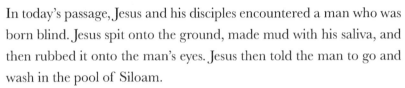

In today's passage, Jesus and his disciples encountered a man who was born blind. Jesus spit onto the ground, made mud with his saliva, and then rubbed it onto the man's eyes. Jesus then told the man to go and wash in the pool of Siloam.

Notice that Jesus didn't just heal this man. Instead, Jesus required him to take a step of faith. He told him to go and wash in the pool of Siloam, and he didn't tell him why. This guy had a choice to make. He could trust the guy who just rubbed spit on his eyes, or he could continue on with his normal life. He chose to trust Jesus. He went and washed in the pool, and he was healed.

Many sit around and claim that they're waiting on God. They claim they're waiting on God to open a door, answer a prayer, or provide for a need. Sometimes, it is necessary to wait on God, but sometimes, God's provision is dependent on your obedience. Maybe you're not waiting on God. Maybe he is waiting on you. Maybe he's waiting on you to be obedient and do whatever he's asked you to do. Like the blind man, you have a choice to make. You can trust Jesus, or you can continue on with your normal life.

Lord, help me trust you and discern your voice. Show me what step you want me to take and give me the courage to take it. Amen.

MAY 15

Now faith is the assurance of things hoped for, the conviction of things not seen. For by it the people of old received their commendation.

Hebrews 11:1-2

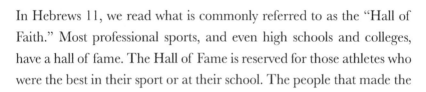

In Hebrews 11, we read what is commonly referred to as the "Hall of Faith." Most professional sports, and even high schools and colleges, have a hall of fame. The Hall of Fame is reserved for those athletes who were the best in their sport or at their school. The people that made the Hall of Faith made it not because of their fame, or success, or wealth, or athletic ability but, as the name suggests, because of their faith.

The book of Hebrews was originally written to the Hebrew Christians. These were Jews who had accepted Christ, but they were falling back into old traditions and routines. Rather than stepping out in faith, they were reverting to what was familiar and comfortable. Paul was encouraging them to imitate those in the Hall of Faith. He was encouraging them to step out in faith and trust God.

Maybe you've gotten comfortable and fallen back to old traditions and routines. Instead of stepping out in faith, perhaps you're reverting to what is familiar and comfortable. If so, be encouraged to imitate those in the Hall of Faith. Remember, you are saved by faith, but you're also called to live by faith.

Lord, thank you for all that you've done for me. Help me live by faith. Help me step away from what is comfortable and familiar to do what you want me to do. Amen.

MAY 16

Jesus answered him, "Truly, truly, I say to you, unless one is born again he cannot see the kingdom of God."

John 3:3

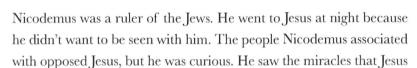

Nicodemus was a ruler of the Jews. He went to Jesus at night because he didn't want to be seen with him. The people Nicodemus associated with opposed Jesus, but he was curious. He saw the miracles that Jesus was performing and knew that he had to be a teacher from God.

He approached Jesus with some small talk, but Jesus got right down to business. Jesus told him that in order to see the kingdom of God, a person must be born again. Nicodemus didn't understand; he thought Jesus was referring to a physical birth, but Jesus was actually referring to a spiritual birth. In order for a person to get to Heaven, they must be born twice. They must have a physical birth and a spiritual birth; they must be born again.

Nicodemus was religious and well-educated in the law, but at this point in his life, he had not been born again. What about you? Have you been born again? Are you sure that you have a relationship with Jesus? If not, you can start a relationship with him right now. You can be born again by confessing your sin, asking for forgiveness, and surrendering your life to him.

Lord, thank you for making a way for me to be born again. Forgive me of my sins. From this moment forward, I will follow you with all of my heart. Amen.

MAY 17

But striking a reef, they ran the vessel aground. The bow stuck and remained immovable, and the stern was being broken up by the surf.

Acts 27:41

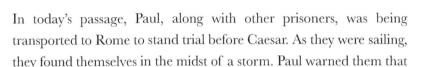

In today's passage, Paul, along with other prisoners, was being transported to Rome to stand trial before Caesar. As they were sailing, they found themselves in the midst of a storm. Paul warned them that it would be dangerous to continue the journey, but they ignored his warning and continued on.

As Paul predicted, the storm put them all in danger. They were forced to throw their cargo overboard in an effort to lighten the load and increase the stability of the ship. An angel ended up appearing to Paul and telling him that everyone on the ship would survive. Although Paul was a prisoner, he quickly became the leader on the ship, and the others listened to what he had to say. Eventually, the ship wrecked, but just as the angel told Paul, everyone survived.

God protected Paul and gave him strength in the midst of the storm, and he will do the same for you. If you listen to and look to God, he will give you the strength to navigate the storms of life. He will give you direction and clarity, even when you're surrounded by panic and chaos. Like Paul, in the midst of the storm, remain calm and trust God.

Lord, thank you for the direction and clarity that you give me. Help me remain calm and trust you in the midst of the storm. Amen.

MAY 18

And the Lord said to Moses, "I have heard the grumbling of the people of Israel. Say to them, 'At twilight you shall eat meat, and in the morning you shall be filled with bread. Then you shall know that I am the Lord your God.'"

Exodus 16:11-12

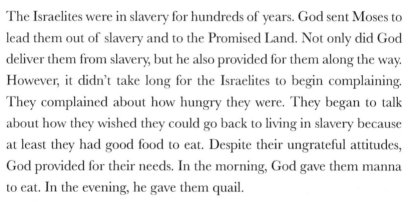

The Israelites were in slavery for hundreds of years. God sent Moses to lead them out of slavery and to the Promised Land. Not only did God deliver them from slavery, but he also provided for them along the way. However, it didn't take long for the Israelites to begin complaining. They complained about how hungry they were. They began to talk about how they wished they could go back to living in slavery because at least they had good food to eat. Despite their ungrateful attitudes, God provided for their needs. In the morning, God gave them manna to eat. In the evening, he gave them quail.

God proved to the Israelites that he would provide for their needs, and they had to learn to trust his provisions. Each day, he gave them just enough quail and manna for that day.

Have you ever wondered where God was? Have you ever felt like your prayers were going unanswered? Have you ever worried that a need would go unmet? You can rest assured that just as God heard the cries of the Israelites, he hears your cry. He knows what you need long before you do, and you can trust his provisions.

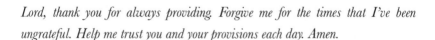

Lord, thank you for always providing. Forgive me for the times that I've been ungrateful. Help me trust you and your provisions each day. Amen.

MAY 19

But the Lord said to Samuel, "Do not look on his appearance or on the height of his stature, because I have rejected him. For the Lord sees not as man sees: man looks on the outward appearance, but the Lord looks on the heart."

1 Samuel 16:7

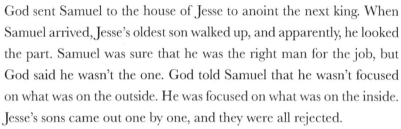

God sent Samuel to the house of Jesse to anoint the next king. When Samuel arrived, Jesse's oldest son walked up, and apparently, he looked the part. Samuel was sure that he was the right man for the job, but God said he wasn't the one. God told Samuel that he wasn't focused on what was on the outside. He was focused on what was on the inside. Jesse's sons came out one by one, and they were all rejected.

Samuel asked Jesse if he had any other sons, and he said his youngest son, David, was out keeping the sheep. They went and got David and brought him before Samuel. Sure enough, he was the one, and Samuel anointed him to be the next king.

We place so much emphasis on appearances. Unfortunately, some people are dismissed and judged solely based on how they appear. Other people are accepted and praised because of the way they appear. Many feel pressured to appear a certain way. The truth is that God cares far more about what's on the inside than what's on the outside. He doesn't turn people away because they dress or appear a certain way. He looks at the heart because that's what truly matters.

Lord, thank you for looking at what truly matters. Help me have the right heart. Give me eyes to see myself and others the way that you do. Amen.

MAY 20

Commit your work to the Lord, and your plans will be established.

Proverbs 16:3

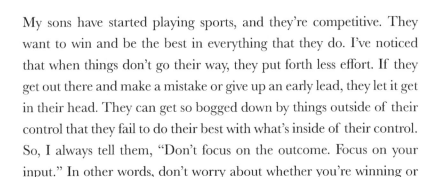

My sons have started playing sports, and they're competitive. They want to win and be the best in everything that they do. I've noticed that when things don't go their way, they put forth less effort. If they get out there and make a mistake or give up an early lead, they let it get in their head. They can get so bogged down by things outside of their control that they fail to do their best with what's inside of their control. So, I always tell them, "Don't focus on the outcome. Focus on your input." In other words, don't worry about whether you're winning or losing. Just focus on putting forth your best effort.

That message also carries over into life. You won't always have control over the outcome, but you do always have control over your input. Regardless of what's going on around you, you can put forth your best effort.

Maybe you're at a place in life where you feel like you're losing. Maybe it seems as if nothing is going your way and you're letting it get in your head. Maybe you're bogged down by things outside of your control. If so, "Commit your work to the Lord, and your plans will be established."

Lord, forgive me for allowing my circumstances to keep me from giving you my best. Help me focus less on the outcome and more on my input. Amen.

MAY 21

Again, if two lie together, they keep warm, but how can one keep warm alone? And though a man might prevail against one who is alone, two will withstand him—a threefold cord is not quickly broken.

Ecclesiastes 4:11-12

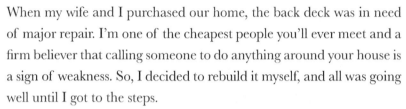

When my wife and I purchased our home, the back deck was in need of major repair. I'm one of the cheapest people you'll ever meet and a firm believer that calling someone to do anything around your house is a sign of weakness. So, I decided to rebuild it myself, and all was going well until I got to the steps.

Our deck has an exterior staircase that leads to a bonus room above our garage. I cut the stringers and attempted to put them in place by myself. Keep in mind, these are 2x12 boards that weigh as much as a small car, and I was on a ladder sixteen feet up in the air. It ended badly. I fell from the ladder, and I don't remember much, but I think the board landed on top of me. I broke my arm and was banged up pretty good, but fortunately, it wasn't much worse.

You probably aren't foolish enough to attempt to hang 2x12 stringers alone, but how often do you attempt to do life alone? One thing that has always stood out to me is the fact that even Jesus surrounded himself with twelve close friends. So, don't be afraid to confide in a friend. Seeking help from others is not a sign of weakness but a sign of strength, and it might just save you from a broken arm.

Lord, thank you for fellowship and community. Help me surround myself with the right people and ask for help when I need it. Amen.

MAY 22

I appeal to you, brothers, by the name of our Lord Jesus Christ, that all of you agree, and that there be no divisions among you, but that you be united in the same mind and the same judgment.

1 Corinthians 1:10

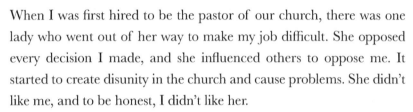

When I was first hired to be the pastor of our church, there was one lady who went out of her way to make my job difficult. She opposed every decision I made, and she influenced others to oppose me. It started to create disunity in the church and cause problems. She didn't like me, and to be honest, I didn't like her.

Eventually, I decided to invite her to the church for a meeting. I listened to her, and then she listened to me. During our conversation, it became clear that we both wanted the same thing, but we had very different approaches. I explained to her why I was doing what I was doing and how I thought it would positively impact the church. Long story short, she apologized for opposing me, we became friends, and she supported me from that moment forward.

People are more divided now than ever before. It's Republicans against Democrats. It's liberals against conservatives. It's rich against poor. It's race against race. It's denomination against denomination. If we're not careful, we can find ourselves arguing over things that don't matter and missing out on the things that do matter. As Christians, we must put away our differences, come together in unity, and work together for a common purpose.

Lord, forgive me for the times I've contributed to disunity. Help me put away my opinions and preferences and partner with others to accomplish your purposes. Amen.

MAY 23

For I know the plans I have for you, declares the Lord, plans for welfare and not for evil, to give you a future and a hope.

Jeremiah 29:11

When our family dog was a puppy, he was bad about wandering off. He would go out and terrorize our neighbors. They would come home to find him swimming in their pool, or we would come home to find shoes, balls, car parts, or something he had brought home. This became an ongoing problem, so I put in an underground fence. I buried the wire, put the collar on his neck, and within a couple of days, he knew his boundaries. After a while, he no longer needed the collar. Without the collar, he is free to go wherever he wants, but he's been conditioned to live within the boundaries of our property.

In that same way, we can allow the enemy to get in our heads. We can begin to believe things that aren't true. We can become conditioned to live within invisible boundaries that keep us from where God wants us.

Today's verse was addressed to the exiles in Babylon, but it still has application today. God has an incredible plan for those who are in Christ. They are promised a future and a hope. If you are a believer, not only do you have a future in Heaven, but you also have a purpose on Earth. Don't allow invisible boundaries to keep you from what God has for you.

Lord, thank you for my purpose. Show me if I'm allowing invisible boundaries to keep me from what you have for me. Help me trust your plan. Amen.

MAY 24

And making a whip of cords, he drove them all out of the temple, with the sheep and oxen. And he poured out the coins of the money-changers and overturned their tables.

John 2:15

The Passover was at hand. People were traveling from all over to come to Jerusalem. Unfortunately, some saw the Passover as an opportunity to profit, not an opportunity to worship. They set up shop in the temple. They sold animals so that people could buy animals to offer a sacrifice to the Lord. They also exchanged currencies because there was only a certain type of currency that was accepted in the temple. They were actually providing necessary services, but it's questionable whether the temple was the appropriate place.

However, the bigger issue was greed. They were taking advantage of people by charging inflated prices. When Jesus saw what was going on, he blew a fuse. He made a whip and literally started driving people out of the temple. He poured out the money and overturned the tables. Jesus was far more concerned with purifying the temple than with enlarging it.

Churches today must be careful not to fall into a similar trap. Obsessing over enlarging the church can lead to compromise. Decisions can be made to appease people, not God. Sermons can be preached that make people feel comfortable without challenging them to live up to biblical standards. Numerical growth is important, but it should always take a backseat to spiritual growth. Like Jesus, we should be far more concerned with purifying the church than with enlarging it.

Lord, thank you for the church. Help me prioritize spiritual growth over numerical growth. Show me what areas of my life need purifying. Amen.

MAY 25

I give them eternal life, and they will never perish, and no one will snatch them out of my hand.

John 10:28

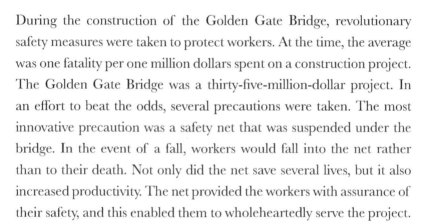

During the construction of the Golden Gate Bridge, revolutionary safety measures were taken to protect workers. At the time, the average was one fatality per one million dollars spent on a construction project. The Golden Gate Bridge was a thirty-five-million-dollar project. In an effort to beat the odds, several precautions were taken. The most innovative precaution was a safety net that was suspended under the bridge. In the event of a fall, workers would fall into the net rather than to their death. Not only did the net save several lives, but it also increased productivity. The net provided the workers with assurance of their safety, and this enabled them to wholeheartedly serve the project.

Over the years, I've witnessed people get saved multiple times. They get saved, but then they sin and fear that maybe they've done something to lose their salvation, so they go back through the process all over again. Jesus tells us that when we are his, we are his. No one can snatch us out of his hand. The truth is that a person cannot lose their salvation. If you are saved, you are eternally secure. This biblical truth should give you assurance and enable you to wholeheartedly serve the Lord.

Lord, thank you for the gift of salvation. Thank you for saving me. Help me rest in your grace and wholeheartedly serve you. Amen.

MAY 26

Why do you see the speck that is in your brother's eye, but do not notice the log that is in your own eye?

Matthew 7:3

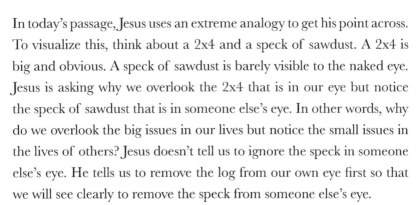

In today's passage, Jesus uses an extreme analogy to get his point across. To visualize this, think about a 2x4 and a speck of sawdust. A 2x4 is big and obvious. A speck of sawdust is barely visible to the naked eye. Jesus is asking why we overlook the 2x4 that is in our eye but notice the speck of sawdust that is in someone else's eye. In other words, why do we overlook the big issues in our lives but notice the small issues in the lives of others? Jesus doesn't tell us to ignore the speck in someone else's eye. He tells us to remove the log from our own eye first so that we will see clearly to remove the speck from someone else's eye.

When there's an issue at work, do you focus on what you can do to better the situation? Or are you too focused on what everybody else did or didn't do to contribute to the problem? When there's a conflict in your marriage or another relationship, do you take responsibility for what you did and work to improve? Are you growing and working to better yourself? Or are you too busy talking about everybody else?

You can waste time critiquing others, or you can work to better yourself. Remember to remove the log from our own eye before trying to remove the speck from your brother's eye.

Lord, forgive me for being hypocritical. Help me be harder on myself than others. Show me the areas I need to work on and make me more aware of my weaknesses. Amen.

MAY 27

"And when she has found it, she calls together her friends and neighbors, saying, 'Rejoice with me, for I have found the coin that I had lost.' Just so, I tell you, there is joy before the angels of God over one sinner who repents."

Luke 15:9-10

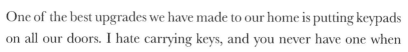

One of the best upgrades we have made to our home is putting keypads on all our doors. I hate carrying keys, and you never have one when you need it. With keypads, you don't have to worry about that.... until the batteries die.

We were recently in a situation where we found ourselves locked out of our bonus room, and we couldn't find a key because we hadn't needed one for years. We searched every drawer, ripped apart couches, and looked in every corner and crevice. We found dozens of keys but not the one we needed. After hours of searching, I was on the verge of breaking the window when my wife finally located the key. We both rejoiced together and made sure to put the key in a safe place for future use.

Have you ever misplaced something of great value? If so, you probably went to great lengths to find it. And if you were fortunate enough to find it, you probably rejoiced and celebrated its return. In that same way, Jesus tells us the angels in Heaven rejoice when one sinner repents. Life change never gets old. If you've been saved, never stop rejoicing. If you have the privilege to witness others get saved, never stop rejoicing. There is nothing sweeter than seeing lost people find Jesus.

Lord, thank you for taking death and turning it into life. Thank you for the gift of salvation. When lost people find you, help me celebrate with the angels in Heaven. Amen.

MAY 28

And the man and his wife were both naked and were not ashamed.

Genesis 2:25

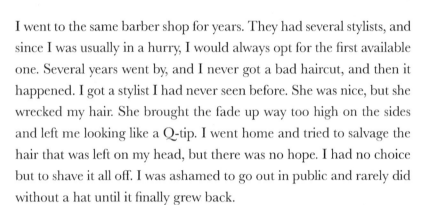

I went to the same barber shop for years. They had several stylists, and since I was usually in a hurry, I would always opt for the first available one. Several years went by, and I never got a bad haircut, and then it happened. I got a stylist I had never seen before. She was nice, but she wrecked my hair. She brought the fade up way too high on the sides and left me looking like a Q-tip. I went home and tried to salvage the hair that was left on my head, but there was no hope. I had no choice but to shave it all off. I was ashamed to go out in public and rarely did without a hat until it finally grew back.

Before Adam and Eve ate the forbidden fruit, shame didn't exist. They were naked, but they weren't ashamed. However, as soon as they ate the fruit, they became ashamed, and they hid from God.

We've all been ashamed. Maybe you're struggling with shame right now. Maybe you're struggling to get past something in your past. Fortunately, you can find freedom from shame through Jesus. When you put your faith in him, you're no longer defined by what you've done but by what he did on the cross. You're no longer defined by who you are but by who he is.

Lord, thank you for what you did on the cross. Forgive me of my sins. Help me get past my shame and find freedom in you. Amen.

MAY 29

Put to death therefore what is earthly in you: sexual immorality, impurity, passion, evil desire, and covetousness, which is idolatry. On account of these the wrath of God is coming.

Colossians 3:5-6

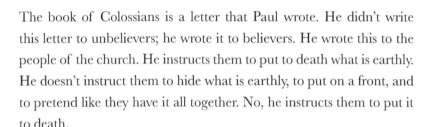

The book of Colossians is a letter that Paul wrote. He didn't write this letter to unbelievers; he wrote it to believers. He wrote this to the people of the church. He instructs them to put to death what is earthly. He doesn't instruct them to hide what is earthly, to put on a front, and to pretend like they have it all together. No, he instructs them to put it to death.

Church is a place where people should feel comfortable bringing their baggage. People should feel comfortable talking about their sin and their struggles. People should feel comfortable sharing their deepest and darkest secrets. The church should be a judgment-free zone. But is it? Or is there more coverup than confession? Is there more concealment than discussion? The unfortunate truth is that most people feel more comfortable being themselves at work on Monday than they do at church on Sunday.

We come to church, put on a front, and pretend to have it all together. A marriage may be falling apart, a person may be struggling with addiction, or someone may be battling depression, but you would never know from the outside looking in. We've become great at hiding what is earthly, but have we put it to death?

Lord, thank you for making a way for me to be set free from sin. Show me what is earthly in me and help me put it to death. Amen.

MAY 30

John answered, "A person cannot receive even one thing unless it is given him from heaven."

John 3:27

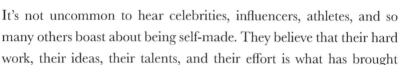

It's not uncommon to hear celebrities, influencers, athletes, and so many others boast about being self-made. They believe that their hard work, their ideas, their talents, and their effort is what has brought them success. This is an easy trap to fall into, but the Bible teaches that "A person cannot receive even one thing unless it is given him from heaven." In other words, if you have it, it's because God gave it to you.

There's nothing wrong with being proud of your hard work. Hard work certainly plays a role in success, but you have to remember who gave you the ability to work hard. There's nothing wrong with being proud of a successful idea, but you have to remember who gave you the ability to think. There's nothing wrong with being proud of an accomplishment, but you have to remember who gave you the talent to accomplish it. There's nothing wrong with being proud of the things that you have, but you have to remember who gave them to you.

God is behind it all. Your upbringing, your work ethic, your brain power, your gifts and talents, he's behind it all. The truth is that none of us are self-made. We're all God-made. Take some time today and acknowledge his goodness in your life. Remember, if you have it, it's because he gave it to you.

Lord, thank you for your goodness in my life. You have given me everything that I have. Help me give you the praise and glory that you deserve. Amen.

MAY 31

Cast your burden on the Lord, and he will sustain you; he will never permit the righteous to be moved.

Psalm 55:22

It's amazing what a new perspective can do. One day, I was driving down the road, going through a mental list of everything I was stressed about. The list was long and included things like paying bills, finishing a project around the house, completing a college assignment, writing a sermon for Sunday morning, etc. Out of nowhere, I felt the Holy Spirit whisper, "Sean, you're blessed." At that moment, it dawned on me that the things I was stressed about were blessings.

As ironic as it sounds, there are a lot of people who would love to be concerned about paying bills. There are a lot of people who would love to own a house and have projects to complete. There are a lot of people who would love to have the opportunity to get a college education. There are a lot of people who would love to have the opportunity to preach God's Word. Driving down the road that day, God gave me a new perspective. I went from stressing about the stuff I had to do to praising God for the things he had entrusted me to do.

You may not be stressed about trivial things, but whatever is weighing you down, it matters to God. If you'll cast your burdens on him, he will give you a new perspective.

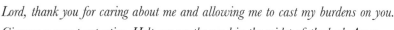

Lord, thank you for caring about me and allowing me to cast my burdens on you. Give me a new perspective. Help me see the good in the midst of the bad. Amen.

JUNE 1

Examine yourselves, to see whether you are in the faith. Test yourselves. Or do you not realize this about yourselves, that Jesus Christ is in you?—unless indeed you fail to meet the test!

2 Corinthians 13:5

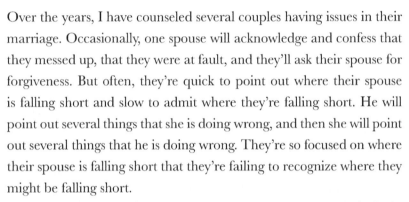

Over the years, I have counseled several couples having issues in their marriage. Occasionally, one spouse will acknowledge and confess that they messed up, that they were at fault, and they'll ask their spouse for forgiveness. But often, they're quick to point out where their spouse is falling short and slow to admit where they're falling short. He will point out several things that she is doing wrong, and then she will point out several things that he is doing wrong. They're so focused on where their spouse is falling short that they're failing to recognize where they might be falling short.

We tend to have this gift where we can quickly identify faults in others while overlooking faults in ourselves. We tend to critique others harshly while making excuses for ourselves.

At the end of your life, you will stand before God. He won't ask you to give an account of the life somebody else lived. He will ask you to give an account of the life you lived. Take some time today to examine yourself. Where are you falling short? What are your weaknesses? What can you do to become a better spouse, parent, employee, employer, or church member?

Lord, help me examine myself. Show me where I am weak and need to improve. Help me focus on improving myself instead of critiquing others. Amen.

JUNE 2

Who comforts us in all our affliction, so that we may be able to comfort those who are in any affliction, with the comfort with which we ourselves are comforted by God.

2 Corinthians 1:4

I remember the first time I watched *Rocky*. It was life-changing. I had never been so inspired in my life. I remember downloading "Eye of the Tiger" to my MP3 player and listening to it on repeat. I never boxed a day in my life, but when I would go running, I couldn't help but airbox just like Rocky did in the movie. My favorite part is in *Rocky IV* when Rocky avenged Creed's loss by taking down the Russian. If you haven't watched that series, stop reading now, go watch, and then come back.

Have you ever heard a story that inspired you? Maybe a story about someone making a drastic physical transformation in a short period of time. Maybe a story about someone who started with nothing and built a valuable company. Maybe a story about someone overcoming their past and making something of themselves. Everybody loves an inspiring story.

What if I told you that God wants to use you to inspire others? I don't know what you're going through, but I do know that God can bring you through it. And not only can he bring you through it, but he can also use it for your good and for his glory. He can take the test and turn it into a testimony. He can take the pain and turn it into a platform. He can take the mess and turn it into a ministry.

Lord, thank you for your inspiring Word. Give me the strength to make it through what I am going through and use my story to inspire others. Amen.

JUNE 3

This is the day that the Lord has made; let us rejoice and be glad in it.

Psalm 118:24

I am a planner. It's not unusual for me to schedule meetings, events, and sermon series several months in advance. I also have goals. I know where I want the church to be in five years. I know where I want my family to be financially in five years. I know what I want to accomplish in the next five years. I know what areas I want to improve over the next five years. I'm a forward-focused person. This is a trait that I am proud of, but it's also one that has held me back at certain times. If I'm not careful, I can become so focused on the future that I fail to give God my best in the present.

Life comes and goes quickly. None of us are guaranteed tomorrow or even another breath, for that matter. Planning and having future goals is great, but you have to be careful. You can become so focused on what's next that you miss what's now.

The reality is that you have no control over the past and little control over the future. You have the most control right now, in the present. Will you enjoy what God has given you? Will you give him your best today? "This is the day the Lord has made; let us rejoice and be glad in it."

Lord, thank you for today. Help me focus on giving you my very best right now. Show me ways that I can serve you today. Amen.

JUNE 4

If possible, so far as it depends on you, live peaceably with all.

Romans 12:18

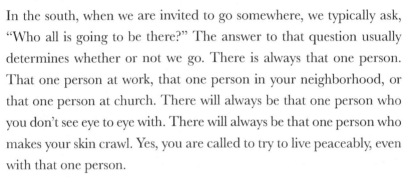

In the south, when we are invited to go somewhere, we typically ask, "Who all is going to be there?" The answer to that question usually determines whether or not we go. There is always that one person. That one person at work, that one person in your neighborhood, or that one person at church. There will always be that one person who you don't see eye to eye with. There will always be that one person who makes your skin crawl. Yes, you are called to try to live peaceably, even with that one person.

I've had my fair share of struggles with others. There have been countless times when I could have chosen peace, but instead, I chose conflict. I wanted to make a point. I wanted to stand up. I wanted to argue. I let my pride get the best of me and ended up doing the opposite of what God calls me to do. I contributed to the conflict and got further away from peace.

What about you? Are you struggling to live peaceably with all? Are there times when you could keep the peace, but instead, you contribute to conflict? Is there anybody that you're not at peace with right now? Peace is not always possible, but the Bible is clear: you should do everything you can to seek it.

Lord, forgive me for the times I've contributed to conflict. Help me get past my pride and live peaceably with all. Amen.

JUNE 5

But Abraham said, 'Child, remember that you in your lifetime received your good things, and Lazarus in like manner bad things; but now he is comforted here, and you are in anguish.'

Luke 16:25

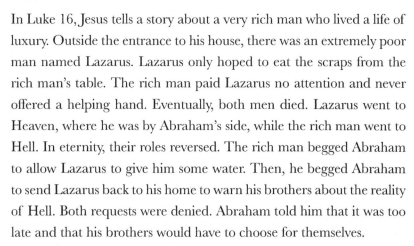

In Luke 16, Jesus tells a story about a very rich man who lived a life of luxury. Outside the entrance to his house, there was an extremely poor man named Lazarus. Lazarus only hoped to eat the scraps from the rich man's table. The rich man paid Lazarus no attention and never offered a helping hand. Eventually, both men died. Lazarus went to Heaven, where he was by Abraham's side, while the rich man went to Hell. In eternity, their roles reversed. The rich man begged Abraham to allow Lazarus to give him some water. Then, he begged Abraham to send Lazarus back to his home to warn his brothers about the reality of Hell. Both requests were denied. Abraham told him that it was too late and that his brothers would have to choose for themselves.

One key takeaway from this story is that Christians should not be indifferent to the less fortunate. God's desire is for us to help those who are hurting and to give to those who are struggling.

It's easy to get caught up in your own agenda and overlook the needs around you. There might be people in your neighborhood, at your place of work, or sitting next to you in church who are in need. Like the rich man, you can keep living your life, or you can learn from his mistake and lend a helping hand.

Lord, thank you for giving me the means to help others. Show me the needs of the people around me and help me lend a helping hand. Amen.

JUNE 6

So if you are offering your gift at the altar and there remember that your brother has something against you, leave your gift there before the altar and go. First be reconciled to your brother, and then come and offer your gift.

Matthew 5:23-24

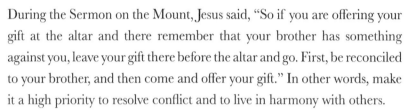

During the Sermon on the Mount, Jesus said, "So if you are offering your gift at the altar and there remember that your brother has something against you, leave your gift there before the altar and go. First, be reconciled to your brother, and then come and offer your gift." In other words, make it a high priority to resolve conflict and to live in harmony with others.

Sadly, there are family members that don't speak with other family members. There are parents that don't speak to their kids and kids that don't speak to their parents. There are siblings that pretend one another doesn't exist. There are many broken and hurting relationships; often, it's over trivial things. Even in situations where real damage has been done, there is no way to biblically justify bitterness and unforgiveness. Jesus makes it clear that reconciliation is important enough to interrupt worship.

There's a common phrase, "Unforgiveness is like drinking poison and expecting it to kill the other person." The truth is that unforgiveness is not only hurting you but also your relationships with others and your relationship with God. This doesn't mean that you don't have a reason to be hurt, but it does mean that the process of healing will not begin until you choose to forgive. If reconciliation is important enough to interrupt worship, it's important enough to interrupt whatever you're doing right now.

Lord, forgive me for bitterness and unforgiveness. Show me if there is anyone I need to make amends with right now. Amen.

JUNE 7

And when they had appointed elders for them in every church, with prayer and fasting they committed them to the Lord in whom they had believed.

Acts 14:23

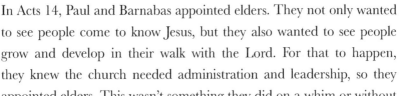

In Acts 14, Paul and Barnabas appointed elders. They not only wanted to see people come to know Jesus, but they also wanted to see people grow and develop in their walk with the Lord. For that to happen, they knew the church needed administration and leadership, so they appointed elders. This wasn't something they did on a whim or without much thought. They knew they were limited in what they could do. They could appoint whoever they felt was best, but the church's health and future was up to God, so they devoted themselves to prayer and fasting.

I wish I could say that I always bathe every decision I make in prayer. I wish I could say that I always spend time fasting and seeking God's will. The truth is that I often make decisions on a whim. Most of the mistakes I have made thus far could have been avoided if I had devoted myself to prayer and fasting.

What about you? Is there a big decision you need to make? A big purchase? An investment opportunity? A new career or promotion? A move to an unfamiliar location? An idea for a ministry? If so, don't make a decision on a whim. Devote yourself to prayer and fasting, and refuse to move forward without God's approval.

Lord, forgive me for the times I've made big decisions on a whim. I pray that you give me clarity and show me the direction you want me to go in. Amen.

JUNE 8

And I tell you, ask, and it will be given to you; seek, and you will find; knock, and it will be opened to you.

Luke 11:9

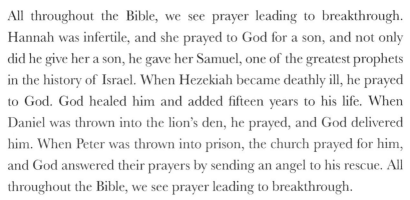

All throughout the Bible, we see prayer leading to breakthrough. Hannah was infertile, and she prayed to God for a son, and not only did he give her a son, he gave her Samuel, one of the greatest prophets in the history of Israel. When Hezekiah became deathly ill, he prayed to God. God healed him and added fifteen years to his life. When Daniel was thrown into the lion's den, he prayed, and God delivered him. When Peter was thrown into prison, the church prayed for him, and God answered their prayers by sending an angel to his rescue. All throughout the Bible, we see prayer leading to breakthrough.

And not only do we read about God answering prayers in the Bible, but we also see God answering prayers today. Our church has a prayer ministry that receives requests on a daily basis. We are blessed to be able to pray for so many people in our community and around the world. Many people who request prayer later send us praise reports, letting us know their prayer has been answered.

Are you praying expectantly and boldly? If your prayers were answered, would it change the world? If not, what should you do differently going forward? Remember, prayer leads to breakthrough.

Lord, thank you for answering prayers. Help me pray expectantly and boldly. I ask for revival and breakthrough. Amen.

JUNE 9

Trust in the Lord with all your heart, and do not lean on your own understanding. In all your ways acknowledge him, and he will make straight your paths.

Proverbs 3:5-6

A few years back, I started bowhunting, and in that process, I learned a lot about trajectories. I learned that very small changes can greatly change the arrow's trajectory. A small change in stance, a small change in grip, a small change in breathing, a small shift in your anchor point, these are small things that can be the difference between hitting the bullseye and missing the target all together.

The same is true when it comes to life. One small decision, good or bad, can greatly change your trajectory. One small habit, good or bad, can greatly change your trajectory. One relationship, good or bad, can greatly change your trajectory. A job change, an investment, a business opportunity, a step of faith. These are small things that can change your trajectory and make a big difference in your life.

It is wise to be more focused on your current trajectory than on your current results. In other words, you should be focused on where you're going rather than where you are. You might not be where you want to be right now, but are you doing the things right now that will get you there in the future? Trust in the Lord with all your heart, and he will make straight your paths.

Lord, thank you for the plan that you have for my life. Help me do the right things now that will get me where you want me to be in the future. Amen.

JUNE 10

Now Thomas, one of the twelve, called the Twin, was not with them when Jesus came. So the other disciples told him, "We have seen the Lord." But he said to them, "Unless I see in his hands the mark of the nails, and place my finger into the mark of the nails, and place my hand into his side, I will never believe."

John 20:24-25

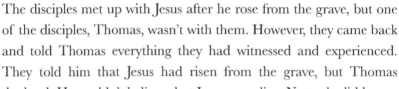

The disciples met up with Jesus after he rose from the grave, but one of the disciples, Thomas, wasn't with them. However, they came back and told Thomas everything they had witnessed and experienced. They told him that Jesus had risen from the grave, but Thomas doubted. He couldn't believe that Jesus was alive. Not only did he say he needed physical evidence to believe what they were telling him, he said he would have to touch Jesus's nail-scarred hands and feel where the spear pierced Jesus's side, or he would never believe.

Eight days later, Jesus appeared to the disciples again, and this time Thomas was with them. Jesus went up to Thomas and let him feel his hands and his side, just as he had requested. Thomas quickly went from doubting God to worshiping God.

In Christian circles, doubt is almost always viewed in a negative context. When doubt sets in, many feel ashamed. They run and hide from their doubt. They put on a front because they fear that other Christians may think less of them. They feel that God will be disappointed in them. The truth is that doubt can be beneficial to your faith. Like Thomas, if you're open and honest about your doubt, God will meet you in the middle of it and help you come out stronger.

Lord, thank you for meeting me in the middle of my doubt. Give me the courage to be open and honest about my doubt and use it to strengthen my faith. Amen.

JUNE 11

But be doers of the word, and not hearers only, deceiving yourselves.

James 1:22

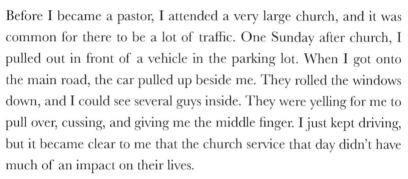

Before I became a pastor, I attended a very large church, and it was common for there to be a lot of traffic. One Sunday after church, I pulled out in front of a vehicle in the parking lot. When I got onto the main road, the car pulled up beside me. They rolled the windows down, and I could see several guys inside. They were yelling for me to pull over, cussing, and giving me the middle finger. I just kept driving, but it became clear to me that the church service that day didn't have much of an impact on their lives.

James instructs us to be doers of the Word and not hearers only. It's one thing to hear a message. It's another thing to apply it. It's one thing to read your Bible. It's another thing to live it out.

Are you a hearer or a doer of the Word? Do you go to church, sing a few songs, listen to a sermon, and then go right back to what you were doing, or do you apply it in your daily life? Do you read your Bible and then go right back to what you were doing, or do you live it out? Be a doer, not a hearer only.

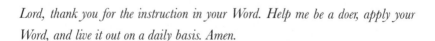

Lord, thank you for the instruction in your Word. Help me be a doer, apply your Word, and live it out on a daily basis. Amen.

JUNE 12

So also faith by itself, if it does not have works, is dead.

James 2:17

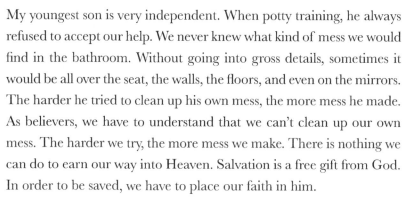

My youngest son is very independent. When potty training, he always refused to accept our help. We never knew what kind of mess we would find in the bathroom. Without going into gross details, sometimes it would be all over the seat, the walls, the floors, and even on the mirrors. The harder he tried to clean up his own mess, the more mess he made. As believers, we have to understand that we can't clean up our own mess. The harder we try, the more mess we make. There is nothing we can do to earn our way into Heaven. Salvation is a free gift from God. In order to be saved, we have to place our faith in him.

We're saved by faith, not by works, but true saving faith is always accompanied by works. The Bible tells us that faith, apart from works, is dead. In other words, when a person puts their faith in Jesus, it's a spiritual impossibility for that person to remain the same.

What evidence is there in your life that you have been saved? Are you the same person you were five years ago, or has there been significant growth? You may not be where you want to be, but you should be a lot closer than you used to be.

Lord, thank you for the gift of salvation. Help me continue to grow and become more like you each day. Amen.

JUNE 13

But if not, be it known to you, O king, that we will not serve your gods or worship the golden image that you have set up.

Daniel 3:18

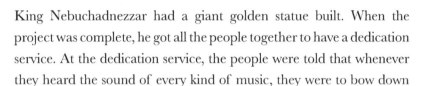

King Nebuchadnezzar had a giant golden statue built. When the project was complete, he got all the people together to have a dedication service. At the dedication service, the people were told that whenever they heard the sound of every kind of music, they were to bow down and worship the golden statue. If anyone refused to comply, they were warned that they would be thrown into the burning fiery furnace.

Despite the severe consequences, Shadrach, Meshach, and Abednego refused to obey the order. King Nebuchadnezzar brought them in and reminded them that if they didn't bow down, they would be thrown into the burning fiery furnace. Unphased by the threat, Shadrach, Meshach, and Abednego told the king they would not worship the golden statue he had built. In a rage, King Nebuchadnezzar had the furnace heated to seven times its normal temperature. Shadrach, Meshach, and Abednego were tied up and thrown inside. Long story short, God was with them inside of the furnace, and not only did they come out alive, but they also came out unharmed.

The story starts with King Nebuchadnezzar ordering the people to bow and worship a golden statue. The story ends with King Nebuchadnezzar giving glory to the God of Shadrach, Meshach, and Abednego. This story proves that it is possible to have unwavering faith in a wavering world.

Lord, forgive me for the times that I have bowed down to the things of this world. Give me the faith of Shadrach, Meshach, and Abednego. Amen.

JUNE 14

Is it a time for you yourselves to dwell in your paneled houses, while this house lies in ruins?

Haggai 1:4

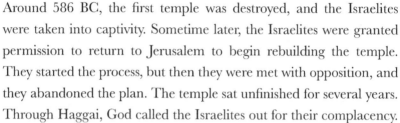

Around 586 BC, the first temple was destroyed, and the Israelites were taken into captivity. Sometime later, the Israelites were granted permission to return to Jerusalem to begin rebuilding the temple. They started the process, but then they were met with opposition, and they abandoned the plan. The temple sat unfinished for several years. Through Haggai, God called the Israelites out for their complacency. He called them out for making excuses and for procrastinating. They were living comfortably in their paneled houses while God's house laid in ruins. Because of Haggai's warning, the Israelites once again began rebuilding the temple.

It's easy to get your priorities out of order. It's easy to put something off temporarily and then forget about it all together. It's easy to become so focused on the little picture and to lose sight of the big picture. That's what happened to the Israelites. They became more concerned about their comfort than about God's calling.

If you're not careful, the same thing can happen to you. Whether you realize it or not, there are opportunities all around you to minister to others and live out the Word of God. Are you capitalizing on those opportunities, or have you become comfortable and complacent like the Israelites?

Lord, forgive me for falling short. Show me if there is any area of my life where I have become complacent. Help me stay focused on the big picture. Amen.

JUNE 15

You believe that God is one; you do well. Even the demons believe—and shudder!

James 2:19

———∽◦∾———

Born in 1824, Charles Blondin grew up to become a famous tightrope walker. Thousands of people would come out to watch him accomplish incredible feats. Without safety equipment, Blondin would walk across ropes that were high off the ground and that spanned long distances. One fall or misstep could have quickly ended his life.

Blondin's most popular feat was crossing a tightrope spanning Niagara Falls. At one point, Blondin was walking across the tightrope, pushing a wheelbarrow. After pushing the wheelbarrow across the rope, he asked the crowd if they thought he could push the wheelbarrow across the rope with someone inside of it. Everyone believed he could, but when he asked for a volunteer, nobody stepped up to the plate. Everybody believed that Blondin could make it across the rope, pushing someone in the wheelbarrow. Still, nobody was willing to take the leap of faith.

There's a big difference between belief and faith. Belief is not enough. James tells us that even the demons believe in God. Being a Christian requires more than a belief in God. It requires faith in God. When it comes to following him, are you standing on the sidelines or sitting in the wheelbarrow?

———∽◦∾———

Lord, thank you for always making a way. Forgive me for the times that I lack faith. Help me trust you and show me where I'm falling short. Amen.

JUNE 16

I have said these things to you, that in me you may have peace. In the world you will have tribulation. But take heart; I have overcome the world.

John 16:33

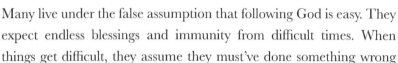

Many live under the false assumption that following God is easy. They expect endless blessings and immunity from difficult times. When things get difficult, they assume they must've done something wrong and God is punishing them. The truth is that the Bible has a lot more to say about the challenges we will face on Earth than the materialistic blessings we will receive.

Jesus tells his disciples, "In the world you will have tribulation." In other words, in this world, there will be times of trouble and suffering. This is true for both believers and unbelievers. However, when those times of tribulation come, believers can have peace because their hope is not in the world but in he who has overcome the world. The disciples went on to prove this true as they faced extreme persecution for living out the gospel without ever being deterred.

When things fail to go your way, do you panic and let anxiety take over, or are you at peace knowing that God is in control? When tragedy strikes, do you lose all hope or press on, knowing that this is only your temporary home? Remember, no matter what happens, Jesus has overcome the world.

Lord, thank you for overcoming the world. Give me peace in the midst of tribulation. Help me place my hope in you, not in this world. Amen.

JUNE 17

He will wipe away every tear from their eyes, and death shall be no more, neither shall there be mourning, nor crying, nor pain anymore, for the former things have passed away.

Revelation 21:4

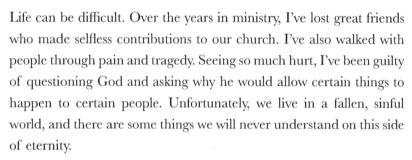

Life can be difficult. Over the years in ministry, I've lost great friends who made selfless contributions to our church. I've also walked with people through pain and tragedy. Seeing so much hurt, I've been guilty of questioning God and asking why he would allow certain things to happen to certain people. Unfortunately, we live in a fallen, sinful world, and there are some things we will never understand on this side of eternity.

The Bible doesn't promise us a life of ease. Instead, the Bible makes it clear that we will face difficult times. Pain and tragedy are inevitable parts of life, but one day, Jesus is coming back, and he is going to make everything that is wrong right.

If you are a Christian, your best days are before you. You can look forward to a day when there will be no more sickness, sorrow, or pain. A day when pain and physical limitations will no longer exist. A day when you will no longer be in the flesh and struggle with sin. A day when stress and worry will be a thing of the past. One day you will spend eternity in Heaven with Jesus. What a day that will be!

Lord, thank you for the gift of eternal life. Thank you for securing my future in Heaven by dying on the cross. I look forward to spending eternity with you. Amen.

JUNE 18

I press on toward the goal for the prize of the upward call of God in Christ Jesus.

Philippians 3:14

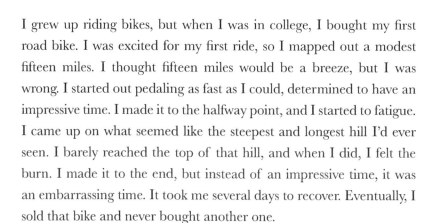

I grew up riding bikes, but when I was in college, I bought my first road bike. I was excited for my first ride, so I mapped out a modest fifteen miles. I thought fifteen miles would be a breeze, but I was wrong. I started out pedaling as fast as I could, determined to have an impressive time. I made it to the halfway point, and I started to fatigue. I came up on what seemed like the steepest and longest hill I'd ever seen. I barely reached the top of that hill, and when I did, I felt the burn. I made it to the end, but instead of an impressive time, it was an embarrassing time. It took me several days to recover. Eventually, I sold that bike and never bought another one.

A lot of times, people start out strong, but then they quickly get weary. A lot of times, people start out enthusiastic, but then they quickly fizzle out. In today's verse, Paul encourages us to press on to reach the end of the race. Starting can be hard, but it's only half the battle. In order to reach the end of the race, a person must persevere long after the initial excitement wears off. I don't know what you're in the middle of but press on to reach the end of the race.

Lord, forgive me for the times that I've quit. Give me the strength to persevere. Help me press on to reach the end of the race. Amen.

JUNE 19

So also the tongue is a small member, yet it boasts of great things. How great a forest is set ablaze by such a small fire!

James 3:5

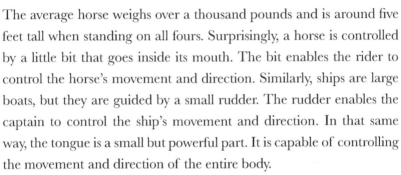

The average horse weighs over a thousand pounds and is around five feet tall when standing on all fours. Surprisingly, a horse is controlled by a little bit that goes inside its mouth. The bit enables the rider to control the horse's movement and direction. Similarly, ships are large boats, but they are guided by a small rudder. The rudder enables the captain to control the ship's movement and direction. In that same way, the tongue is a small but powerful part. It is capable of controlling the movement and direction of the entire body.

Your tongue is dangerous, it's evil, it's full of deadly poison. If you just let it go, it's going to lead you in the wrong direction. And it's going to cause uncontrollable damage to yourself and others. The solution is simple but far from easy: you must learn to tame your tongue. This is a difficult task but possible with the Holy Spirit. With the help of the Holy Spirit, your speech can become uplifting and God-honoring.

The words you speak are capable of doing good or causing harm. The words you speak are capable of leading you in the right direction or leading you astray. The words you speak are capable of building others up or tearing others down. Today, choose your words wisely.

Lord, thank you for this day. Help me tame my tongue and use my words to build others up. Show me when my words aren't honoring to you. Amen.

JUNE 20

And the Lord said, "Behold, they are one people, and they have all one language, and this is only the beginning of what they will do. And nothing that they propose to do will now be impossible for them."

Genesis 11:6

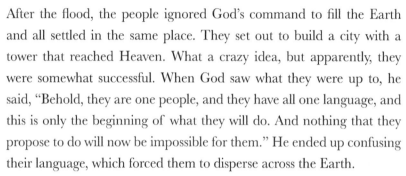

After the flood, the people ignored God's command to fill the Earth and all settled in the same place. They set out to build a city with a tower that reached Heaven. What a crazy idea, but apparently, they were somewhat successful. When God saw what they were up to, he said, "Behold, they are one people, and they have all one language, and this is only the beginning of what they will do. And nothing that they propose to do will now be impossible for them." He ended up confusing their language, which forced them to disperse across the Earth.

One thing that has always fascinated me about this passage is the fact that the people were able to do something so improbable by working together. They were on their way toward building a tower that reached Heaven until God confused their language. What makes this even more fascinating is the fact that the improbable thing they were doing was in disobedience to God.

Imagine what we could accomplish if we worked together, not in disobedience, but in obedience to God. What if we worked together to feed the hungry, to house the homeless, or to reach the unreached? There is power in numbers and unity. Will you put away your preferences and desires to be a part of something bigger than yourself?

Lord, thank you for using people like me to accomplish your purposes. Help me partner with others to further your kingdom. Show me the power of unity. Amen.

JUNE 21

Brothers, if anyone is caught in any transgression, you who are spiritual should restore him in a spirit of gentleness. Keep watch on yourself, lest you too be tempted. Bear one another's burdens, and so fulfill the law of Christ.

Galatians 6:1-2

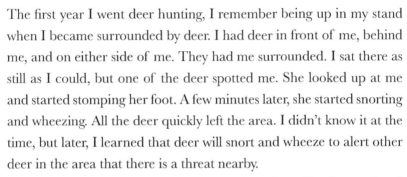

The first year I went deer hunting, I remember being up in my stand when I became surrounded by deer. I had deer in front of me, behind me, and on either side of me. They had me surrounded. I sat there as still as I could, but one of the deer spotted me. She looked up at me and started stomping her foot. A few minutes later, she started snorting and wheezing. All the deer quickly left the area. I didn't know it at the time, but later, I learned that deer will snort and wheeze to alert other deer in the area that there is a threat nearby.

I'm thankful to have people in my life who will tell me what I need to hear, even when it's not what I want to hear. They alert me when I'm in danger or when there's a threat nearby. They hold me accountable and have the courage to call me out when I am wrong. They tell me the truth and restore me in a spirit of gentleness.

Who's alerting you when you get off course? Who's alerting you when there's danger or a threat nearby? Who's there to restore you in a spirit of gentleness? Have you invited accountability into your life?

Lord, thank you for placing others in my life to hold me accountable. Help me listen to advice and heed warnings when they are given. Amen.

JUNE 22

Pride goes before destruction, and a haughty spirit before a fall.

Proverbs 16:18

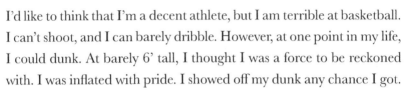

I'd like to think that I'm a decent athlete, but I am terrible at basketball. I can't shoot, and I can barely dribble. However, at one point in my life, I could dunk. At barely 6' tall, I thought I was a force to be reckoned with. I was inflated with pride. I showed off my dunk any chance I got.

One year, I went to a children's camp with a group from our church. I was playing basketball in sandals with a group of third graders. For whatever reason, I felt the need to impress these kids and show off my dunking skills. I went up, I think I missed the dunk, and then I came back down and landed awkwardly on my ankle. Within a few minutes, it swelled up like a balloon. Within a few hours, I could barely walk. Fortunately, it was toward the end of the week, but I spent the remainder of that camp limping from place to place.

"Pride goes before destruction." Just when you think you have arrived, you are reminded of how far away you still are. Just when you think you've beaten a sin, you are reminded just how weak you still are. Just when you think that relationship couldn't be any stronger, you are reminded how quickly it can fall apart. Is there an area of your life that you have become overly confident in? If so, repent, humble yourself and recognize that without God, you would be nothing and have nothing.

Lord, forgive me for my arrogance. Without you, I would be nothing and have nothing. Help me walk in humility and remember how weak I really am. Amen.

JUNE 23

And if I go and prepare a place for you, I will come again and will take you to myself, that where I am you may be also.

John 14:3

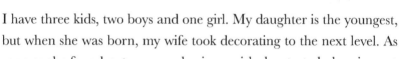

I have three kids, two boys and one girl. My daughter is the youngest, but when she was born, my wife took decorating to the next level. As soon as she found out we were having a girl, she started planning out the nursery. She made me paint, put up wallpaper, and hang pictures. She had the carpet cleaned and custom bedding and curtains made. Long before our daughter arrived, we spent hours preparing her room.

Isn't it comforting to know that Jesus is in Heaven doing the same for us? He has gone to prepare a place for us. We fear and mourn death. We do everything we can to prolong our lives here on Earth. I recently heard about a man that invested a ridiculous amount of money to have his body frozen after death with hope that he could be resurrected in the future. What's this world coming to?

Death isn't something we like to think or talk about, but the truth is that death is only the beginning for those who have a relationship with Jesus. We should value and make the most of the time we have on Earth but also remember that the best is yet to come. One day, we will spend an eternity in Heaven. That's not something we should fear but something we should anticipate.

Lord, thank you for preparing a place for me. I look forward to spending an eternity in Heaven with you. Amen.

JUNE 24

Set your minds on things that are above, not on things that are on earth.

Colossians 3:2

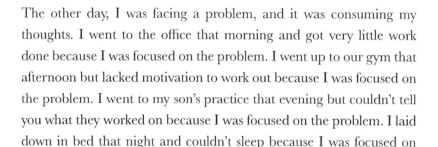

The other day, I was facing a problem, and it was consuming my thoughts. I went to the office that morning and got very little work done because I was focused on the problem. I went up to our gym that afternoon but lacked motivation to work out because I was focused on the problem. I went to my son's practice that evening but couldn't tell you what they worked on because I was focused on the problem. I laid down in bed that night and couldn't sleep because I was focused on the problem. I wish I could say that's abnormal, but it's the norm. My thoughts are often consumed by what's going on around me.

"Set your minds on things that are above, not on things that are on earth." What does that mean? It means that our thoughts shouldn't be consumed by the things of the Earth but by the things of God.

What is consuming your thoughts? What do you think about the most? Your career or business? Money? Your kids? Your marriage? Your favorite team? We all think about different things, but most of us must admit that we are guilty of setting our minds on things that are on Earth. Today, strive to set your mind on things that are above.

Lord, thank you for who you are. Help me set my mind on things that are above, not on things that are on Earth. Help me focus on you, not on the problems. Amen.

JUNE 25

But Moses said to the Lord, "Oh, my Lord, I am not eloquent, either in the past or since you have spoken to your servant, but I am slow of speech and of tongue."

Exodus 4:10

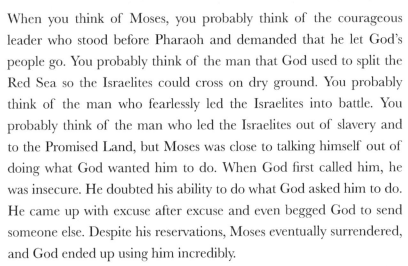

When you think of Moses, you probably think of the courageous leader who stood before Pharaoh and demanded that he let God's people go. You probably think of the man that God used to split the Red Sea so the Israelites could cross on dry ground. You probably think of the man who fearlessly led the Israelites into battle. You probably think of the man who led the Israelites out of slavery and to the Promised Land, but Moses was close to talking himself out of doing what God wanted him to do. When God first called him, he was insecure. He doubted his ability to do what God asked him to do. He came up with excuse after excuse and even begged God to send someone else. Despite his reservations, Moses eventually surrendered, and God ended up using him incredibly.

In that same way, God calls all of us to do certain things, and if we're not careful, we can talk ourselves out of doing what he wants us to do. We can focus on our lack of ability, qualifications, or experience. We can come up with excuses and let insecurity get the best of us.

You are incapable when you rely on your abilities, but when you put your faith and trust in God, nothing is impossible. What step is he calling you to take? Say yes to him today.

Lord, thank you for using me. Show me what step your calling me to take and give me the courage to take it. Amen.

JUNE 26

But the Lord answered her, "Martha, Martha, you are anxious and troubled about many things, but one thing is necessary. Mary has chosen the good portion, which will not be taken away from her."

Luke 10:41-42

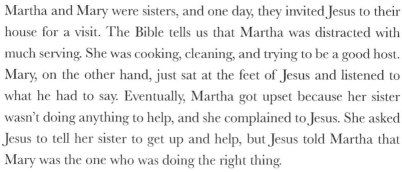

Martha and Mary were sisters, and one day, they invited Jesus to their house for a visit. The Bible tells us that Martha was distracted with much serving. She was cooking, cleaning, and trying to be a good host. Mary, on the other hand, just sat at the feet of Jesus and listened to what he had to say. Eventually, Martha got upset because her sister wasn't doing anything to help, and she complained to Jesus. She asked Jesus to tell her sister to get up and help, but Jesus told Martha that Mary was the one who was doing the right thing.

Martha wasn't doing anything wrong. She was serving. The Bible commends serving. She was doing a good thing. The problem was she allowed a good thing to distract her from a God thing. Jesus was right in front of her, but she was too distracted to spend quality time in his presence.

Sometimes, the most difficult choices in life are not choices between good and bad but choices between good and God. Like Martha, you can allow good things to distract you from God things. Is there anything in your life, maybe even a good thing, that is keeping you from a God thing?

Lord, thank you for all the opportunities you have given me. Help me discern between what's good and what's from you. Amen.

JUNE 27

And give no opportunity to the devil.

Ephesians 4:27

There's a lady in our church who is hands down the best cook I've ever encountered. Even her coffee tastes like it was shipped straight from Heaven. There is nothing this woman can't do in the kitchen, but her specialty is desserts. I was never a big fan of desserts until I tasted her chocolate pie. It was unlike anything I ever tasted before, and it quickly became my favorite dessert. She usually brings me one for my birthday, and I always look forward to it. The only problem is that I can't have just one piece. I don't have that much will power. When I start to eat that chocolate pie, I lose control and end up consuming the whole thing.

Temptation is a lot like that pie. It has a way of sucking you in. One bite leads to another bite. One piece leads to another piece. Before long, you've eaten the whole thing and done what you said you wouldn't do.

You're likely not as strong as you think you are and certainly not strong enough to linger in the midst of temptation. If you play with fire, sooner or later, you're going to get burnt. The best policy is to give no opportunity to the devil because if you give him an inch, he will take a mile.

Lord, thank you for giving me the power to resist temptation. Help me keep my guard up and give no opportunity to the devil. Amen.

JUNE 28

Search me, O God, and know my heart! Try me and know my thoughts! And see if there be any grievous way in me, and lead me in the way everlasting!

Psalm 139:23-24

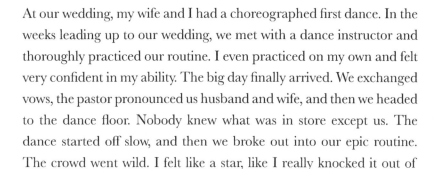

At our wedding, my wife and I had a choreographed first dance. In the weeks leading up to our wedding, we met with a dance instructor and thoroughly practiced our routine. I even practiced on my own and felt very confident in my ability. The big day finally arrived. We exchanged vows, the pastor pronounced us husband and wife, and then we headed to the dance floor. Nobody knew what was in store except us. The dance started off slow, and then we broke out into our epic routine. The crowd went wild. I felt like a star, like I really knocked it out of the park until I watched the video a few days later. In reality, I looked ridiculous, like a fish out of water, and I felt bad for everyone who had to witness that performance.

Nobody can deceive you better than you can deceive yourself. There are probably things in your life that you're unaware of, things that are holding you back. There are probably areas that you think are strong, but they could actually use some improvement.

It might be painful, it might be humbling, but invite God to search your heart. Ask him if there is any sin in your life that you're not aware of. Ask him to show you where you're weak and how you can improve. Right now, invite him to search you and lead you in the way everlasting.

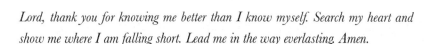

Lord, thank you for knowing me better than I know myself. Search my heart and show me where I am falling short. Lead me in the way everlasting. Amen.

JUNE 29

"But God said to him, 'Fool! This night your soul is required of you, and the things you have prepared, whose will they be?' So is the one who lays up treasure for himself and is not rich toward God."

Luke 12:20-21

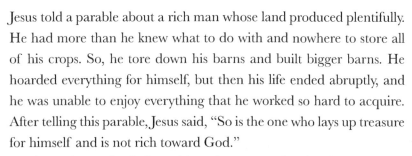

Jesus told a parable about a rich man whose land produced plentifully. He had more than he knew what to do with and nowhere to store all of his crops. So, he tore down his barns and built bigger barns. He hoarded everything for himself, but then his life ended abruptly, and he was unable to enjoy everything that he worked so hard to acquire. After telling this parable, Jesus said, "So is the one who lays up treasure for himself and is not rich toward God."

Several years back, I was blessed to meet a family of missionaries in Haiti. They are some of the most kind, generous and faithful people I've ever had the privilege to know. They told me a story about a time when, right after answering the call to become missionaries, they lost everything to a natural disaster. They explained that they lost all of their stuff, but they still had everything that really mattered. It was a tragic situation, but through it all, their faith never wavered.

The harsh reality is that stuff comes and goes, sometimes in an instant. It becomes apparent how strong a person's faith is when everything else is stripped away. Those who live to acquire earthly treasure will be devastated. But those who live to acquire heavenly treasure will remain steadfast. Remember, what really matters is what you have in Heaven, not what you have on this Earth.

Lord, forgive me for not laying up treasure in Heaven. Help me understand what truly matters and live my life to further your kingdom. Amen.

JUNE 30

He who loves money will not be satisfied with money, nor he who loves wealth with his income; this also is vanity.

Ecclesiastes 5:10

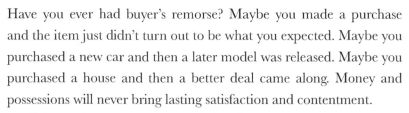

Have you ever had buyer's remorse? Maybe you made a purchase and the item just didn't turn out to be what you expected. Maybe you purchased a new car and then a later model was released. Maybe you purchased a house and then a better deal came along. Money and possessions will never bring lasting satisfaction and contentment.

I have always been a sucker for the latest and greatest tech, especially phones. I recently bought a new phone, the best of the best, or at least that's what I thought. A few months later, I went to a family gathering, and my brother broke out the sleekest phone I've ever laid my eyes on. This thing had three screens, was foldable, and doubled as a tablet. Immediately, I felt differently about my phone. Suddenly, it seemed insignificant, outdated, and boring.

Stuff always over-promises and under-delivers. That next purchase might satisfy temporarily, but eventually, the newness will wear off. That new car eventually becomes an old car. That new piece of tech quickly becomes outdated. That new house eventually needs a remodel. If you continue looking for satisfaction in materialistic things, you will continue to be miserable. True, lasting satisfaction and contentment can only be found in Christ. Remember, he who loves money will never be satisfied.

Lord, thank you for everything that you've blessed me with. Help me stop looking for satisfaction in stuff and start looking for it in you. Amen.

JULY 1

For the righteous falls seven times and rises again, but the wicked stumble in times of calamity.

Proverbs 24:16

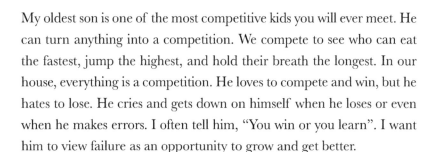

My oldest son is one of the most competitive kids you will ever meet. He can turn anything into a competition. We compete to see who can eat the fastest, jump the highest, and hold their breath the longest. In our house, everything is a competition. He loves to compete and win, but he hates to lose. He cries and gets down on himself when he loses or even when he makes errors. I often tell him, "You win or you learn". I want him to view failure as an opportunity to grow and get better.

Success will not happen without failure. Walt Disney was fired by a newspaper editor for lack of creativity. He also went bankrupt before he built Walt Disney. Albert Einstein didn't speak until he was four, didn't read until he was seven, and one of his teachers said he would never amount to much. Michael Jordan was cut from his high school's varsity basketball team in his sophomore year for a lack of skill.

Some of our greatest life lessons come in the form of losses. When you fail, you can stay down, or you can get back up, learn, and come back stronger. View failure as an opportunity to grow and get better. Remember, you win or you learn.

Lord, thank you for turning losses into lessons. Thank you for using failure to make me better. Give me the strength to get back up and keep going. Amen.

JULY 2

There is therefore now no condemnation for those who are in Christ Jesus.

Romans 8:1

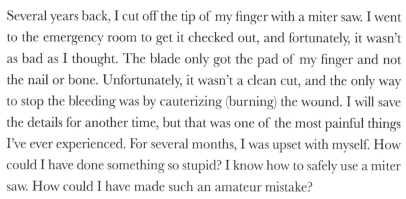

Several years back, I cut off the tip of my finger with a miter saw. I went to the emergency room to get it checked out, and fortunately, it wasn't as bad as I thought. The blade only got the pad of my finger and not the nail or bone. Unfortunately, it wasn't a clean cut, and the only way to stop the bleeding was by cauterizing (burning) the wound. I will save the details for another time, but that was one of the most painful things I've ever experienced. For several months, I was upset with myself. How could I have done something so stupid? I know how to safely use a miter saw. How could I have made such an amateur mistake?

Have you ever done something and struggled to forgive yourself? Maybe you confessed and repented, but for some reason, you just couldn't move on. And maybe it was something much more serious than cutting your finger. Maybe it was something life-altering. Maybe you're still dealing with it now and trying to move on, but you can't seem to shake it.

The enemy has a way of bringing up your past and making you feel inadequate, but there is no condemnation for those who are in Christ Jesus. By his grace, you are forgiven.

Lord, thank you for your grace. Help me recognize the difference between conviction and condemnation. Help me get over the mistakes that I have made. Amen.

JULY 3

Remember not the former things, nor consider the things of old. Behold, I am doing a new thing; now it springs forth, do you not perceive it? I will make a way in the wilderness and rivers in the desert.

Isaiah 43:18-19

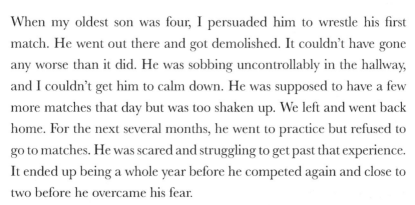

When my oldest son was four, I persuaded him to wrestle his first match. He went out there and got demolished. It couldn't have gone any worse than it did. He was sobbing uncontrollably in the hallway, and I couldn't get him to calm down. He was supposed to have a few more matches that day but was too shaken up. We left and went back home. For the next several months, he went to practice but refused to go to matches. He was scared and struggling to get past that experience. It ended up being a whole year before he competed again and close to two before he overcame his fear.

In Isaiah 43, God is speaking to the Israelites. He had done a lot for them in the past. He delivered them from slavery, provided for them, and performed miracles. He tells them not to remember the former things and reminds them that he is doing a new thing.

Past experiences can be traumatizing. Maybe you tried before and failed, and now you are afraid of trying again. Or maybe you feel like you have peaked and that your best days are behind you. If so, let me remind you that in Christ, the best is yet to come.

Lord, thank you for doing a new thing. Help me stop focusing on what I have or have not accomplished in the past and start focusing on what you have for me right now. Amen.

JULY 4

For freedom Christ has set us free; stand firm therefore, and do not submit again to a yoke of slavery.

Galatians 5:1

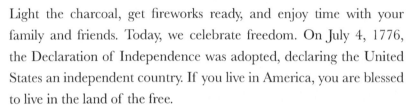

Light the charcoal, get fireworks ready, and enjoy time with your family and friends. Today, we celebrate freedom. On July 4, 1776, the Declaration of Independence was adopted, declaring the United States an independent country. If you live in America, you are blessed to live in the land of the free.

The freedom we enjoy as citizens is a blessing, but it's nothing compared to the freedom we enjoy as Christians. We are no longer slaves to sin. We are no longer defined by the mistakes we've made. We can leave the past in the past and begin a new life in Christ. Jesus came to set us free from our sin. He came to Earth, took our place on the cross, and paid the penalty for our sin.

We enjoy freedom, not because of something we have done, but because of what he did. You're not free from sin because you're religious. You're not free from sin because you go to church. You're not free from sin because you read your Bible. You're not free from sin because you're generous. You're free from sin, not because of something you've done, but because of what he did. Take some time today to celebrate freedom.

Lord, thank you for freedom. Thank you for taking my place on the cross and paying the penalty for my sin. Forgive me for taking my salvation for granted. Amen.

JULY 5

And then will I declare to them, 'I never knew you; depart from me, you workers of lawlessness.'

Matthew 7:23

One day, I went to the gym to work out. I had been going to the same small-town gym for years. Most days looked the same. However, on this particular day, something exciting happened. As I walked into the gym, I saw "Stone Cold" Steve Austin working out in the corner. I did a double take, and sure enough, it was him. He happened to be filming a TV show in our town and had come to the gym for a workout. I immediately recognized him because I had seen him on TV for years. I knew some facts about his life and career. I knew of him, but I didn't know him personally.

In Matthew 7, Jesus warns us that many know of him, but they don't know him personally. They go through the right motions and do the right things, but they've neglected the most important part: a relationship with him.

What about you? Maybe you know the Bible stories and have the answers. Maybe you serve your church and are respected in your community. Maybe you know of Jesus, but do you know him personally? Do you have a genuine relationship with him? If there's any doubt, now is the time to get it right.

Lord, thank you for your Word. Show me if I don't have a genuine relationship with you. I don't just want to know of you, I want to know you. Amen.

JULY 6

And the King will answer them, 'Truly, I say to you, as you did it to one of the least of these my brothers, you did it to me.'

Matthew 25:40

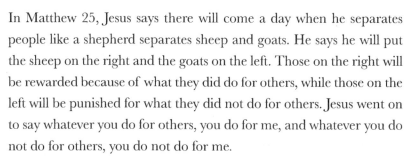

In Matthew 25, Jesus says there will come a day when he separates people like a shepherd separates sheep and goats. He says he will put the sheep on the right and the goats on the left. Those on the right will be rewarded because of what they did do for others, while those on the left will be punished for what they did not do for others. Jesus went on to say whatever you do for others, you do for me, and whatever you do not do for others, you do not do for me.

One of the best ways to live out the gospel is simply by serving others. When someone is hungry, give them something to eat. When someone is thirsty, give them something to drink. When someone lacks clothing or shelter, give it to them. When you encounter a stranger, welcome them. When someone is sick or hurting, visit them. When someone is in need, do what you can to help.

This passage of scripture should make you think twice before ignoring the needs around you. Whatever you do for others, you do for Jesus. And whatever you do not do for others, you do not do for Jesus. Today, go find someone to serve.

Lord, thank you for going out of your way to serve me. Help me be more aware of the needs around me. In the midst of the busyness, give me a heart to serve. Amen.

JULY 7

Therefore, since we are surrounded by so great a cloud of witnesses, let us also lay aside every weight, and sin which clings so closely, and let us run with endurance the race that is set before us.

Hebrews 12:1

When I was in middle school, I was on the cross-country team. I never enjoyed running, but I was good at it, so I continued to participate. I actually hated it and still do. I run occasionally to stay in shape, but I will never understand people who do it for fun. I would get through those cross-country races by telling myself, "The faster I run, the faster this will be over." I envisioned crossing the finish line, and that's what kept my legs moving until I actually crossed the finish line.

In today's verse, Paul compares life to a race. He encourages us to run the race of life with endurance by looking to Jesus, the founder and perfecter of our faith.

In the midst of life, it's easy to become winded. It's easy to get exhausted. It's easy to become weighed down by your circumstances. It's easy to get caught up in what is going on around you and to take your eyes off Jesus. However, looking to him is what will enable you to run with endurance the race that is set before you. So, before you stop running, remember who you're running for.

Lord, thank you for enduring the cross. Help me run the race that is set before me with endurance. Help me keep my eyes fixed on you. Amen.

JULY 8

Finally, all of you, have unity of mind, sympathy, brotherly love, a tender heart, and a humble mind.

1 Peter 3:8

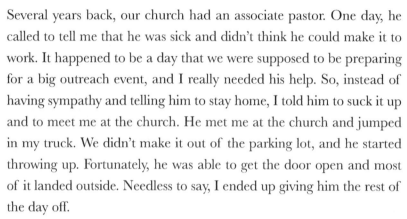

Several years back, our church had an associate pastor. One day, he called to tell me that he was sick and didn't think he could make it to work. It happened to be a day that we were supposed to be preparing for a big outreach event, and I really needed his help. So, instead of having sympathy and telling him to stay home, I told him to suck it up and to meet me at the church. He met me at the church and jumped in my truck. We didn't make it out of the parking lot, and he started throwing up. Fortunately, he was able to get the door open and most of it landed outside. Needless to say, I ended up giving him the rest of the day off.

When we go through challenging things, we expect others to understand and be sympathetic toward us, but then we may struggle to be sympathetic toward others. Instead of extending compassion, we may extend judgment. Instead of offering to help, we may ignore the need.

Unless you walk in their shoes, you have no idea what the people around you are going through. One of the best ways to change the world is simply to be sympathetic toward others.

Lord, thank you for being sympathetic toward me. Help me extend that same kind of sympathy to others. Help me be slow to judge and quick to help. Amen.

JULY 9

And the Lord said to Gideon, "With the 300 men who lapped I will save you and give the Midianites into your hand, and let all the others go every man to his home."

Judges 7:7

The Israelites were being overpowered by the Midianites. The Midianites would come into Israel's land and wipe out all their food supply. They would destroy their livestock and their crops. The Israelites became crippled by fear and started hiding in caves.

God called Gideon to lead the Israelites into battle. Gideon was hesitant. He made excuses and asked God for signs, which God gave him. Eventually, Gideon surrendered to God and rounded up 32,000 men to take into battle, but there was one problem. Although the Midianites had more, God told Gideon he had too many men. Gideon thinned the men out by allowing several thousand to return home. This reduced the number of men to 22,000. God told Gideon that there were still too many men. In the end, God narrowed the number of men down to just 300, and he used them to deliver the Israelites from the hands of the Midianites.

God usually doesn't do things the way you want or expect, but he always has a plan. His ways are higher than your ways. There is nothing that he can't do, but you have to trust him. You can allow fear to cripple you and continue living in a cave, or you can step out in faith and do what he's leading you to do. Remember, when he's on your side, the odds are always in your favor.

Lord, thank you for always having a plan. Forgive me for allowing fear to hold me back. Help me step out in faith and trust you. Amen.

JULY 10

And whatever you do, in word or deed, do everything in the name of the Lord Jesus, giving thanks to God the Father through him.

Colossians 3:17

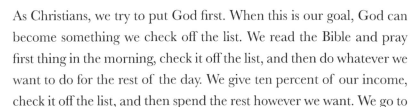

As Christians, we try to put God first. When this is our goal, God can become something we check off the list. We read the Bible and pray first thing in the morning, check it off the list, and then do whatever we want to do for the rest of the day. We give ten percent of our income, check it off the list, and then spend the rest however we want. We go to church on Sunday morning, check it off the list, and then do whatever we want for the rest of the week.

God shouldn't just be first on your list. He should be at the very center of everything on your list. You should do everything in the name of the Lord Jesus. You shouldn't just spend time with him in the morning but all throughout the day. You shouldn't just honor him with a percentage of your income but with all of your income. You shouldn't just worship him at church on Sunday but all throughout the week.

He should be at the center of your job or business. He should be at the center of your relationships. He should be at the center of your hobbies. He should be at the center of your home. He should be at the center of your finances. He shouldn't just be first on your list. He should be at the very center of everything on your list.

Lord, thank you for being present in my life. Help me put you at the center and do everything in the name of the Lord Jesus. Amen.

JULY 11

She came and told the man of God, and he said, "Go, sell the oil and pay your debts, and you and your sons can live on the rest."

2 Kings 4:7

In 2 Kings 4, there is a story about a woman who lost her husband and found herself in some financial trouble. She couldn't pay what she owed, so the lender was going to take her two sons as slaves to satisfy the debt. She went to Elisha for help. She explained to him that she had nothing except a small jar of oil. He instructed her to borrow as many containers as she could from her neighbors. He told her to go inside her house, close the door, and begin pouring oil from her container into the borrowed containers. Miraculously, the oil never ran out, and she filled all the containers. She was able to sell the oil, pay off the debt, and have money left over to support her family.

Have you ever made excuses? Here's a few examples: I can't grow my business because I don't have good employees. I can't step out in faith and start that ministry because I don't have the resources. I can't get more involved in the church because I don't have time. I can't save for retirement because I don't have enough money. I can't overcome this addiction because I don't have enough strength.

God didn't use what the widow didn't have. He used the one thing she did have. Today, stop waiting around for what you want, and start working with what you have.

Lord, thank you for what you have given me. Help me be a good steward and make the most of what I do have instead of waiting around for what I don't have. Amen.

JULY 12

And they all ate and were satisfied. And they took up twelve baskets full of the broken pieces left over. And those who ate were about five thousand men, besides women and children.

Matthew 14:20-21

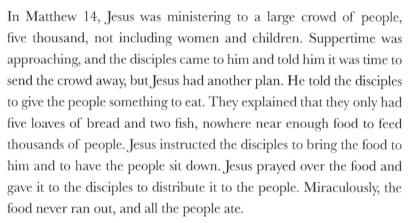

In Matthew 14, Jesus was ministering to a large crowd of people, five thousand, not including women and children. Suppertime was approaching, and the disciples came to him and told him it was time to send the crowd away, but Jesus had another plan. He told the disciples to give the people something to eat. They explained that they only had five loaves of bread and two fish, nowhere near enough food to feed thousands of people. Jesus instructed the disciples to bring the food to him and to have the people sit down. Jesus prayed over the food and gave it to the disciples to distribute it to the people. Miraculously, the food never ran out, and all the people ate.

Jesus performed the miracle, but it took place in the hands of the disciples. Jesus gave them the food and told them to distribute it to the people. As they were distributing the food, it began to multiply, and all the people were able to eat.

What has Jesus put in your hands? If you will see past your limitations and relinquish control of whatever he has given you, there is no limit to what he can accomplish through you. He's not a God of addition but a God of multiplication.

Lord, thank you for what you have put in my hands. Help me see past my limitations, relinquish control, and be obedient with what you have given me. Amen.

JULY 13

He said, "Do not lay your hand on the boy or do anything to him, for now I know
that you fear God, seeing you have not withheld your son, your only son, from me."

Genesis 22:12

Abraham waited decades to have a son with his wife, Sarah. Finally, they conceived, and she gave birth to their son, Isaac. They spent time together, Isaac grew up, and one day God instructed Abraham to offer Isaac as a burnt offering. In other words, God wanted Abraham to sacrifice what he loved the most: his son Isaac. Abraham packed everything up and traveled to the place where the sacrifice would take place. He put Isaac up on the altar and was about to slaughter him when an angel of the Lord stopped him. In the end, God provided a ram for Abraham to sacrifice in lieu of his son.

Almost everything you do is to achieve a desired outcome. You go to sleep at night so that you feel rested in the morning. You brush your teeth so that they don't turn yellow and fall out. You wake up and go to work every day so that you can pay the bills. You go to the gym and eat healthily so that you can look good on the beach. You put money away each month so that one day, you can retire.

You do things to achieve a desired outcome, but true significance is not found in an outcome. It's found in obedience to God. Like Abraham, will you be obedient to God, even if it doesn't result in the outcome you want?

Lord, thank you for your sovereignty. Give me the faith to be obedient to you, even
when it doesn't result in the outcome I want. Amen.

JULY 14

When the people saw that Moses delayed to come down from the mountain, the people gathered themselves together to Aaron and said to him, "Up, make us gods who shall go before us. As for this Moses, the man who brought us up out of the land of Egypt, we do not know what has become of him."

Exodus 32:1

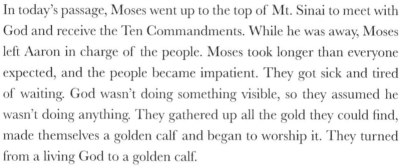

In today's passage, Moses went up to the top of Mt. Sinai to meet with God and receive the Ten Commandments. While he was away, Moses left Aaron in charge of the people. Moses took longer than everyone expected, and the people became impatient. They got sick and tired of waiting. God wasn't doing something visible, so they assumed he wasn't doing anything. They gathered up all the gold they could find, made themselves a golden calf and began to worship it. They turned from a living God to a golden calf.

It's easy to read this passage and critique the foolish decision that the Israelites made, but don't be so quick to judge. How often do you do something similar? You become impatient. You get sick and tired of waiting. You don't see God doing something visible, so you assume he's not doing anything, and you take matters into your own hands. You turn from a living God to your idol of choice.

Maybe you are currently in a waiting season. Maybe you're wondering where God is and questioning if he's there? Maybe you're on the verge of taking matters into your own hands. If so, let me encourage you to be patient. God knows what you don't know, and he sees what you don't see. His timing is always right on time.

Lord, thank you for your perfect timing. Show me if there are any idols in my life. Help me trust you, even when I don't see you doing something visible. Amen.

JULY 15

For whoever has despised the day of small things shall rejoice, and shall see the plumb line in the hand of Zerubbabel. "These seven are the eyes of the Lord, which range through the whole earth."

Zechariah 4:10

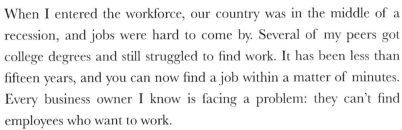

When I entered the workforce, our country was in the middle of a recession, and jobs were hard to come by. Several of my peers got college degrees and still struggled to find work. It has been less than fifteen years, and you can now find a job within a matter of minutes. Every business owner I know is facing a problem: they can't find employees who want to work.

I'm thankful for a booming economy and the opportunity many have had to earn higher wages, but I've also noticed a trend. Many are afraid to start small, and if they have to start small, they'd rather just not start at all. People no longer want to work their way up to the top; they want to start at the top. That might be a nice fantasy, but the truth is that nothing worth having in this world will come without hard work.

In today's verse, through the prophet Zechariah, God encouraged the Israelites as they were rebuilding the temple. He reminded them not to despise small beginnings. This is also something we need to be reminded of from time to time. There will be times in life when you have to start small and persevere through difficult times to get to where God wants you to be.

Lord, thank you for using small things. Help me be obedient to you, even if it means starting small. Show me if there's anything that you want me to start right now. Amen.

JULY 16

And then as a widow until she was eighty-four. She did not depart from the temple, worshiping with fasting and prayer night and day.

Luke 2:37

In Luke 2, we learn about a woman named Anna. She was married young, her husband quickly passed away, and she spent most of her life as a widow. She was dealt a bad hand, but we read that she didn't depart from the temple. She spent her time fasting and praying. Amidst tragedy, she found a way to grow and turn a negative into a positive.

You can't control everything that happens to you, but you can control the way that you respond. When things don't go according to plan, you can grow bitter, or you can get better and come out stronger. When you get laid off, you can get angry, become complacent, and grow bitter. Or you can re-strategize, get better, and come out stronger. When there is a hiccup in your marriage, you can play the blame game, push each other away, and grow bitter. Or you can refuse to give up, get better, and come out stronger. When tragedy strikes, you can throw in the towel, rebel, and grow bitter. Or you can trust God, get better, and come out stronger.

When the unexpected happens, how will you respond? Will you grow bitter or get better? Remember, you can't control everything that happens to you, but you can control the way that you respond.

Lord, thank you for always being present. Help me respond to whatever life throws my way in a way that brings glory and honor to you. Help me get better, not grow bitter. Amen.

JULY 17

And we know that for those who love God all things work together for good, for those who are called according to his purpose.

Romans 8:28

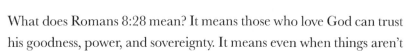

What does Romans 8:28 mean? It means those who love God can trust his goodness, power, and sovereignty. It means even when things aren't going your way, even when life is miserable, you can trust that God has a plan. It means that God can use all things, even bad things, for good.

This is one of those things that we usually only comprehend in hindsight. Take Jesus, for example. He came to Earth; he lived a perfect, sinless life. He performed miracles and healed the sick. People started following him and listening to his teachings. And then, he was arrested, beaten, tortured, and crucified on a cross. That wasn't a happy time. Jesus told people what was going to happen, and they still didn't understand. His followers thought it was all over. Jesus was dead and gone. In the middle of that circumstance, it seemed as if no good could ever come out of it. But then, three days later, he rose from the grave, once and for all overcoming and defeating death. Now, in hindsight, it's easy to recognize that his death is the greatest gift we have ever received and that it was all part of God's master plan.

I don't know what you're going through, or what mistakes you've made, or what's been done to you, but I do know that there is nothing God can't use for your good and for his glory.

Lord, thank you for bringing good from bad. Thank you for always having a plan. Help me trust you in this season of life that I'm in. Amen.

JULY 18

Whoever walks with the wise becomes wise, but the companion of fools will suffer harm.

Proverbs 13:20

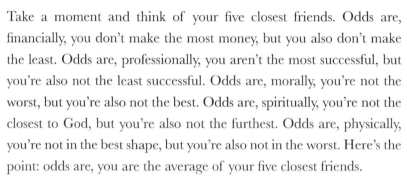

Take a moment and think of your five closest friends. Odds are, financially, you don't make the most money, but you also don't make the least. Odds are, professionally, you aren't the most successful, but you're also not the least successful. Odds are, morally, you're not the worst, but you're also not the best. Odds are, spiritually, you're not the closest to God, but you're also not the furthest. Odds are, physically, you're not in the best shape, but you're also not in the worst. Here's the point: odds are, you are the average of your five closest friends.

"Whoever walks with the wise becomes wise, but the companion of fools will suffer harm." In other words, the people you surround yourself with will either set you up for success or failure.

Are the people you're surrounding yourself with helping you to grow in your walk with the Lord? Or are they hindering you from growing? Are the people you're surrounding yourself with making you better? Or are they holding you back? Have you intentionally surrounded yourself with the right people? Or have you unintentionally surrounded yourself with the wrong people? Maybe it's time to get involved in a church, join a small group, or invite someone to lunch. Remember, you are the average of your five closest friends, so choose your friends wisely.

Lord, thank you for my friends. Help me surround myself with the right people. I ask that you place people in my life that will help me grow in my relationship with you. Amen.

JULY 19

For the moment all discipline seems painful rather than pleasant, but later it yields the peaceful fruit of righteousness to those who have been trained by it.

Hebrews 12:11

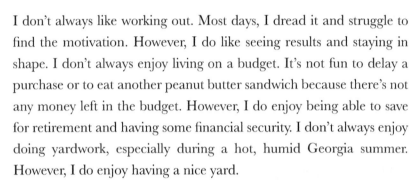

I don't always like working out. Most days, I dread it and struggle to find the motivation. However, I do like seeing results and staying in shape. I don't always enjoy living on a budget. It's not fun to delay a purchase or to eat another peanut butter sandwich because there's not any money left in the budget. However, I do enjoy being able to save for retirement and having some financial security. I don't always enjoy doing yardwork, especially during a hot, humid Georgia summer. However, I do enjoy having a nice yard.

There's the pain of discipline or the pain of regret. What does that mean? That means you can be disciplined now. It might be uncomfortable at the moment, but it will pay off later. Or you can be undisciplined now, do what's comfortable at the moment, and deal with regret later. The choice is yours.

None of us enjoy discipline; it seems painful rather than pleasant, but we do enjoy the fruit that discipline yields. In other words, we don't like discipline, but we do like the results that it brings. Where are you lacking discipline? Maybe you're not disciplined financially. Maybe you're not disciplined physically. Maybe you're not disciplined spiritually. What steps can you begin taking today to live a more disciplined life?

Lord, thank you for loving me unconditionally. Show me where I am lacking discipline. Show me what steps I can begin taking to live a more disciplined life. Amen.

JULY 20

Do not be deceived: God is not mocked, for whatever one sows, that will he also reap.

Galatians 6:7

One person eats unhealthy, drinks excessively, and abuses their body. Eventually, they have health problems. Another person exercises, diets, and takes care of themselves. They live a long, healthy life. One person buys a big house that they can barely afford. They finance a new car, max out their credit cards, and live beyond their means. Eventually, they end up in a financial hole. Another person lives below their means and saves a large portion of their income. They make sacrifices in the short run that pay dividends in the long run. They retire early and enjoy financial freedom. I could go on with examples, but the point is simple: you reap what you sow.

I've noticed the areas of my life that I am most proud of are the areas I've worked at the most. I've been intentional in those areas for a long time. On the other hand, the areas that I'm least proud of, or even ashamed of, are the areas I've been complacent in.

Where you're at today is the result of the decisions you made and the actions you took in the past. The decisions you make and the actions you take today will determine where you're at in the future. Remember, you reap what you sow.

Lord, forgive me for the areas I've been complacent in. Help me make the right decisions and take the right actions today. Amen.

JULY 21

'For this my son was dead, and is alive again; he was lost, and is found.' And they began to celebrate.

Luke 15:24

In Luke 15, Jesus told a story about a wealthy man who had two sons. The younger son was ready to leave the house and asked his father if he could receive his inheritance early. This was an insulting question, but the father agreed. He divided his property between his two sons, and the younger son left home. He traveled to a distant country and blew everything that his father gave him. He partied, spent recklessly, and lived it up for a while, but eventually, he ran out of money.

To make matters worse, there was a famine in the land, and he found himself in a desperate situation. Eventually, he came to his senses and decided to go back home and beg his father to take him back as one of his servants. To his surprise, when he was a long way off, his father ran out to meet him. He welcomed his son with open arms and threw him a party. He didn't welcome him back as his servant but as his son.

This story is less about the son and more about the father. It's a story about his grace and mercy. It's a story about his unconditional love. And it's proof that you haven't wandered too far to come back home. Despite what you might think, the Father is waiting for you with open arms.

Lord, thank you for your unconditional love. Show me if I have wandered from you and give me the courage to come back home. Amen.

JULY 22

"But he answered his father, 'Look, these many years I have served you, and I never disobeyed your command, yet you never gave me a young goat, that I might celebrate with my friends.'"

Luke 15:29

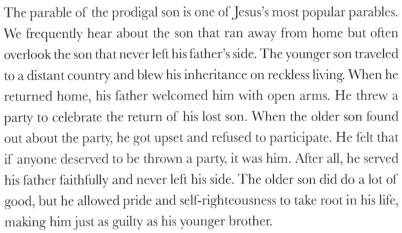

The parable of the prodigal son is one of Jesus's most popular parables. We frequently hear about the son that ran away from home but often overlook the son that never left his father's side. The younger son traveled to a distant country and blew his inheritance on reckless living. When he returned home, his father welcomed him with open arms. He threw a party to celebrate the return of his lost son. When the older son found out about the party, he got upset and refused to participate. He felt that if anyone deserved to be thrown a party, it was him. After all, he served his father faithfully and never left his side. The older son did do a lot of good, but he allowed pride and self-righteousness to take root in his life, making him just as guilty as his younger brother.

What is self-righteousness? Self-righteousness is the belief that you have done something to deserve something from God. Here are some self-righteous thoughts: "Since I attend church faithfully, I deserve to be in a leadership position. Since I tithe, I deserve to be blessed materialistically. Since I do the right things, I deserve to go to Heaven."

The truth is that we are not declared righteous because of anything we have done, but because of what Christ did on the cross. Be on guard, and refuse to allow pride and self-righteousness to take root in your life.

Lord, thank you for making a way for me to be declared righteous. Forgive me for the times that I've relied on my own effort and help me be on guard against self-righteousness. Amen.

JULY 23

They profess to know God, but they deny him by their works. They are detestable, disobedient, unfit for any good work.

Titus 1:16

Throughout my life, I have been blessed to know many people who have influenced me greatly. Without those people, I wouldn't be where I am today. As I reflect on how they've influenced me, I recognize that it was less the things they said and more the things they did. I've also had the privilege to influence others. I've had people write me cards, send me emails, and pull me aside to thank me for making a difference in their life. I preach sermons every week, but they almost always thank me for something I did, not something I said. I guess it's true. Actions really do speak louder than words.

In today's verse, Paul talks about people who claim to know God, yet they live contrary to his Word. In other words, their mouths say one thing, and their actions say another thing. Paul writes, "They are detestable, disobedient, unfit for any good work." That may seem like a harsh assessment, but it's true.

Do your actions prove your words to be true, or do your actions prove otherwise? If you took words out of the equation, would others conclude that you're a Christian simply by observing the way you live your life? Remember, actions really do speak louder than words.

Lord, forgive me for the times I've said one thing and done another thing. Help me align my actions with my words and live in a way that points others to you. Amen.

JULY 24

But he answered, 'Truly, I say to you, I do not know you.' Watch therefore, for you know neither the day nor the hour.

Matthew 25:12-13

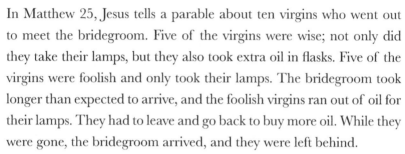

In Matthew 25, Jesus tells a parable about ten virgins who went out to meet the bridegroom. Five of the virgins were wise; not only did they take their lamps, but they also took extra oil in flasks. Five of the virgins were foolish and only took their lamps. The bridegroom took longer than expected to arrive, and the foolish virgins ran out of oil for their lamps. They had to leave and go back to buy more oil. While they were gone, the bridegroom arrived, and they were left behind.

When you are really anticipating something, not only do you get prepared for it, but you also stay prepared for it. So, here's the big question: are you prepared for the return of Jesus? If you knew he was going to return next week, would you begin to change the way that you're living? Would you scramble to get your life in the right order? Would you go out looking to buy more oil? Or are you prepared? Are you looking forward to and anticipating his return?

Like the five foolish virgins, it is easy to get caught up in the busyness of life and to get your priorities out of order. If that describes you, what changes do you need to start making today?

Lord, forgive me for the times I've gotten my priorities out of order. Help me get and stay prepared for your return. Amen.

JULY 25

Be patient, therefore, brothers, until the coming of the Lord. See how the farmer waits for the precious fruit of the earth, being patient about it, until it receives the early and the late rains.

James 5:7

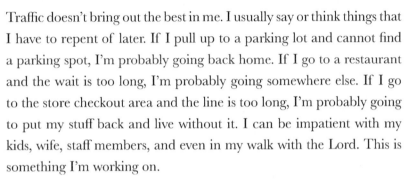

Traffic doesn't bring out the best in me. I usually say or think things that I have to repent of later. If I pull up to a parking lot and cannot find a parking spot, I'm probably going back home. If I go to a restaurant and the wait is too long, I'm probably going somewhere else. If I go to the store checkout area and the line is too long, I'm probably going to put my stuff back and live without it. I can be impatient with my kids, wife, staff members, and even in my walk with the Lord. This is something I'm working on.

We live in a fast-paced society. We want it here, we want it fast, and we want it now. The microwave is a must-have appliance because it cooks food in a matter of minutes. Drive-throughs are so profitable because they save time and provide a quick meal. Cell phones are so popular because they allow us to communicate instantly with people all across the world.

We are accustomed to immediate gratification, but if we're not careful, our impatience can keep us and distract us from the main thing. Just as a farmer is patient and waits for a seed to produce a crop, we should be patient and wait for the Lord.

Lord, forgive me for being impatient. Help me slow down and surrender to your will. Amen.

JULY 26

Would not God discover this? For he knows the secrets of the heart.

Psalm 44:21

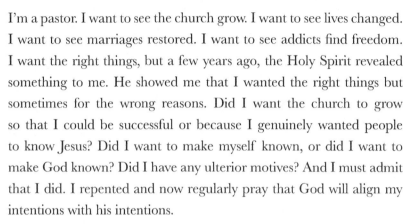

I'm a pastor. I want to see the church grow. I want to see lives changed. I want to see marriages restored. I want to see addicts find freedom. I want the right things, but a few years ago, the Holy Spirit revealed something to me. He showed me that I wanted the right things but sometimes for the wrong reasons. Did I want the church to grow so that I could be successful or because I genuinely wanted people to know Jesus? Did I want to make myself known, or did I want to make God known? Did I have any ulterior motives? And I must admit that I did. I repented and now regularly pray that God will align my intentions with his intentions.

Evaluate not only what you're doing but the intentions behind what you're doing. Are you going to church because you're hungry to learn God's Word or because you want to gain status? Are you serving in leadership within the church because you want to see it grow or because you want to have power? Are you writing that tithe check because you're eager to contribute to the kingdom or because you want others to see how generous you are?

If you are doing the right things with any sort of ulterior motive, repent. Ask God to align your intentions with his intentions. Be honest with yourself. Remember, God knows the secrets of your heart.

Lord, show me if I am doing any of the right things for the wrong reasons. Show me if I have any ulterior motives and forgive me if I do. Amen.

JULY 27

What shall we say then? Are we to continue in sin that grace may abound? By no means! How can we who died to sin still live in it?

Romans 6:1-2

This summer, my family went on vacation to the beach. One night, my wife and I went out, just the two of us. We got something to eat, and then we went into a few different stores because we wanted to buy shirts for our kids. As we were shirt shopping, we came across a shirt that said, "If you don't sin, Jesus died for nothing." What a terrible thing to say, even worse, to put it on a shirt. But we must be careful because even as Christians, we can drift into this mindset. We can begin to use God's grace as an excuse to continue living in sin. We can begin to knowingly indulge in sin because we know that God will forgive us. This is the dangerous mindset that Paul addressed in Romans 6.

God's grace is not an excuse to continue living in sin. It's a reason to change. How can we say that we love God and continue to knowingly do things that hurt him? All sin separates us from God, and all sin leads to death.

Is there any sin in your life that you've overlooked? Perhaps you've been guilty of using God's grace as an excuse to continue living in sin. If so, there's no better time to ask for forgiveness than right now.

Lord, thank you for your amazing grace. Forgive me for the times that I've used your grace as an excuse to continue living in sin. Help me see my sin for what it really is. Amen.

JULY 28

Beware of practicing your righteousness before other people in order to be seen by them, for then you will have no reward from your Father who is in heaven.

Matthew 6:1

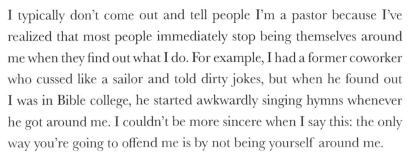

I typically don't come out and tell people I'm a pastor because I've realized that most people immediately stop being themselves around me when they find out what I do. For example, I had a former coworker who cussed like a sailor and told dirty jokes, but when he found out I was in Bible college, he started awkwardly singing hymns whenever he got around me. I couldn't be more sincere when I say this: the only way you're going to offend me is by not being yourself around me.

None of us want to admit it, but we've all been guilty of putting on a show for others. You might get into an argument with your spouse on the way to church or yell at your kids in the parking lot, but then put a smile on your face before going inside. You might struggle with a secret addiction while others applaud your faith. You might be upside down in a mountain of debt but drive a luxury car or live in the nicest house in your neighborhood.

You might fool people, but you will not fool God. He knows you better than you know yourself. He sees what you do behind closed doors. Being popular, well-liked, and respected by others might be rewarding, but you must remember that the greatest reward is awaiting you in Heaven.

Lord, forgive me for putting on a show for others. Help me be genuine in all that I do and all that I say. Thank you for the reward that is awaiting me in Heaven. Amen.

JULY 29

If my people who are called by my name humble themselves, and pray and seek my face and turn from their wicked ways, then I will hear from heaven and will forgive their sin and heal their land.

2 Chronicles 7:14

Today's verse is not addressed to Hollywood, politicians, or atheists. It is addressed to Christians. It says, "If my people who are called by my name humble themselves, and pray and seek my face and turn from their wicked ways, then I will hear from Heaven and will forgive their sin and heal their land." This verse of scripture gives us the recipe for revival.

We tend to sit in our comfortable church facilities and talk about how bad things are on the outside. We talk about politicians and the media. We talk about how rampant sin has become. We talk about how evil and corrupt the world is. The truth is that we are the ones who can bring about positive change.

Revival doesn't start outside of the church; it starts inside of the church. We must humble ourselves. We must recognize that it is only by his mercy and grace that we are saved. We must pray. Revival is always preceded and sustained by prayer. We must seek his face. He must be front and center of everything that we do. And we must turn from our wicked ways. We must repent and stop justifying sin in our own lives. That's the recipe for revival.

Lord, thank you for never turning your back on me. Help me walk in humility, spend time in prayer, seek your face, and turn from my wicked ways. Heal our land. Amen.

JULY 30

For where your treasure is, there your heart will be also.

Matthew 6:21

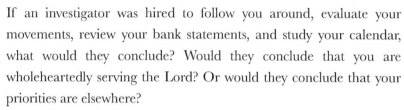

If an investigator was hired to follow you around, evaluate your movements, review your bank statements, and study your calendar, what would they conclude? Would they conclude that you are wholeheartedly serving the Lord? Or would they conclude that your priorities are elsewhere?

I love my kids, and I'm obsessed with sports. I'm determined to give my kids every opportunity to become the best athletes they can be. So, we drive several thousand miles a year to take our kids to the best training facilities and to compete in the best events. We value having a place to relax and entertain. For several years, we drove older vehicles so we could afford a nicer house. We have always tried to stay in shape. So, when it became difficult to go to the gym after having kids, we invested in a home gym. We love our church and believe in the work that is being done. So, we try our best to give generously to support the mission. Here's the point: we invest in the things that matter to us.

Many say that they love God and that furthering the kingdom is their priority, but their bank statements would prove otherwise. What about you? The greatest investment you can make is an investment into the kingdom of God. Remember, where your treasure is, there your heart will be also.

Lord, thank you for allowing me to invest in your kingdom. Show me if my priorities are in the wrong place, and help me put my money where my mouth is. Amen.

JULY 31

For the love of money is a root of all kinds of evils. It is through this craving that some have wandered away from the faith and pierced themselves with many pangs.

1 Timothy 6:10

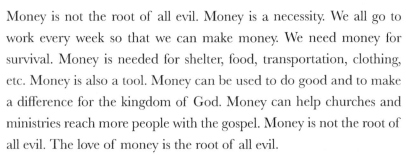

Money is not the root of all evil. Money is a necessity. We all go to work every week so that we can make money. We need money for survival. Money is needed for shelter, food, transportation, clothing, etc. Money is also a tool. Money can be used to do good and to make a difference for the kingdom of God. Money can help churches and ministries reach more people with the gospel. Money is not the root of all evil. The love of money is the root of all evil.

There is nothing wrong with wealth or having money. However, when money begins to control you, it becomes a problem. The love of money has led people to lie, cheat, steal, and make other compromises. The love of money has destroyed homes and broken up families. The love of money has led people to wander away from the faith and pierce themselves with many pangs. In other words, the love of money has prevented many from wholeheartedly serving the Lord.

What about you? Is money distracting you from the things that really matter? Are you working nonstop to make more money but missing irreplaceable time with your family? Are you growing a company but not playing a role in growing the church? Are you building wealth but missing what God has for you? Remember, the love of money is the root of all evil.

Lord, thank you for the money you've entrusted me with. Help me see it as a tool and nothing more. Help me stay focused on the things that really matter. Amen.

AUGUST 1

O Lord, you have searched me and known me!

Psalm 139:1

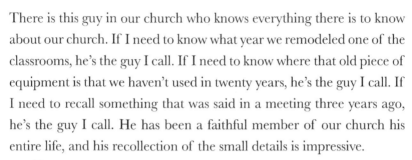

There is this guy in our church who knows everything there is to know about our church. If I need to know what year we remodeled one of the classrooms, he's the guy I call. If I need to know where that old piece of equipment is that we haven't used in twenty years, he's the guy I call. If I need to recall something that was said in a meeting three years ago, he's the guy I call. He has been a faithful member of our church his entire life, and his recollection of the small details is impressive.

Have you ever met a person that knew everything about something? Maybe you know someone who is an expert in their field, and their knowledge is incredible. Maybe you know someone who is a dedicated sports fan, and they know every stat there is to know about their favorite player or team.

What if I told you that God knows everything there is to know about you? He sees every move you make and action you take. He knows every thought that goes through your mind. He hears every word that comes out of your mouth. This shouldn't scare you but comfort you. God knows everything there is to know about you, and yet he still loves you unconditionally.

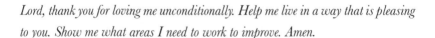

Lord, thank you for loving me unconditionally. Help me live in a way that is pleasing to you. Show me what areas I need to work to improve. Amen.

AUGUST 2

Draw near to God, and he will draw near to you. Cleanse your hands, you sinners, and purify your hearts, you double-minded.

James 4:8

The thought of having a daughter scared me to death, so I was excited when our first two children turned out to be boys. When our third child turned out to be a girl, I needed time to process it. I didn't know how to raise a daughter, and I was scared. However, I will never forget the moment I first laid eyes on her. She melted my heart in a way that the boys never did.

Two years later, I still find it difficult to discipline her and give her practically anything she wants. It makes my day when I come home and find her excited to see me. There is no better feeling in this world than to see her running toward me, holding out her arms to give me a hug.

Your heavenly Father feels the same way about you. He loves you and cares for you in a way you can't even begin to fathom, and he longs to spend time in fellowship with you. Think about it: the creator of the universe wants to have a personal relationship with you. If you draw near to him, he will draw near to you. Take some time today to spend in his presence.

Lord, thank you for being the perfect Father. Thank you for making it possible for me to have a personal relationship with you. Help me draw near to you. Amen.

AUGUST 3

But he said to me, "My grace is sufficient for you, for my power is made perfect in weakness." Therefore I will boast all the more gladly of my weaknesses, so that the power of Christ may rest upon me.

2 Corinthians 12:9

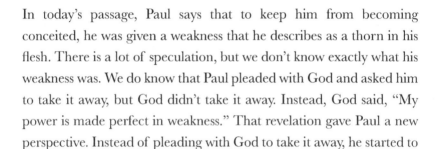

In today's passage, Paul says that to keep him from becoming conceited, he was given a weakness that he describes as a thorn in his flesh. There is a lot of speculation, but we don't know exactly what his weakness was. We do know that Paul pleaded with God and asked him to take it away, but God didn't take it away. Instead, God said, "My power is made perfect in weakness." That revelation gave Paul a new perspective. Instead of pleading with God to take it away, he started to boast about it so that God's power could work through him.

There are so many things that I would change about myself if I could. There are things that I wish God would take away, but this passage reminds me that God can work through my weaknesses.

This doesn't mean that you should become okay with sin in your life or stop trying to improve yourself. It simply means that God can reveal himself through your weaknesses. Like Paul, your weaknesses keep you from becoming conceited and remind you of your need for God's intervention. Your weaknesses also bring glory to God. When he works through your weaknesses, his strength becomes the only explanation. Instead of pleading with God to take away a weakness, boast about it so that God's power can work through you.

Lord, thank you for my weaknesses. Help me see my weaknesses in the same light as Paul. I will boast about my weaknesses so that your power can work through me. Amen.

AUGUST 4

For I tell you, none of those men who were invited shall taste my banquet.

Luke 14:24

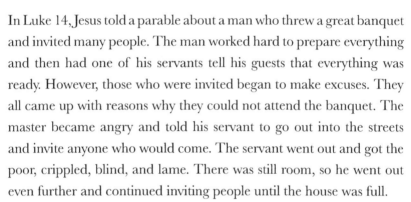

In Luke 14, Jesus told a parable about a man who threw a great banquet and invited many people. The man worked hard to prepare everything and then had one of his servants tell his guests that everything was ready. However, those who were invited began to make excuses. They all came up with reasons why they could not attend the banquet. The master became angry and told his servant to go out into the streets and invite anyone who would come. The servant went out and got the poor, crippled, blind, and lame. There was still room, so he went out even further and continued inviting people until the house was full.

At this time, many believed that only the Jews would enter the kingdom of God. Jesus used this parable to address that misconception. The Jews were God's chosen people, but sadly, many of them were too preoccupied with religion and tradition to follow Jesus.

The truth is that Jesus didn't come to die for a certain group of people. He came to die for all. All are invited into the kingdom of God. Those who ignore the invitation will miss out, but those who accept will spend an eternity in Heaven.

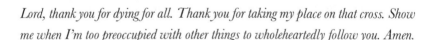

Lord, thank you for dying for all. Thank you for taking my place on that cross. Show me when I'm too preoccupied with other things to wholeheartedly follow you. Amen.

AUGUST 5

And as they continued to ask him, he stood up and said to them, "Let him who is without sin among you be the first to throw a stone at her."

John 8:7

In John 8, a woman was caught in the act of adultery. According to the law, this woman should have been stoned to death. However, Jesus came to her defense and said, "Let him who is without sin among you be the first to throw a stone at her." The people dropped their stones and walked away. Jesus was the only one without sin, the only one that could have condemned her, but he extended grace.

We tend to rank sin. We tolerate some sin but consider other sin unacceptable. We overlook some sin but judge other sin harshly. The truth is that sin is sin. It all separates us from God. If Jesus chose not to throw stones, we should probably follow suit. After all, he was perfect, and we are far from it.

This doesn't mean that you should accept and condone sin. Jesus extended grace to the adulterous woman, but he also told her to go and sin no more. This does mean that you should recognize that you are not without sin. You may not struggle with the same thing as someone else, but you struggle with something. So, before you pick up a stone, thoroughly evaluate your own heart.

Lord, thank you for your grace. Please help me extend your grace to others. Show me where I am falling short and when I judge others too harshly. Amen.

AUGUST 6

And he said to them, "Follow me, and I will make you fishers of men." Immediately they left their nets and followed him.

Matthew 4:19-20

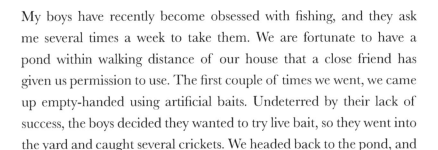

My boys have recently become obsessed with fishing, and they ask me several times a week to take them. We are fortunate to have a pond within walking distance of our house that a close friend has given us permission to use. The first couple of times we went, we came up empty-handed using artificial baits. Undeterred by their lack of success, the boys decided they wanted to try live bait, so they went into the yard and caught several crickets. We headed back to the pond, and sure enough, the crickets did the trick. They were able to catch several fish, and they had the time of their lives.

Simon and Peter were fishermen by trade, but Jesus invited them to follow him and told them that he would make them fishers of men. Those who follow Jesus are called to win people for him.

Sometimes, this can be discouraging. There will be times when you share the gospel and people don't respond. There will be times when you invite a person to church and they don't show up. However, it can also be rewarding. If you are persistent, there will be times when people do respond, times when God allows you to play a small role in changing someone's life. Regardless of the outcome, you are called to fish.

Lord, thank you for calling me to fish. Give me the courage to share the gospel with others. Help me be undeterred by the rejection that will inevitably come. Amen.

AUGUST 7

To the weak I became weak, that I might win the weak. I have become all things to all people, that by all means, I might save some.

1 Corinthians 9:22

Paul met people where they were. He got into their world. He went into their territory. He didn't wait around for people to come to him. He went and sought them out. This verse shouldn't be taken out of context. Paul wasn't condoning or accepting sin. He was sharing the gospel and extending grace.

Unfortunately, the average church has no strategy for reaching the lost. Of those churches that do have a strategy, it's usually lacking. It may involve building new facilities, having energetic services, or handing out free gifts to visitors. There's nothing wrong with those things. However, we're not called to sit around and wait. We're called to go and tell. Like Paul, we should strive to meet people where they are. We should get into their world. We should go into their territory. We should not condone or accept sin, but we should share the gospel and extend grace.

Almost every week, we encourage those who attend our church to invite others to join them for our next service. Inviting people to church is a great thing, but it shouldn't replace evangelism. Remember, we're not called to sit around and wait. We're called to go and tell. Today, who do you need to share the gospel with?

Lord, thank you for the gospel. Help me play an active role in fulfilling the Great Commission. Give me an opportunity to share the gospel with someone today. Amen.

AUGUST 8

Walk in wisdom toward outsiders, making the best use of the time.

Colossians 4:5

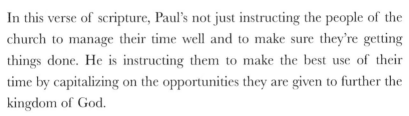

In this verse of scripture, Paul's not just instructing the people of the church to manage their time well and to make sure they're getting things done. He is instructing them to make the best use of their time by capitalizing on the opportunities they are given to further the kingdom of God.

I'm a task-oriented person. If I'm writing a sermon in my office, my mind is on my sermon. If I'm doing a project around the house, my mind is on the project. But some of the greatest opportunities I've had to minister have come in the form of interruptions. Maybe I'm sitting in my office and somebody walks in who needs someone to talk to. I can rush them out of my office so I can get back to writing, or I can stop and make the best use of my time. Maybe I run to the hardware store to pick up something for a project and bump into somebody who is having a bad week. I can rush out of there so I can get back to my project, or I can stop and make the best use of my time.

If you're not careful, your to-do list can keep you from making the best use of your time. Don't let what is most urgent keep you from doing what is most important. Capitalize on the opportunities you are given to further the kingdom of God.

Lord, thank you for the opportunities you give me to further your kingdom. Help me slow down and make the best use of my time. Amen.

AUGUST 9

I have fought the good fight, I have finished the race, I have kept the faith. Henceforth there is laid up for me the crown of righteousness, which the Lord, the righteous judge, will award to me on that day, and not only to me but also to all who have loved his appearing.

2 Timothy 4:7-8

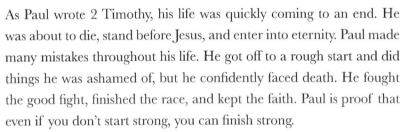

As Paul wrote 2 Timothy, his life was quickly coming to an end. He was about to die, stand before Jesus, and enter into eternity. Paul made many mistakes throughout his life. He got off to a rough start and did things he was ashamed of, but he confidently faced death. He fought the good fight, finished the race, and kept the faith. Paul is proof that even if you don't start strong, you can finish strong.

If you were to receive the news today that you only have a week left to live, how would you respond? Would you look back over your life and wish you could go back and do things differently? Would you be full of regret? Would you fear standing before Jesus? Or would you look back over your life knowing you made mistakes but confident that you gave God your best? Would you be excited to stand before Jesus and enter into eternity?

Maybe you can echo the words of Paul and say I have fought the good fight, finished the race, and kept the faith. If not, you have no control over what has happened in the past, but you do have some control over what happens from this moment forward. Even if you didn't start strong, today can be the first day of a strong finish.

Lord, thank you for second chances. Forgive me for the times I have fallen short and settled for less than your best. Help me finish strong. Amen.

AUGUST 10

After this many of his disciples turned back and no longer walked with him.

John 6:66

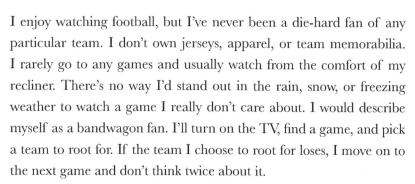

I enjoy watching football, but I've never been a die-hard fan of any particular team. I don't own jerseys, apparel, or team memorabilia. I rarely go to any games and usually watch from the comfort of my recliner. There's no way I'd stand out in the rain, snow, or freezing weather to watch a game I really don't care about. I would describe myself as a bandwagon fan. I'll turn on the TV, find a game, and pick a team to root for. If the team I choose to root for loses, I move on to the next game and don't think twice about it.

In John 6, Jesus is speaking to bandwagon Christians. These were people who were following him simply because of what he had to offer them. They had witnessed him perform miracles and wanted to see more. They were curious, but they weren't committed. Jesus explained that following him would be costly, and many turned around and went back home.

Are you a bandwagon or die-hard Christian? Are you half-heartedly or wholeheartedly following him? Do you have one foot in and one foot out? Are you in it for the rewards, or have you counted the cost? Remember, he's either Lord of all, or he's not Lord at all.

Lord, thank you for making it possible for me to follow you. Show me if there's any area of my life that I haven't fully surrendered to you. Help me become a die-hard Christian. Amen.

AUGUST 11

The kingdom of heaven is like treasure hidden in a field, which a man found and covered up. Then in his joy he goes and sells all that he has and buys that field.

Matthew 13:44

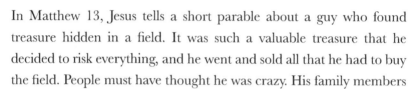

In Matthew 13, Jesus tells a short parable about a guy who found treasure hidden in a field. It was such a valuable treasure that he decided to risk everything, and he went and sold all that he had to buy the field. People must have thought he was crazy. His family members probably questioned him and warned him that he was making a big mistake, but he didn't care. He knew what he had.

Not only did he sell everything that he had, he sold everything joyfully so that he could buy the field. He wasn't reluctant. He didn't get hung up on the cost. He didn't view it as a major sacrifice. He sold everything with a smile on his face because he knew he was receiving something far more valuable. That's what Jesus says the kingdom of Heaven is like.

The reality of Heaven should absolutely change the way that you live your life. It should make you willing to sacrifice and go without things that society deems as important. The truth is that everything on this Earth is temporary, and it all pales in comparison to an eternity in Heaven. What are you holding on to? What is preventing you from surrendering all? What is keeping you from buying that field? Remember, Jesus is worth risking everything.

Lord, thank you for the treasure that is awaiting me in Heaven. Give me the courage to risk everything. Show me what is holding me back. Amen.

AUGUST 12

He said, "Come." So Peter got out of the boat and walked on the water and came to Jesus.

Matthew 14:29

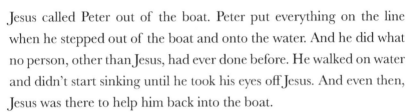

Jesus called Peter out of the boat. Peter put everything on the line when he stepped out of the boat and onto the water. And he did what no person, other than Jesus, had ever done before. He walked on water and didn't start sinking until he took his eyes off Jesus. And even then, Jesus was there to help him back into the boat.

My youngest son loves to race other kids on the playground at school. He comes home on a weekly basis and brags to me about how he won a race. The problem is that he only wants to race kids he knows he can beat. One day, I suggested that he race a kid I knew was faster than him, and he immediately shied away from the idea because he didn't want to risk failure. I explained to him that seeking out the fastest kids in his grade would only make him faster, even if it meant losing.

As adults, how often do we have this same mindset? Instead of putting ourselves out there and taking risks, we stick with what we know we're good at. It's nearly impossible to grow inside your comfort zone. If you want to excel, grow, and get better, you must learn to risk failure. What step of faith is Jesus asking you to take? Don't let fear of failure keep you from taking action.

Lord, forgive me for playing it safe. Stretch me and help me step out of my comfort zone. Show me what step you want me to take right now. Amen.

AUGUST 13

For am I now seeking the approval of man, or of God? Or am I trying to please man? If I were still trying to please man, I would not be a servant of Christ.

Galatians 1:10

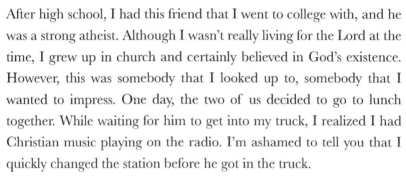

After high school, I had this friend that I went to college with, and he was a strong atheist. Although I wasn't really living for the Lord at the time, I grew up in church and certainly believed in God's existence. However, this was somebody that I looked up to, somebody that I wanted to impress. One day, the two of us decided to go to lunch together. While waiting for him to get into my truck, I realized I had Christian music playing on the radio. I'm ashamed to tell you that I quickly changed the station before he got in the truck.

It's easy to begin living your life to please others. You can begin to make decisions based on what others will approve or disapprove of. You can begin buying things you don't need to impress others. You can begin to alter yourself to appease others.

You were not put on this Earth to please people; you were put on this Earth to please God. It's impossible to do both. You can stand with God and be judged by the world, or you can stand with the world and be judged by God. The choice is yours. Will you seek the approval of man or God?

Lord, forgive me for being a people pleaser. Help me please you at all costs. Show me if there is any area where I am living for others and not for you. Amen.

AUGUST 14

Then Samson called to the Lord and said, "O Lord God, please remember me and please strengthen me only this once, O God, that I may be avenged on the Philistines for my two eyes."

Judges 16:28

Samson was set apart at birth. He was talented and gifted. God blessed him with supernatural strength. As long as he kept his hair, he would keep his strength. Samson made a lot of mistakes, but his biggest downfall was his choice of women. His story really began to unfold and unravel when he met a woman named Delilah. She was a prostitute. That should have been a red flag. She was a Philistine. That should have been another red flag, but Samson was head over heels in love with her.

Delilah couldn't have cared less about Samson. She was paid off by the head Philistines to seduce him and figure out the secret of his strength. Samson should have known better, but eventually, he told her the secret of his strength. When he fell asleep, she cut his hair, he lost his strength, and the Philistines captured him. Fortunately, in the final moments of his life, Samson called out to God, and God gave him his strength back to destroy the Philistines, but it did cost him his life.

Samson chose his path. God blessed him with gifts and talents and set him apart, but Samson was his own worst enemy. His poor choices destroyed his potential. Similarly, God has blessed you, but if you're not careful, you can become your own worst enemy. Remember, the choices you make matter.

Lord, thank you for blessing me. Forgive me for the poor choices that I have made. Help me avoid becoming my own worst enemy. Amen.

AUGUST 15

Therefore be imitators of God, as beloved children. And walk in love, as Christ loved us and gave himself up for us, a fragrant offering and sacrifice to God.

Ephesians 5:1-2

There are many small habits that I'm glad I started over the years. Shortly after high school, I started working out consistently. Exercise has become one of my outlets, and it's very rare that I miss a week in the gym. In 2012, I started going to church, and little did I know that I would eventually become a pastor. In the last decade, I've only missed church a handful of times. Around that same time, I started reading my Bible. God's Word has become what I've built my life, family, and church around. In 2014, my wife and I agreed to start budgeting. Budgeting saved us from getting into financial trouble and enabled us to save and make investments. As I reflect on my life thus far, I realize that it's not one big thing that shaped me into who I am but the culmination of several small habits.

What's one thing you need to start? What's one thing that will help you become a better imitator of Christ? Maybe you need to start going to church regularly. Maybe you need to start tithing. Maybe you need to start saving money for retirement. Maybe you need to start exercising. Maybe you need to start spending more time with your spouse. What's one thing you need to start today?

Lord, thank you for giving me the perfect example. Help me imitate you and build good habits. Show me one thing I need to start today. Amen.

AUGUST 16

Therefore put away all filthiness and rampant wickedness and receive with meekness the implanted word, which is able to save your souls.

James 1:21

When I first became the pastor of my church, I was the only full-time staff member. I was overwhelmed. I had a long list of homebound members that I needed to visit on a regular basis. There was always someone in the hospital that I needed to go and pray with. There were always fires to put out, meetings to attend, and problems to solve.

The first two years, I didn't manage my time well and almost always spent the weekend writing my sermon. This cut into our family time and eventually became a problem. So, I made a commitment to manage my time better. I made a commitment to stop bringing work home on the weekends. That ended up being one of the best decisions I've ever made. It has enabled me to spend time with my family, take a mental break, and refresh on the weekends.

What's one thing you need to stop? Maybe you need to stop a particular sin. Maybe you need to stop smoking, drinking, looking at porn, or gossiping. Or maybe it's not something that's sinful or directly prohibited by scripture, but it's something that is self-destructing. Stopping a bad habit might end up being one of the best decisions you ever make.

Lord, forgive me for my bad habits. Show me if there is anything I need to stop doing and give me the strength to be obedient. Amen.

AUGUST 17

But one day, when he went into the house to do his work and none of the men of the house was there in the house, she caught him by his garment, saying, "Lie with me." But he left his garment in her hand and fled and got out of the house.

Genesis 39:11-12

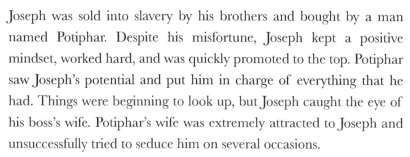

Joseph was sold into slavery by his brothers and bought by a man named Potiphar. Despite his misfortune, Joseph kept a positive mindset, worked hard, and was quickly promoted to the top. Potiphar saw Joseph's potential and put him in charge of everything that he had. Things were beginning to look up, but Joseph caught the eye of his boss's wife. Potiphar's wife was extremely attracted to Joseph and unsuccessfully tried to seduce him on several occasions.

One day, Potiphar's wife caught Joseph in the house alone. She grabbed his clothing and demanded that he have sex with her. Joseph could have attempted to justify it. After all, he wasn't the one initiating the affair. He wasn't the one married. She wasn't taking no for an answer. They were alone, and he could have probably gotten away with it. It's likely that these thoughts went through his mind, but he refused to sin against God and betray Potiphar's trust. Instead, he ran out of the house as fast as he could. Potiphar's wife lied and said that Joseph was the one who tried to seduce her, so Potiphar had Joseph thrown into prison.

Like Joseph, are you willing to do the right thing, even when the consequences are severe? When temptation comes your way, do you entertain it, or do you run from it as fast as you can?

Lord, forgive me for entertaining temptation. When temptation comes my way, help me follow Joseph's example and run as fast as I can in the opposite direction. Amen.

AUGUST 18

Yet the chief cupbearer did not remember Joseph, but forgot him.

Genesis 40:23

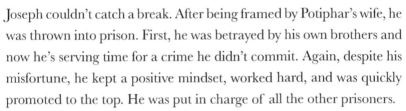

Joseph couldn't catch a break. After being framed by Potiphar's wife, he was thrown into prison. First, he was betrayed by his own brothers and now he's serving time for a crime he didn't commit. Again, despite his misfortune, he kept a positive mindset, worked hard, and was quickly promoted to the top. He was put in charge of all the other prisoners.

One day, Joseph got two new inmates, the chief cupbearer and the chief baker. While in prison, the cupbearer and the baker both had disturbing dreams that Joseph interpreted. Joseph told the cupbearer that in three days, he would be released from prison and restored to his previous position. Unfortunately, things weren't as positive for the baker. Joseph explained that in three days, he would be killed. Joseph asked the cupbearer to remember him when he was released and to share with Pharaoh how he had been wrongly accused of a crime he didn't commit. Three days after interpreting the dreams, the cupbearer was released from prison and restored to his previous position, while the baker was killed. Unfortunately, the cupbearer forgot about Joseph, and Joseph remained in prison for two additional years.

There will be times in life when you feel forgotten, overlooked, or unimportant. Times when it seems as if nothing is going your way. During those times, it's important to remain faithful and to remember that God is always working, even when you can't see it.

Lord, thank you for always working. Help me be faithful, even when I feel forgotten. Give me the fortitude and resilience of Joseph. Amen.

AUGUST 19

Then Pharaoh said to Joseph, "Since God has shown you all this, there is none so discerning and wise as you are. You shall be over my house, and all my people shall order themselves as you command. Only as regards the throne will I be greater than you."

Genesis 41:39-40

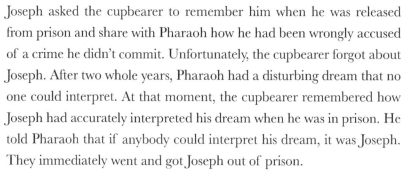

Joseph asked the cupbearer to remember him when he was released from prison and share with Pharaoh how he had been wrongly accused of a crime he didn't commit. Unfortunately, the cupbearer forgot about Joseph. After two whole years, Pharaoh had a disturbing dream that no one could interpret. At that moment, the cupbearer remembered how Joseph had accurately interpreted his dream when he was in prison. He told Pharaoh that if anybody could interpret his dream, it was Joseph. They immediately went and got Joseph out of prison.

Pharaoh shared his dream with Joseph, and he quickly interpreted it. Joseph explained to Pharaoh that there would be seven years of plenty followed by seven years of famine. Joseph took it a step further and advised Pharaoh on what must be done during the seven years of plenty to prepare for the seven years of famine. Pharaoh was so impressed with Joseph's proposal that he placed Joseph in charge of the entire kingdom. In an instant, Joseph's situation turned around for the better. He moved out of the prison and into the palace.

No matter what you go through or may be going through, there is always hope. Remember, there's not a situation that God can't turn around for the better in an instant.

Lord, thank you for your power. Help me keep a positive attitude in the middle of negative circumstances. I ask that you turn my situation around for the better. Amen.

AUGUST 20

Now Joseph was governor over the land. He was the one who sold to all the people of the land. And Joseph's brothers came and bowed themselves before him with their faces to the ground.

Genesis 42:6

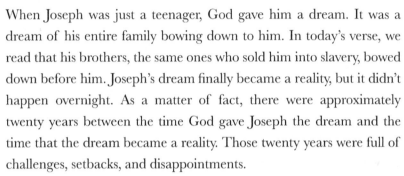

When Joseph was just a teenager, God gave him a dream. It was a dream of his entire family bowing down to him. In today's verse, we read that his brothers, the same ones who sold him into slavery, bowed down before him. Joseph's dream finally became a reality, but it didn't happen overnight. As a matter of fact, there were approximately twenty years between the time God gave Joseph the dream and the time that the dream became a reality. Those twenty years were full of challenges, setbacks, and disappointments.

Often, people underestimate what it will take to get to where God wants them to go. When God gives them a dream, they get excited, but that excitement quickly wears off as soon as they face adversity. Many give up and call it quits long before reaching their destination.

Joseph's story is proof that delayed doesn't mean denied. Something may not happen as quickly as you want or expect, but that doesn't mean it's not going to happen. There will be challenges, setbacks, and disappointments along the way. Like Joseph, continue pressing forward, and keep your eyes on the prize. Don't let anyone or anything take out of you what God has put in you.

Lord, thank you for having a plan for my life. Give me the strength to press forward in the midst of adversity. Help me keep my eyes on the prize. Amen.

AUGUST 21

As for you, you meant evil against me, but God meant it for good, to bring it about that many people should be kept alive, as they are today.

Genesis 50:20

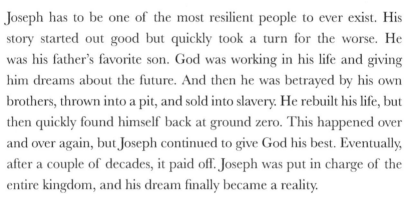

Joseph has to be one of the most resilient people to ever exist. His story started out good but quickly took a turn for the worse. He was his father's favorite son. God was working in his life and giving him dreams about the future. And then he was betrayed by his own brothers, thrown into a pit, and sold into slavery. He rebuilt his life, but then quickly found himself back at ground zero. This happened over and over again, but Joseph continued to give God his best. Eventually, after a couple of decades, it paid off. Joseph was put in charge of the entire kingdom, and his dream finally became a reality.

In hindsight, Joseph recognized that everything he went through was preparation for the destination. Those setbacks were actually setups for something much greater. God used all the bad to prepare Joseph for what he had in store. How would your life change if you had the same perspective as Joseph?

Maybe you're going through a difficult time. Maybe you've been treated unfairly. Maybe you've been cheated. Maybe it seems as if nothing good could ever come out of your current circumstance. You can roll over, give up, and abandon the dream. Or you can get up, press on, and refuse to settle for less than God's best. Maybe it's all preparation for the destination. Maybe what seems to be a setback is actually a setup for something much greater.

Lord, thank you for my current circumstance. Use the challenges, setbacks, and failures to prepare me for what you have in store for me. Amen.

AUGUST 22

Not neglecting to meet together, as is the habit of some, but encouraging one another, and all the more as you see the Day drawing near.

Hebrews 10:25

We live in a time where we can virtually attend a church service from our living rooms. It's common for people to tell me that they watch our services online. We have people from different states and even different countries who watch our services each week. I am thankful for the internet and the global impact that it has enabled our church to have. However, there is one thing we will never be able to replace with a computer, and that is fellowship. The Bible instructs us to regularly meet with one another because fellowship is a crucial aspect of Christianity.

I think about baseball. I can be a baseball fan from my living room. I can tune in and watch every game. I can wear the jersey, cheer, and even invite friends to join me. I can be a fan from a distance but not a member of the team. As a Christian, you're not called to be a fan; you're called to be a member of the team, and that's only possible when you are present.

Every Christian should be actively involved in a local church. The music is great, the preaching is important, but the fellowship is irreplaceable. Are you trying to do church from a distance? Or are you actively involved in a church and regularly engaging in fellowship?

Lord, thank you for the gift of fellowship. Help me prioritize spending time with like-minded people. Show me how to encourage others and place people in my life to encourage me. Amen.

AUGUST 23

No temptation has overtaken you that is not common to man. God is faithful, and he will not let you be tempted beyond your ability, but with the temptation he will also provide the way of escape, that you may be able to endure it.

1 Corinthians 10:13

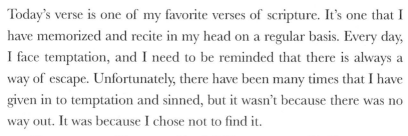

Today's verse is one of my favorite verses of scripture. It's one that I have memorized and recite in my head on a regular basis. Every day, I face temptation, and I need to be reminded that there is always a way of escape. Unfortunately, there have been many times that I have given in to temptation and sinned, but it wasn't because there was no way out. It was because I chose not to find it.

Have you ever felt trapped in sin? Have you ever felt like you were backed into a corner? Have you ever felt like you just couldn't say no? If so, you're not alone. We all have our struggles. We all face temptation, but God is faithful. He promises that he will never let us be tempted beyond our ability. In other words, there is always an alternative to sin.

Maybe you're struggling with something right now. Maybe you've accepted defeat and you're settling for less than God's best. Maybe you feel powerless and continue to give in, although you know that it's wrong. Let me remind you that God will never let you be tempted beyond your ability. He will always provide a way of escape; you just have to find it.

Lord, thank you for always providing a way out of temptation. Help me see sin for what it is and find the way of escape. Amen.

AUGUST 24

For the wages of sin is death, but the free gift of God is eternal life in Christ Jesus our Lord.

Romans 6:23

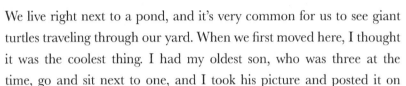

We live right next to a pond, and it's very common for us to see giant turtles traveling through our yard. When we first moved here, I thought it was the coolest thing. I had my oldest son, who was three at the time, go and sit next to one, and I took his picture and posted it on social media. Apparently, it was a snapping turtle. You can imagine the backlash I received. I felt like a terrible parent for putting my child in a dangerous situation. Needless to say, we stay away from the turtles now.

The Bible teaches us that all sin leads to death. You've probably heard the phrase, "Sin always takes you further than you want to go, keeps you longer than you want to stay, and costs you more than you want to pay." We tend to categorize sin, but this is true of all sin. If the Bible calls it sin, it is dangerous, and it leads to death.

I'm afraid that Christians are becoming far too lax about sin. We tend to put ourselves in dangerous situations over and over without even realizing it. So, I encourage you to take inventory. Is there any sin in your life that you've become comfortable with? Or that you're overlooking?

Lord, forgive me for being lax about sin. Show me if there is any sin in my life that I've become comfortable with or that I'm overlooking. Amen.

AUGUST 25

He gives power to the faint, and to him who has no might he increases strength.

Isaiah 40:29

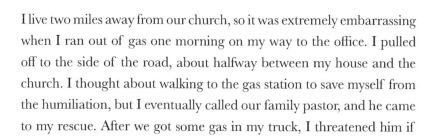

I live two miles away from our church, so it was extremely embarrassing when I ran out of gas one morning on my way to the office. I pulled off to the side of the road, about halfway between my house and the church. I thought about walking to the gas station to save myself from the humiliation, but I eventually called our family pastor, and he came to my rescue. After we got some gas in my truck, I threatened him if he ever told anyone what had happened.

Maybe you've heard the phrase, "If the devil can't make you bad, he will make you busy." How often do we run around on E and convince ourselves that we're fine? We get caught up in the busyness and chaos of life. We pack our schedules to the max and run around like chickens with our heads cut off. A lot of times, we foolishly keep going without stopping, and we run ourselves dry.

Are you burnt out? What about overwhelmed? How about exhausted? If so, it's probably time to stop and refuel. It's probably time to slow down, rest, pray, and read the Bible. Remember, God gives power to the faint and strength to those who are lacking. He will give you power and strength if you just stop and ask.

Lord, thank you for giving me power and strength. Thank you for coming to my rescue when I find myself burnt out and depleted. Amen.

AUGUST 26

For we are his workmanship, created in Christ Jesus for good works, which God prepared beforehand, that we should walk in them.

Ephesians 2:10

When I turned 16, my dad gifted me a truck. It was a 1990 Nissan pickup. It had a manual transmission and no A/C. It had been sitting in our driveway for several years and was covered in rust, but to me, it was the greatest thing in the world. My dad made me a deal. He told me that if I sanded and primed the truck, he would pay for the paint job. I spent an entire summer sanding that truck by hand and finally got it ready for paint. We took it to the body shop, and I picked out a shade of my favorite color, blue.

When the truck came out of the body shop, it looked far better than I ever imagined. I was so proud of my truck, but people started calling it a purple truck. For the record, it was blue, but I let people get in my head. I started to think differently about my truck. At one time, I was proud of it, but I started to become insecure about it.

How often do you allow people to define you? How often do you forget what God has to say about you and focus on what the world has to say about you? Maybe others have torn you down, or perhaps you're struggling with insecurity. Remember, you are his workmanship, created in Christ Jesus for good works.

Lord, thank you for creating me in your image. Thank you for loving and caring for me. Help me cling to what you say about me, not what the world says about me. Amen.

AUGUST 27

And when you fast, do not look gloomy like the hypocrites, for they disfigure their faces that their fasting may be seen by others. Truly, I say to you, they have received their reward.

Matthew 6:16

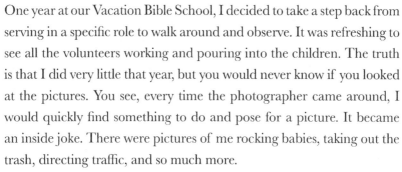

One year at our Vacation Bible School, I decided to take a step back from serving in a specific role to walk around and observe. It was refreshing to see all the volunteers working and pouring into the children. The truth is that I did very little that year, but you would never know if you looked at the pictures. You see, every time the photographer came around, I would quickly find something to do and pose for a picture. It became an inside joke. There were pictures of me rocking babies, taking out the trash, directing traffic, and so much more.

In Matthew 6, Jesus addressed hypocrisy. He addressed people who appeared to be one thing when they were actually something else. People who did some of the right things but for the wrong reasons. People who were more concerned with recognition on Earth than a reward in Heaven.

You can go to church. You can read your Bible. You can tithe. You can serve. You can fast. You can look like you are close to God. You can fool others, but you can't fool God. Are you appearing to be one thing when you're actually something else, or are you the real deal?

Lord, help me be genuine in all that I do. Forgive me for the times that I have fallen short and show me if there is any hypocrisy in my life. Amen.

AUGUST 28

And you will know the truth, and the truth will set you free.

John 8:32

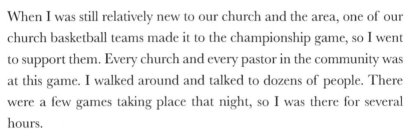

When I was still relatively new to our church and the area, one of our church basketball teams made it to the championship game, so I went to support them. Every church and every pastor in the community was at this game. I walked around and talked to dozens of people. There were a few games taking place that night, so I was there for several hours.

Finally, when the game was over and I was getting up to leave, someone pulled me off to the side and discreetly said, "Sean, your fly is down." I looked down and my zipper was wide open, and it had been wide open the entire time I was at the game. The truth could have saved me from a lot of embarrassment, but no one except that loyal friend had the courage to tell me.

We live in a time where truth is being watered down and even avoided all together. People want to hear what they want to hear, not what they need to hear. It's not politically correct to stand firm in your convictions. But the truth, not lies or half-truths, is what has the power to set us free. No, you shouldn't go around throwing the Bible in people's faces and condemning them to Hell. But you also shouldn't be afraid to stand in your convictions and on the truth of God's Word. After all, if you don't, who will?

Lord, thank you for your Word. Give me the courage to stand in my convictions and on the truth of your Word. Amen.

AUGUST 29

He said to them, "Because of your little faith. For truly, I say to you, if you have faith like a grain of mustard seed, you will say to this mountain, 'Move from here to there,' and it will move, and nothing will be impossible for you."

Matthew 17:20

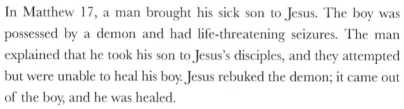

In Matthew 17, a man brought his sick son to Jesus. The boy was possessed by a demon and had life-threatening seizures. The man explained that he took his son to Jesus's disciples, and they attempted but were unable to heal his boy. Jesus rebuked the demon; it came out of the boy, and he was healed.

Later, the disciples asked Jesus why they were unable to cast the demon out. After all, he had given them the power and authority to do so. Jesus answered, "Because of your little faith. For truly, I say to you, if you have faith like a grain of mustard seed, you will say to this mountain, 'Move from here to there,' and it will move, and nothing will be impossible for you."

Your doubt can create mountains that only faith can move. Maybe you're in the middle of a season of doubt. Maybe you're struggling with addiction and doubting that God can deliver you. Maybe your marriage is falling apart and you're doubting that God can restore it. Maybe someone close to you is going down a dangerous path and you're doubting that God can save them. It is easy to let doubt set in and get the best of you, but today, you can choose to trust God. You don't need a lot, just faith like a grain of a mustard seed.

Lord, thank you for being patient with me. Forgive me for my doubt. Help me act on the faith that I have, even when it's not a lot. Amen.

AUGUST 30

But those who desire to be rich fall into temptation, into a snare, into many senseless and harmful desires that plunge people into ruin and destruction.

1 Timothy 6:9

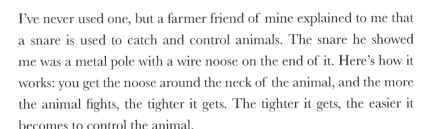

I've never used one, but a farmer friend of mine explained to me that a snare is used to catch and control animals. The snare he showed me was a metal pole with a wire noose on the end of it. Here's how it works: you get the noose around the neck of the animal, and the more the animal fights, the tighter it gets. The tighter it gets, the easier it becomes to control the animal.

The Bible tells us that those who desire to be rich fall into a snare that leads to ruin and destruction. It's not wrong to want to increase your income, but you have to be careful not to fall into the enemy's snare. Many waste their lives pursuing money, trying to live out the American dream, and buying things they can't afford to impress people they don't like. They aren't controlling their money; their money is controlling them. Unfortunately, these people will eventually look back over their lives and realize that they missed the point.

Have you fallen into a snare? Are you controlling your money, or is your money controlling you? This is a question that you need to ask yourself on a regular basis because it's easy to get off track. If you have fallen into a snare, there is no better time to get out than right now.

Lord, thank you for all of your provisions. Help me stay out of the enemy's snare and forgive me for the times that I've failed. Amen.

AUGUST 31

And he said, "Truly, I tell you, this poor widow has put in more than all of them. For they all contributed out of their abundance, but she out of her poverty put in all she had to live on."

Luke 21:3-4

In today's passage of scripture, Jesus was sitting down and watching people as they put their money into the offering box. Many rich people came along and put in large sums of money. And then, a poor widow came along and put in two small copper coins. When I read this story, I always envision people looking at, whispering about, and chuckling at her as she gave her contribution. I'm not sure if that actually happened, but the amount of her offering was insignificant when compared to everybody else's. But Jesus said, "Truly, I tell you, this poor widow has put in more than all of them. For they all contributed out of their abundance, but she, out of her poverty, put in all she had to live on."

Many people don't give simply because they feel they don't have anything significant to give. They think things like, "I don't have anything to offer," or "My small contribution won't make a difference." The truth is that God is far more concerned with how you give than with how much you give. The poor widow wasn't focused on how small her offering was. She was focused on being faithful with what she had.

What do you have? It might feel insignificant. You might feel insecure giving so little. You might think that it's just a drop in the bucket. Give it anyway.

Lord, thank you for allowing me to give back to you. Help me give with the right heart and be generous with what I have. Amen.

SEPTEMBER 1

Repent therefore, and turn back, that your sins may be blotted out.

Acts 3:19

We were never those responsible parents who baby-proofed their house. I don't recall which one, but one of our boys, when he became mobile, was obsessed with touching our electrical outlets. Several times a day, we corrected him and told him not to touch the outlets. We slapped his hand when he reached for the outlets and tried everything. As his parents, we knew that the outlets would hurt him, but to him, they seemed enticing. And the one day it happened, he got shocked, and he hasn't touched an outlet since.

God knows what's best for you. You might find something enticing, but he sees what you don't see. He knows what you don't know. You might think you're not affected by sin, but he knows best. If you play with fire, sooner or later, you're going to get burnt. Or if you stick your finger in an electrical outlet, sooner or later, you're going to get shocked.

Repentance is more than admitting you're wrong, saying sorry, and going right back to do the same thing. Repentance is turning around and going in the opposite direction. It's agreeing with God that your sin is bad and that he knows best. If there is something that you are struggling with, there's no better time to repent than right now.

Lord, thank you for your mercy and grace. Forgive me of my sins. Give me strength to resist temptation. Help me turn around and go in the opposite direction. Amen.

SEPTEMBER 2

And Jesus said, "Father, forgive them, for they know not what they do." And they
cast lots to divide his garments.

Luke 23:34

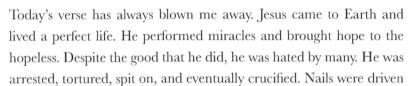

Today's verse has always blown me away. Jesus came to Earth and
lived a perfect life. He performed miracles and brought hope to the
hopeless. Despite the good that he did, he was hated by many. He was
arrested, tortured, spit on, and eventually crucified. Nails were driven
through his hands and feet, and then the cross was erected.

As he hung on the cross, people were standing around laughing
at him, mocking him, taunting him, and yelling degrading comments.
He could have climbed down from the cross and opened up a can of
you know what. He could have given them what they deserved, but he
didn't. Instead, he interceded on their behalf. He asked God to forgive
them for what they were doing to him as they were doing it.

There is no grace like God's grace. The truth is that all of our sin
put him on the cross. We're just as guilty as the ones who drove the
nails, but that's why he came to Earth. He knew it was the only way.
We were dead in our sin. We were destined for Hell. We were doomed,
but he made a way. It's mind-boggling. He paid the penalty for the sin
we committed against him. I don't know what you've done, but I do
know his sacrifice is more than enough to cover your sin.

Lord, thank you for your sacrifice on the cross. Thank you for taking my place and
paying the penalty for my sin. I owe all to you. Amen.

SEPTEMBER 3

Wretched man that I am! Who will deliver me from this body of death? Thanks be to God through Jesus Christ our Lord! So then, I myself serve the law of God with my mind, but with my flesh I serve the law of sin.

Romans 7:24-25

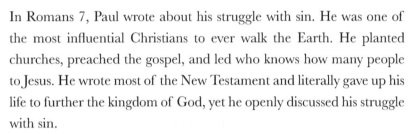

In Romans 7, Paul wrote about his struggle with sin. He was one of the most influential Christians to ever walk the Earth. He planted churches, preached the gospel, and led who knows how many people to Jesus. He wrote most of the New Testament and literally gave up his life to further the kingdom of God, yet he openly discussed his struggle with sin.

There is a lot that we can learn from this example. Unfortunately, we tend to conceal our sin. We want to appear as if we have it all together. We fear that if others knew the truth about us, they would think less of us. We might come across as weak or ruin our Christian influence. This mindset has resulted in many living their lives crippled by hidden sin. No one can find freedom in the dark. We must care more about growth than appearance. We must care more about what God knows than what people think.

Don't be afraid to follow Paul's example. When you're ready to talk openly about your sin, that's when you're ready to begin the process of recovery. Remember, it's only by his grace that you can live in victory.

Lord, thank you for allowing me to live in victory. Help me be vulnerable and genuine. Help me care more about what you know than what people think. Amen.

SEPTEMBER 4

And they came to Jesus and saw the demon-possessed man, the one who had had the legion, sitting there, clothed and in his right mind, and they were afraid.

Mark 5:15

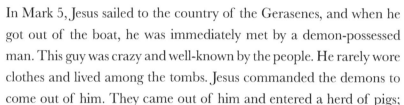

In Mark 5, Jesus sailed to the country of the Gerasenes, and when he got out of the boat, he was immediately met by a demon-possessed man. This guy was crazy and well-known by the people. He rarely wore clothes and lived among the tombs. Jesus commanded the demons to come out of him. They came out of him and entered a herd of pigs; the herd of pigs rushed down a steep bank and into the lake, and they drowned. When the people from the town saw the crazy guy sitting there, in his right mind, wearing clothes, they were afraid. They were so afraid they asked Jesus to leave their region.

This demon-possessed man was written off as a lost cause. No one thought that there was any hope for him. He was crazy, delusional, and too far gone to be helped, but then he met Jesus.

Is there anybody that you have written off as a lost cause? Someone that you think is too far gone to be helped? Someone you've cut off and given up on? You must recognize that the only thing separating you from that person is Jesus. Instead of judging that person, why not commit to praying for that person's salvation? Remember, there's no one too far gone for Jesus.

Lord, thank you for never giving up on me. Forgive me for the times I've given up on others. I pray that you would save those who have been written off by others. Amen.

SEPTEMBER 5

And he went away and began to proclaim in the Decapolis how much Jesus had done for him, and everyone marveled.

Mark 5:20

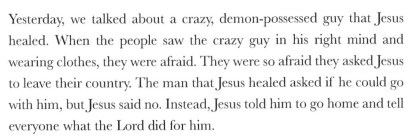

Yesterday, we talked about a crazy, demon-possessed guy that Jesus healed. When the people saw the crazy guy in his right mind and wearing clothes, they were afraid. They were so afraid they asked Jesus to leave their country. The man that Jesus healed asked if he could go with him, but Jesus said no. Instead, Jesus told him to go home and tell everyone what the Lord did for him.

Sometime later, Jesus returned to this same area. Remember, this was the place that he was asked to leave. He was previously unwelcome but something changed. This time, the people were excited to see him. They brought a man to him who needed to be healed, and they rejoiced when Jesus healed him. What changed? Why did the people ask Jesus to leave and then welcome him back? Apparently, that crazy, demon-possessed guy did exactly what Jesus asked him to do. He went and told everybody what the Lord did for him, and because of his testimony, lives were changed.

Are you sharing with others what the Lord has done for you? Are you telling others how he has changed your life? Are you telling others how he has blessed you beyond measure? Your greatest evangelical tool is your testimony.

Lord, thank you for what you have done for me. Help me celebrate what you have done and what you are doing in my life. Help me share my testimony with others. Amen.

SEPTEMBER 6

For he knows our frame; he remembers that we are dust.

Psalm 103:14

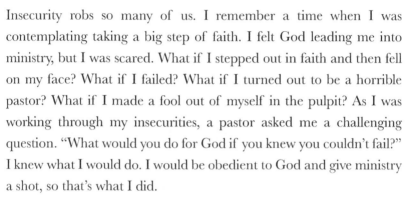

Insecurity robs so many of us. I remember a time when I was contemplating taking a big step of faith. I felt God leading me into ministry, but I was scared. What if I stepped out in faith and then fell on my face? What if I failed? What if I turned out to be a horrible pastor? What if I made a fool out of myself in the pulpit? As I was working through my insecurities, a pastor asked me a challenging question. "What would you do for God if you knew you couldn't fail?" I knew what I would do. I would be obedient to God and give ministry a shot, so that's what I did.

Obedience to God doesn't guarantee that you won't fail, but it does take your insecurity out of the equation. When you stop thinking about everything that could go wrong and start thinking about everything that could go right, it changes your perspective.

I've had my fair share of failures, but through it all, God has been faithful. Taking that step of faith was one of the best things that I've ever done. I'm now more certain than ever that I'm doing exactly what God wants me to do. So, let me ask you, what would you do for God if you knew you couldn't fail? Whatever your answer is, let me encourage you to go and do it.

Lord, thank you for leading me to do things bigger than me. Give me a new perspective. Help me get past my insecurities and be obedient to you. Amen.

SEPTEMBER 7

And the men said to her, "Our life for yours even to death! If you do not tell this business of ours, then when the Lord gives us the land we will deal kindly and faithfully with you."

Joshua 2:14

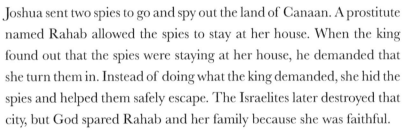

Joshua sent two spies to go and spy out the land of Canaan. A prostitute named Rahab allowed the spies to stay at her house. When the king found out that the spies were staying at her house, he demanded that she turn them in. Instead of doing what the king demanded, she hid the spies and helped them safely escape. The Israelites later destroyed that city, but God spared Rahab and her family because she was faithful.

Rahab was put in a dangerous situation. She chose to take a big risk by hiding the spies. If she were caught, she would have likely been killed along with the spies. She heard about the God of the Israelites and how he had provided for them along the way, and ultimately, she chose to trust him. Ironically, taking that big risk is what ended up saving her life. God rewarded her faith and courage.

As you follow God, he will often call you to take risks. When he does, you can allow fear to hold you back, or like Rahab, you can step out in faith and trust him. Taking a big risk might just be the best decision you make.

Lord, show me what risk you want me to take and give me the courage to take it. Help me trust you, even when there seems to be a lot at stake. Amen.

SEPTEMBER 8

Jesus said to him, "No one who puts his hand to the plow and looks back is fit for the kingdom of God."

Luke 9:62

In Luke 9, there was a guy who wanted to follow Jesus, but first, he wanted to go and tell his family goodbye. Jesus replied, "No one who puts his hand to the plow and looks back is fit for the kingdom of God." This may seem like a harsh reply, but Jesus is making it clear that following him requires commitment. When you commit to follow him, he must come before everything else. He must be the top priority.

We live in a time when people have commitment phobia. More and more couples are opting to live together and play house because they don't want to commit to marriage. More and more people are jumping from job to job because they don't want to commit to one company. Many churches are doing away with church membership because many are scared away by the commitment it requires.

Unfortunately, we tend to bring this commitment phobia into our walk with the Lord. We want to follow him, but we're scared to fully commit because we also want to hold on to things of this world. So, we end up surrendering some but not all. Let today's passage serve as a warning: it's impossible to follow Jesus without fully committing. He must come before everything else. He must be your top priority.

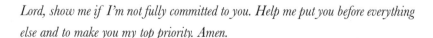

Lord, show me if I'm not fully committed to you. Help me put you before everything else and to make you my top priority. Amen.

SEPTEMBER 9

He must increase, but I must decrease.

John 3:30

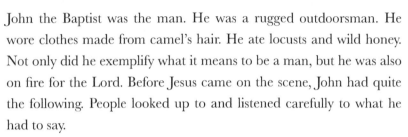

John the Baptist was the man. He was a rugged outdoorsman. He wore clothes made from camel's hair. He ate locusts and wild honey. Not only did he exemplify what it means to be a man, but he was also on fire for the Lord. Before Jesus came on the scene, John had quite the following. People looked up to and listened carefully to what he had to say.

However, when Jesus came on the scene, John started to lose some of his thunder. John's disciples noticed that more people were going to Jesus to be baptized and less were coming to him. They expressed their concern to John, and he replied, "He must increase, but I must decrease." John got it. He understood that his purpose was not to make a name for himself but to point others to Jesus, and that's exactly what he did.

We've all been guilty of self-centeredness. There have probably been many times when you've promoted your preferences before considering God's purposes. Like John, you must realize it's not about what you want. It's about what he wants. You weren't put on this Earth to make a name for yourself. You were put on this Earth to point others to Jesus. Take some time today and evaluate your life. Are you living for him, or are you living for you?

Lord, forgive me for being self-centered. Help me care more about your purposes than my preferences. Show me when I begin to get my priorities out of order. Amen.

SEPTEMBER 10

Even as the Son of Man came not to be served but to serve, and to give his life as a ransom for many.

Matthew 20:28

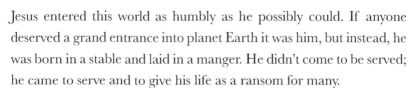

Jesus entered this world as humbly as he possibly could. If anyone deserved a grand entrance into planet Earth it was him, but instead, he was born in a stable and laid in a manger. He didn't come to be served; he came to serve and to give his life as a ransom for many.

The world today is full of selfishness. The example Jesus set is often overshadowed by a worldly agenda. Jesus tells us to be selfless, while the world tells us to be selfish. Jesus tells us to put others before ourselves, while the world tells us to put ourselves before others. Jesus tells us that our purpose is to serve, while the world tells us that our purpose is to reach a place where others are serving us.

As a believer, you have the power to make a difference, but only when you transition from a self-serving mindset to a kingdom-serving mindset. Do you primarily make your decisions based on what's best for you or based on what's best for the kingdom of God? Are you seeking to bring glory to your name or glory to his name? Are you looking to be served, or are you anxious to serve others? How can you use your time, money, gifts, and talents for the betterment of his kingdom?

Lord, thank you for sending your son to serve and give his life as a ransom for many. Help me follow his example, serve others, and further your kingdom. Amen.

SEPTEMBER 11

Greater love has no one than this, that someone lay down his life for his friends.

John 15:13

I was sitting in my fifth-grade class when the first plane crashed into the North Tower of the World Trade Center. I remember my teacher rolling the TV into our classroom, and for the remainder of the day, we watched tragedy unfold. At the time, I couldn't fully grasp what was taking place, and it wasn't until years later that I realized the severity of the attack. Almost 3,000 people lost their lives, and many are still affected to this day.

September 11th is a day I will never forget. I mourn with those who lost loved ones, and I am inspired by the heroic actions of so many. I think about the first responders who risked, and many who lost, their lives trying to help others. I think about the passengers and the crew on Flight 93. When their plane was hijacked, they decided to fight back. The plane ended up crashing in a field, killing all those on board, but countless lives were saved because of their courage. I think about the thousands of people who volunteered their time to go to ground zero to assist with rescue, recovery and cleanup.

Take some time today to remember the lives that were lost on 9/11 and to celebrate the heroes. Pray and ask God to give you the courage to replicate their heroic actions.

Lord, thank you for laying your life down for me. Today, I pray for all who were affected by 9/11. Thank you for the heroes who laid down their lives for others. Amen.

SEPTEMBER 12

But he answered, "It is written, "'Man shall not live by bread alone, but by every word that comes from the mouth of God."'

Matthew 4:4

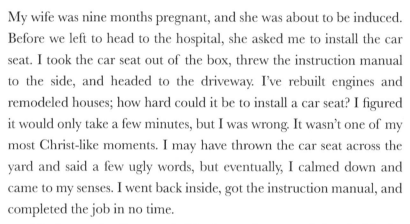

My wife was nine months pregnant, and she was about to be induced. Before we left to head to the hospital, she asked me to install the car seat. I took the car seat out of the box, threw the instruction manual to the side, and headed to the driveway. I've rebuilt engines and remodeled houses; how hard could it be to install a car seat? I figured it would only take a few minutes, but I was wrong. It wasn't one of my most Christ-like moments. I may have thrown the car seat across the yard and said a few ugly words, but eventually, I calmed down and came to my senses. I went back inside, got the instruction manual, and completed the job in no time.

Maybe you're frustrated. Maybe you're overwhelmed. Maybe you're exerting a lot of effort and energy, but you're making little to no progress. Maybe you're wasting valuable time because you're attempting to go through life without God's Word.

The Bible contains the answers to life's most difficult questions. There is no book in the world that can replace the inerrant Word of God. As a believer, you should spend some time reading life's "instruction manual" every single day. There's no better time to start than right now.

Lord, thank you for the Bible. I pray that you will give me a hunger and desire to read it daily. Help me approach your Word with humility. Amen.

SEPTEMBER 13

And let us not grow weary of doing good, for in due season we will reap, if we do not give up.

Galatians 6:9

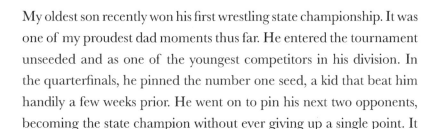

My oldest son recently won his first wrestling state championship. It was one of my proudest dad moments thus far. He entered the tournament unseeded and as one of the youngest competitors in his division. In the quarterfinals, he pinned the number one seed, a kid that beat him handily a few weeks prior. He went on to pin his next two opponents, becoming the state champion without ever giving up a single point. It was great to see his hard work pay off in a big way.

One thing that God has shown me over the last decade is the power of consistency. We exert so much effort looking for hacks, shortcuts, and instant results, but consistency is the key. This is true professionally, physically, relationally, and spiritually.

As I reflect on my life, I realize that the areas I've been most successful in are the areas I've been the most consistent in. Maybe you're discouraged and on the verge of moving on to the next thing. Maybe you're ready to close that business, abandon that project, leave that church, or walk away from that relationship. If so, I encourage you to spend time praying before making any rash decisions. Maybe God wants you to persevere and stay consistent. Remember, in due season, you will reap if you do not give up.

Lord, forgive me for the times I've lacked consistency. Help me persevere and stay consistent in all that I do. Amen.

SEPTEMBER 14

Therefore I tell you, do not be anxious about your life, what you will eat or what you will drink, nor about your body, what you will put on. Is not life more than food, and the body more than clothing?

Matthew 6:25

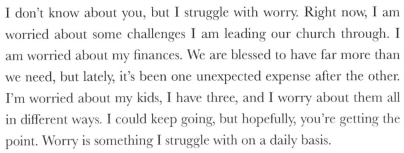

I don't know about you, but I struggle with worry. Right now, I am worried about some challenges I am leading our church through. I am worried about my finances. We are blessed to have far more than we need, but lately, it's been one unexpected expense after the other. I'm worried about my kids, I have three, and I worry about them all in different ways. I could keep going, but hopefully, you're getting the point. Worry is something I struggle with on a daily basis.

Can you relate? Are you stressed about something going on at work? Are you worried about one of your kids, or a relationship, or your finances? Are you anxious about an upcoming meeting, an appointment, or a difficult conversation that you will have?

What you worry about the most usually reveals where you trust God the least. That's a convicting statement because it's true. Worry is a tool of the enemy. If he can get you to worry, he can divert your attention away from your calling and purpose. Is worry consuming and distracting you from the main thing? If so, confess your worry to him and seek first the kingdom of God.

Lord, forgive me for not trusting you in certain areas of my life. Help me overcome worry and seek first your kingdom. Amen.

SEPTEMBER 15

Indeed, we felt that we had received the sentence of death. But that was to make us rely not on ourselves but on God who raises the dead.

2 Corinthians 1:9

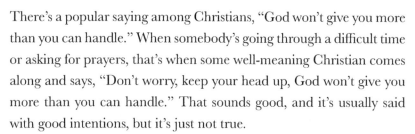

There's a popular saying among Christians, "God won't give you more than you can handle." When somebody's going through a difficult time or asking for prayers, that's when some well-meaning Christian comes along and says, "Don't worry, keep your head up, God won't give you more than you can handle." That sounds good, and it's usually said with good intentions, but it's just not true.

I have been through countless situations in life that were bigger than me. Situations where I wanted to give up. Situations where I wanted to run and hide, but through prayer, God gave me the strength to face them head-on. There's no way I would have been able to make it through without him. It was far more than I could handle on my own, but thankfully, I wasn't alone. God was with me.

God will give you or at least allow you to go through more than you can handle, and that's why you so desperately need him. If you're feeling powerless or weak, remember he gives power to the faint and strength to the weak. It might be bigger than you, but rest assured, it's not bigger than him. Thankfully, you're not alone. God is with you.

Lord, thank you for always being with me. Give me the strength to face the challenges that are in front of me. Help me face difficult situations head-on. Amen.

SEPTEMBER 16

Casting all your anxieties on him, because he cares for you.

1 Peter 5:7

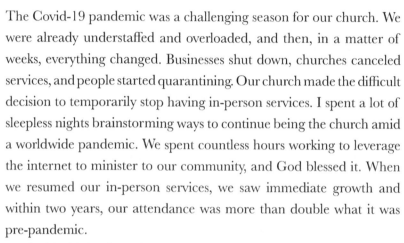

The Covid-19 pandemic was a challenging season for our church. We were already understaffed and overloaded, and then, in a matter of weeks, everything changed. Businesses shut down, churches canceled services, and people started quarantining. Our church made the difficult decision to temporarily stop having in-person services. I spent a lot of sleepless nights brainstorming ways to continue being the church amid a worldwide pandemic. We spent countless hours working to leverage the internet to minister to our community, and God blessed it. When we resumed our in-person services, we saw immediate growth and within two years, our attendance was more than double what it was pre-pandemic.

In hindsight, I see how God used that season of uncertainty to benefit our church and grow my faith. However, in the middle of that season, my anxiety was at an all-time high, and I lived in a constant state of worry. I had to learn to cast my anxieties on him, and he made it evident that he cares for me and for our church.

What are you anxious about? What is consuming your thoughts? Are you living in a constant state of worry? Cast your anxieties on him because he cares for you.

Lord, thank you for caring for me. Help me trust you with all the things that are causing me anxiety. Amen.

SEPTEMBER 17

Everyone then who hears these words of mine and does them will be like a wise man who built his house on the rock.

Matthew 7:24

In Matthew 7, Jesus talks about two builders, a wise builder and a foolish builder. What separates the two of them is obedience. The wise builder hears the Word of God and does it. He builds his house on the rock. The foolish builder hears the Word of God but does not do it. He builds his house on the sand. When the storm comes, the house built on the rock stands strong, but the house built on the sand is destroyed.

A person can look like the real deal. They can have all the right answers. They can appear as if they have it all together. They can put up a front, but when the storm comes, their true foundation will be revealed.

It's easy to follow God when everything is falling into place. It's easy to follow God when everyone is healthy. It's easy to follow God when everyone is happy. It's easy to follow God when the bills are paid. It's easy to follow God when everything is good. It's much more difficult to follow God when everything seems to be falling apart. It's much more difficult to follow God when the world is crashing down on you. When the storm comes, what will it reveal? Have you built your life upon the rock or the sand?

Lord, thank you for being a firm foundation. Help me live out your Word and build my foundation on the rock. Amen.

SEPTEMBER 18

Two are better than one, because they have a good reward for their toil. For if they fall, one will lift up his fellow. But woe to him who is alone when he falls and has not another to lift him up!

Ecclesiastes 4:9-10

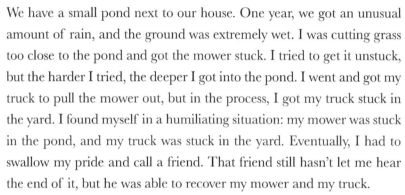

We have a small pond next to our house. One year, we got an unusual amount of rain, and the ground was extremely wet. I was cutting grass too close to the pond and got the mower stuck. I tried to get it unstuck, but the harder I tried, the deeper I got into the pond. I went and got my truck to pull the mower out, but in the process, I got my truck stuck in the yard. I found myself in a humiliating situation: my mower was stuck in the pond, and my truck was stuck in the yard. Eventually, I had to swallow my pride and call a friend. That friend still hasn't let me hear the end of it, but he was able to recover my mower and my truck.

There will be times in life when you get stuck. You may find that the harder you try to get unstuck, the more stuck you get. You may struggle to admit that you need help, or you may be too embarrassed to ask, but sometimes, asking for help is the only way to get unstuck.

The Bible tells us that two are better than one. As a Christian, it is important to have friends that you can call, people that will help you and hold you accountable. If you're stuck, maybe it's time to call a friend.

Lord, thank you for my friends. Help me be humble and admit when I need help from others. Place people in my life that will help me get unstuck. Amen.

SEPTEMBER 19

May the God of endurance and encouragement grant you to live in such harmony with one another, in accord with Christ Jesus.

Romans 15:5

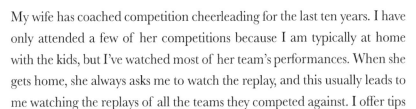

My wife has coached competition cheerleading for the last ten years. I have only attended a few of her competitions because I am typically at home with the kids, but I've watched most of her team's performances. When she gets home, she always asks me to watch the replay, and this usually leads to me watching the replays of all the teams they competed against. I offer tips and suggestions, like I know something about cheerleading.

One thing that has always impressed me is how in-sync the teams are during their performances. When they move, they move in unison. They have their timing down to hundredths of a second. Some of the performances could even pass as computer-generated.

That's what comes to mind when I think about living in harmony. A group of people putting away their differences and coming together to work toward a common goal. When one person wins, the whole team wins. When one person struggles, the whole team struggles. They move in unison. Their hearts and desires are in-sync with one another. That's what God has in mind for the church. Instead of arguing over petty things, God wants us to come together in unison to further his kingdom.

Are you contributing to harmony within the church, or are you contributing to disunity? Are you being a team player, or are you too focused on your own preferences?

Lord, thank you for the church. Help me contribute to harmony within the church. Help us come together in unison to further your kingdom. Amen.

SEPTEMBER 20

Do not be conformed to this world, but be transformed by the renewal of your mind, that by testing you may discern what is the will of God, what is good and acceptable and perfect.

Romans 12:2

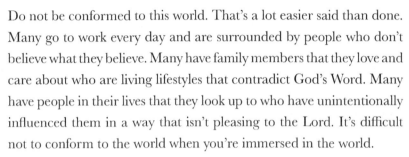

Do not be conformed to this world. That's a lot easier said than done. Many go to work every day and are surrounded by people who don't believe what they believe. Many have family members that they love and care about who are living lifestyles that contradict God's Word. Many have people in their lives that they look up to who have unintentionally influenced them in a way that isn't pleasing to the Lord. It's difficult not to conform to the world when you're immersed in the world.

Today, we see so much compromise within the church. There are Christians that stand for things that Jesus never stood for. There are entire denominations that are altering their beliefs to appease people.

It's easy to stop viewing sin as sin when everybody is doing it. Is there any sin in your life that you've become okay with? It's easy to accept and condone sin in the lives of others when it's considered socially acceptable. Have you justified the sinful lifestyles that others may be living? It's easy to find yourself in a pile of debt trying to impress others. Have you got caught up in the never-ending pursuit of more? "Do not be conformed to this world, but be transformed by the renewal of your mind." In other words, empty yourself of worldly thinking and fill yourself with God's Word.

Lord, thank you for the gift of life. Help me live boldly for you. Show me if I have conformed to this world and forgive me if I have. Amen.

SEPTEMBER 21

*Be sober-minded; be watchful. Your adversary the devil prowls around like a roaring
lion, seeking someone to devour.*

1 Peter 5:8

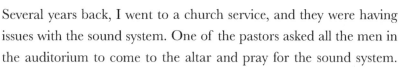

Several years back, I went to a church service, and they were having
issues with the sound system. One of the pastors asked all the men in
the auditorium to come to the altar and pray for the sound system.
Men started walking toward the altar, and they proceeded to audibly
yell at the devil for the next ten minutes. They blamed him for their
sound issues, but I think it turned out to be the sound guy who forgot to
unmute one of the channels. It was an interesting and scary experience.

I've never been one to blame the devil for every little thing. Sometimes,
things just don't go our way. Sometimes, we bring things upon ourselves.
Sometimes, other people are to blame. But make no mistake, the devil
is a roaring lion seeking someone to devour. And the more you pursue
God, the more he will pursue you. I've noticed in my own life that the
enemy usually attacks me most when God has something in store. For
instance, maybe the weeks leading up to Easter are especially difficult for
me, and then on Easter, God saves dozens of people.

If you feel under attack, maybe God has something in store. If
nothing is going your way, maybe you're on the verge of a breakthrough.
Stay the course, keep your guard up, and don't let the devil keep you
from what God has for you.

*Lord, thank you for what you have in store for me. Help me be on guard against the
attacks of the enemy. Give me strength to stay the course. Amen.*

SEPTEMBER 22

A hot-tempered man stirs up strife, but he who is slow to anger quiets contention.

Proverbs 15:18

The other day, I lost my cool with my seven-year-old son. We were at wrestling practice, and I felt, from the comfort of my seat, that he wasn't giving it his all during the live wrestling. I yelled at him during practice. And then I spent the hour-long car ride home lecturing him and critiquing everything he did wrong. When we got home, I took him upstairs to our wrestling room, and I showed him everything he could have and should have done differently. Eventually, I calmed down, realized I had gone overboard, and apologized to him. I believe in pushing my kids to be their best, but I don't think that approach is going to get them there.

Often, we get angry and then respond impulsively. We end up doing and saying things that we aren't proud of. In the end, without realizing it, we are angrier about the way we handled the situation than we are about the situation itself. Anger only makes the situation worse.

Would you describe yourself as patient? Or can you go from zero to hot in a quick minute? Do you regularly catch yourself losing your cool with your spouse, kids, employees, or coworkers? You can allow your temper to stir up strife, or you can be slow to anger and quiet contention.

Lord, thank you for the patience that you have extended to me. Help me extend that same patience to others. Help me be slow to anger and quiet contention. Amen.

SEPTEMBER 23

So neither he who plants nor he who waters is anything, but only God who gives the growth.

1 Corinthians 3:7

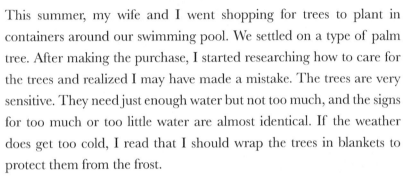

This summer, my wife and I went shopping for trees to plant in containers around our swimming pool. We settled on a type of palm tree. After making the purchase, I started researching how to care for the trees and realized I may have made a mistake. The trees are very sensitive. They need just enough water but not too much, and the signs for too much or too little water are almost identical. If the weather does get too cold, I read that I should wrap the trees in blankets to protect them from the frost.

I'll go out on a limb and say the trees won't make it long. I'm just not willing to invest that much time and effort into trees. But even if I was, even if I did everything right, I don't have the power to make those trees grow. I can plant and water, but God is the one who brings the growth.

Today's verse is one that has meant much to my ministry. The truth is that I can do all the right things, but I have to trust God. I can lead the church, launch ministries, preach sermons, visit the sick, and do everything else that needs to be done, but I have to trust God to bring growth. And the same is true for you. You want growth, but are you trusting him?

Lord, thank you for the growth you have already brought into my life. Show me if there is any area of my life where I'm not fully trusting you. Amen.

SEPTEMBER 24

The fear of man lays a snare, but whoever trusts in the Lord is safe.

Proverbs 29:25

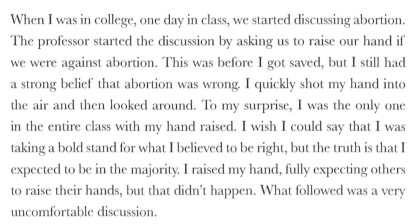

When I was in college, one day in class, we started discussing abortion. The professor started the discussion by asking us to raise our hand if we were against abortion. This was before I got saved, but I still had a strong belief that abortion was wrong. I quickly shot my hand into the air and then looked around. To my surprise, I was the only one in the entire class with my hand raised. I wish I could say that I was taking a bold stand for what I believed to be right, but the truth is that I expected to be in the majority. I raised my hand, fully expecting others to raise their hands, but that didn't happen. What followed was a very uncomfortable discussion.

The majority of people are living contrary to God's Word. The majority of people are not only accepting sin but encouraging it. Being in the minority can be uncomfortable. It can even be humiliating and embarrassing, but that should be the norm for those who are following Christ.

Today, you can go with the crowd and blend in, or you can take a stand for what you believe to be right. You can be in the majority with people's approval, or you can be in the minority with God's approval. The choice is yours.

Lord, forgive me for the times that I have chosen to go with the crowd. Give me the courage to stand for what's right, even if that means being in the minority. Amen.

SEPTEMBER 25

The man who had died came out, his hands and feet bound with linen strips, and his face wrapped with a cloth. Jesus said to them, "Unbind him, and let him go."

John 11:44

In John 11, Jesus did the impossible. Lazarus was deathly ill. As odd as it may seem, when Jesus heard the news, he delayed. Instead of going directly to Lazarus, he waited two days longer in the place where he was. By the time Jesus arrived, Lazarus had already been dead for four days. Undeterred by the news of Lazarus's death, Jesus wanted to know where his body was laid. They took him to the tomb; it was a cave with a large stone covering the opening. Jesus asked them to take away the stone. Reluctantly, they removed the stone, and Jesus yelled for Lazarus to come out. Sure enough, Lazarus walked out of the tomb on his own two feet.

This is one of many stories that prove nothing is impossible for God. There is no circumstance that he can't turn around. There's no person that he can't save. There's no sickness that he can't heal. There is nothing that is out of his hands.

No matter what you may be going through, remember that God is still on the throne. That doesn't mean that he will work things out the way you hope, but it does mean that he has a plan. That doesn't mean that you won't struggle, but it does mean that you don't have to struggle alone.

Lord, thank you for being a way maker. Help me look to you when life gets the best of me. Give me the strength to trust your plan. Amen.

SEPTEMBER 26

Nevertheless, many even of the authorities believed in him, but for fear of the Pharisees they did not confess it, so that they would not be put out of the synagogue; for they loved the glory that comes from man more than the glory that comes from God.

John 12:42-43

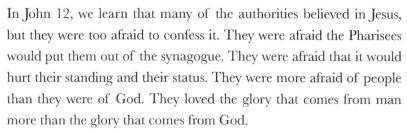

In John 12, we learn that many of the authorities believed in Jesus, but they were too afraid to confess it. They were afraid the Pharisees would put them out of the synagogue. They were afraid that it would hurt their standing and their status. They were more afraid of people than they were of God. They loved the glory that comes from man more than the glory that comes from God.

What about you? Do you fear people more than you fear God? Do you do things in private that you would never do in public? Are there things in your life that you hide from others but do right in front of God?

Maybe you have a secret sin that nobody knows about. Maybe you're cutting some corners in business, and you wouldn't want anyone else to find out because it could cost you everything. Maybe you don't speak up when you know you should, or maybe you don't stand for what you believe to be right. Like the authorities in John 12, maybe you love the glory that comes from man more than the glory that comes from God. As a Christian, you must stop being more concerned about saving face with people than being in a right standing with God.

Lord, forgive me for being a hypocrite. Help me care more about pleasing you than people. Show me where I'm falling short. Amen.

SEPTEMBER 27

I will instruct you and teach you in the way you should go; I will counsel you with my eye upon you.

Psalm 32:8

I've coached flag football for the last two seasons. Throughout the season, I make it a priority to give every kid at least one opportunity to run the ball. The biggest challenge is getting five and six-year-olds to run the ball in the right direction. Some get the ball, take off, and run straight to their parents, who are on the sidelines. Some get the ball, take off, and run backward before running forward. And some get the ball, take off, and sprint in the opposite direction, toward their own endzone, as fast as they can. This usually results in a safety, giving the other team two points.

My youngest son recently got his first opportunity to run the ball. In the huddle, I told him to run to the right. As we broke out of the huddle, he was obviously still confused. He pointed toward our endzone and asked if that was the direction I wanted him to run. At that point, I didn't care if he ran left or right. I just told him to move the ball forward. Fortunately, he went on to score a touchdown.

There will be countless times in life when you are confused and unsure of what direction to go in. If you look to God, he will instruct you and teach you the way that you should go. If you seek him, he will lead, guide, and direct you.

Lord, thank you for being patient with me. Teach me and show me the way that I should go. Lead, guide, and direct me in all that I do. Amen.

SEPTEMBER 28

When Jesus heard this, he said to him, "One thing you still lack. Sell all that you have and distribute to the poor, and you will have treasure in heaven; and come, follow me." But when he heard these things, he became very sad, for he was extremely rich.

Luke 18:22-23

A ruler came up to Jesus and asked him what a person must do to inherit eternal life. Jesus listed off several commandments, and the guy quickly responded by saying that he had kept all of them since he was a child. Jesus said, "One thing you still lack. Sell all that you have and distribute it to the poor, and you will have treasure in Heaven; and come, follow me." This guy went away sad because he was extremely rich. Evidently, he didn't want to give up everything that he had to begin to follow Jesus.

There's a phrase, "God doesn't care if you have stuff. He cares if stuff has you." In other words, there is nothing wrong with having stuff, but stuff should never become the focus of your life. Jesus didn't want this guy to sell his stuff and give away his money because his stuff and money was bad. He wanted him to sell his stuff and give away his money because it had become a problem. It wasn't that he had stuff. It was that stuff had him.

Does stuff have you? If God were to tell you to sell everything that you have, would you do it? Your answer to that question will tell you if you have stuff or if stuff has you.

Lord, forgive me for placing too much emphasis on stuff, money, and possessions. Show me if anything is holding me back from following you. Amen.

SEPTEMBER 29

No one can serve two masters, for either he will hate the one and love the other, or he will be devoted to the one and despise the other. You cannot serve God and money.

Matthew 6:24

The Bible has a lot to say about money. There are hundreds of verses that address the topics of money, possessions, and stewardship. Why does the Bible talk so much about money? Because money is the number one thing that competes for our hearts.

I believe so many people miss their God-given purpose in life because they get caught up in the never-ending pursuit of money. I wonder how many fathers have failed to be there for their children because they were more dedicated to their jobs than their families. And they justified it by telling themselves they were doing it to give their children a better life. I wonder how many marriages have ended in divorce because somewhere along the way, money took precedence over God. I wonder how many people always meant to get more involved in the church but never got around to it because they were more interested in boosting their income than serving their God.

We all need money to live and to support our families. Money is necessary for survival, but if we are not careful, it can become an idol. Are you serving God or money? Because you can't serve them both.

Lord, thank you for the money that you have entrusted me with. Help me be a good steward and remember who my master is. Amen.

SEPTEMBER 30

Bring the full tithe into the storehouse, that there may be food in my house. And thereby put me to the test, says the Lord of hosts, if I will not open the windows of heaven for you and pour down for you a blessing until there is no more need.

Malachi 3:10

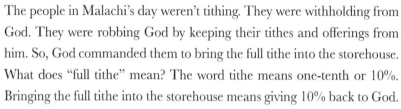

The people in Malachi's day weren't tithing. They were withholding from God. They were robbing God by keeping their tithes and offerings from him. So, God commanded them to bring the full tithe into the storehouse. What does "full tithe" mean? The word tithe means one-tenth or 10%. Bringing the full tithe into the storehouse means giving 10% back to God.

Many push back on this command and make excuses for not tithing. They say, "God doesn't need my money." The truth is that he doesn't need their money, but he does ask them to trust him. They say, "I work hard for my money. I'm not going to give it away." The truth is that God is the one that gave them the ability to work hard. They say, "I can't afford to tithe." The truth is that they can't afford not to tithe.

This is one of the only times in scripture that God challenges us to test him. And he makes it clear that if we are faithful, we will be blessed. That doesn't mean that if you tithe, God is going to bless you with materialistic things, but it does mean that it is impossible to outgive God. Have you been faithful with your finances? Have you made a commitment to give 10% of your income to further the kingdom of God? If not, will you take God at his word and surrender your finances to him?

Lord, thank you for what you have blessed me with financially. Thank you for allowing me to give back to you. Help me give eagerly, not reluctantly. Amen.

OCTOBER 1

Judge not, and you will not be judged; condemn not, and you will not be condemned; forgive, and you will be forgiven.

Luke 6:37

We all tend to quickly find faults in the lives of others while overlooking the faults in our own lives. When we have an argument, we usually focus on everything the other person did wrong while ignoring what we did wrong. When problems arise at work, we usually point out where others fell short while ignoring where we fell short. When something goes south, we usually shift the blame and make ourselves out to be the victim.

In today's verse, Jesus instructs us to "judge not." He goes on to tell us that we will be judged by the same standard we judge others. This verse should make you think twice before judging others too harshly. Instead of judging others, you should extend the same grace you would like to receive.

We tend to spend our time looking out of the window instead of looking in the mirror. In other words, we spend more time evaluating others than ourselves. Often, we are blind to our own weaknesses and shortcomings. The truth is that we would accomplish a lot more if we stopped trying to improve everybody else's weaknesses and started trying to improve our own. Today is a good day to stop looking out the window and start looking in the mirror.

Lord, thank you for your grace. Help me extend that same grace to others. Show me where I am falling short and how I can improve myself. Amen.

OCTOBER 2

Then Simon Peter, having a sword, drew it and struck the high priest's servant and cut off his right ear. (The servant's name was Malchus.) So Jesus said to Peter, "Put your sword into its sheath; shall I not drink the cup that the Father has given me?"

John 18:10-11

Jesus went with his disciples to the Garden of Gethsemane. This must have been a place that he frequently visited with his disciples because Judas knew where to find him. Judas was one of Jesus's disciples, but he decided to betray him for a payout. While Jesus and his disciples were hanging out in the garden, Judas showed up with a group of Roman soldiers. Jesus knew they were there to arrest him, and he voluntarily surrendered himself.

Peter wasn't ready to give up so easily. He pulled out his sword and cut off the right ear of one of the men. Jesus commanded Peter to put the sword away. Violence wasn't his method. He knew that what was about to happen to him would lead to the deliverance of many. They ended up arresting Jesus and taking him away.

Jesus didn't come to Earth and die accidentally. He died intentionally. He wasn't taken against his will. He went willingly. At any moment, he could have put an end to it. He could have broken free and escaped. He could have given Judas and those soldiers what they deserved, but he didn't. He voluntarily surrendered himself because he knew it would lead to the deliverance of many.

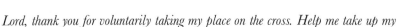

Lord, thank you for voluntarily taking my place on the cross. Help me take up my cross each day to follow you. Amen.

OCTOBER 3

When the Lord first spoke through Hosea, the Lord said to Hosea, "Go, take to yourself a wife of whoredom and have children of whoredom, for the land commits great whoredom by forsaking the Lord."

Hosea 1:2

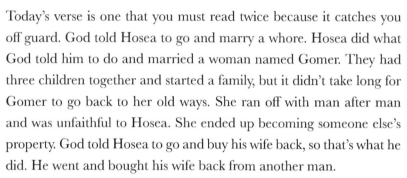

Today's verse is one that you must read twice because it catches you off guard. God told Hosea to go and marry a whore. Hosea did what God told him to do and married a woman named Gomer. They had three children together and started a family, but it didn't take long for Gomer to go back to her old ways. She ran off with man after man and was unfaithful to Hosea. She ended up becoming someone else's property. God told Hosea to go and buy his wife back, so that's what he did. He went and bought his wife back from another man.

Why did God ask Hosea to marry a whore? Because he wanted to provide a real-life illustration of his relationship with the Israelites. God pursued a relationship with the Israelites, foreknowing every mistake they would ever make. They were unfaithful, but he continued to love them. Despite their unfaithfulness, God was still faithful.

The same is true for you. You have been unfaithful to God. You have turned your back on him. Through it all, he has continued to love you. He even sent his only son to die on the cross for you. You were a slave to sin, and he bought you back. Despite your unfaithfulness, God is still faithful.

Lord, thank you for your faithfulness. Thank you for continuing to love me. Forgive me for the times that I've been unfaithful and turned my back on you. Amen.

OCTOBER 4

And when Jesus saw their faith, he said to the paralytic, "Son, your sins are forgiven."

Mark 2:5

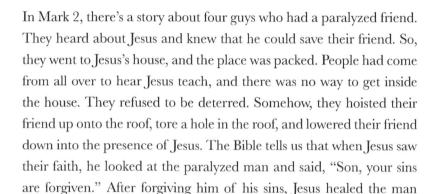

In Mark 2, there's a story about four guys who had a paralyzed friend. They heard about Jesus and knew that he could save their friend. So, they went to Jesus's house, and the place was packed. People had come from all over to hear Jesus teach, and there was no way to get inside the house. They refused to be deterred. Somehow, they hoisted their friend up onto the roof, tore a hole in the roof, and lowered their friend down into the presence of Jesus. The Bible tells us that when Jesus saw their faith, he looked at the paralyzed man and said, "Son, your sins are forgiven." After forgiving him of his sins, Jesus healed the man physically, and he was able to get up and walk home.

You don't have the ability to save anyone, but you can introduce people to the one who can. Who is someone in your life that doesn't know Jesus? Who is someone you need to share the gospel with? Who is someone you need to invite to church? Whose salvation do you need to start praying for right now? Like these four courageous friends, will you commit to doing everything in your power to get them into the presence of Jesus?

Lord, thank you for entrusting me to share the gospel. Help me identify people that need you. Help me go out of my way to get people into your presence. Amen.

OCTOBER 5

And Jesus said to them, "Follow me, and I will make you become fishers of men."

Mark 1:17

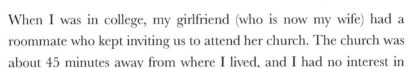

When I was in college, my girlfriend (who is now my wife) had a roommate who kept inviting us to attend her church. The church was about 45 minutes away from where I lived, and I had no interest in church, so I came up with an excuse. However, the invitations kept coming and eventually, I ran out of excuses.

When I went for the first time, I was skeptical and wanted to hate it, but I felt God speaking to me in a way I never had before. I went back the next week and then the next week and then the next week. A few months later, I surrendered my life to Jesus and got baptized. God used a simple invitation to change my life.

In Mark 1, Jesus invited the disciples to follow him. In that same way, he invites you to follow him. There is always an open invitation. It will require leaving your former life behind, but it will be more than worth it. If you have accepted his invitation, he calls you to invite others. Who in your life do you need to invite to follow Jesus? Who in your life do you need to invite to church? Remember, God can use a simple invitation to change someone's life.

Lord, thank you for inviting me to follow you. Give me the courage to go out and invite others to follow you. Place someone in my path today. Amen.

OCTOBER 6

Then he said to his disciples, "The harvest is plentiful, but the laborers are few; therefore pray earnestly to the Lord of the harvest to send out laborers into his harvest."
Matthew 9:37-38

The first time I went on a foreign mission trip, I was asked to lead a group to go out in the streets and tell people about Jesus. They gave us a translator and off we went. I had preached the gospel in front of hundreds of people, but for some reason, I found it difficult to share the gospel in the streets that day. I fumbled my words, got nervous, and was extremely uncomfortable. Despite my poor delivery, people listened, and some even prayed to receive Christ. I returned to the states determined to be bolder in sharing my faith.

We wear the shirt, invite people to church, and make posts on social media, but are we out in the streets telling people about Jesus? We talk about our kids, our favorite teams, issues at work, and so much more. Why is it that we can comfortably talk about everything under the sun, but then find it uncomfortable to talk about Jesus? The truth is that we can all be bolder in sharing our faith.

The harvest is plentiful, but the laborers are few. God is looking for people who will step out of their comfort zones and tell others about him. Will you be one of those people?

Lord, forgive me for not being bolder in sharing my faith. Help me step out of my comfort zone and tell others about you. Amen.

OCTOBER 7

But Peter and the apostles answered, "We must obey God rather than men."

Acts 5:29

Peter and the apostles were repeat offenders. They were arrested for preaching and teaching about Jesus. They were warned to never mention the name of Jesus again, but they didn't listen. As soon as they escaped, they went right back to preaching and teaching about Jesus. They were arrested again and asked why they didn't listen the first time. Their response was, "We must obey God rather than men." Peter and the apostles refused to let people get in their way of serving God. They were arrested, threatened, and beaten but chose to obey God rather than men. Because of their faithfulness, the church grew, people were saved, and lives were changed.

There are probably several people that you want to make proud, and there's nothing wrong with that. Others can push you and help you reach your potential. We all want to be liked and approved of by others, but we can't let that get in our way of serving God.

Will you do what God wants you to, even if it means doing it alone? Will you do what God wants you to do, even if there are severe consequences? Will you do what God wants you to do, even if it means losing status? Will you stand strong and obey God rather than men?

Lord, thank you for always being with me. Help me seek your approval at all costs. Show me if I'm allowing people to get in my way of serving you. Amen.

OCTOBER 8

Now the word of the Lord came to Jonah the son of Amittai, saying, "Arise, go to Nineveh, that great city, and call out against it, for their evil has come up before me."

Jonah 1:1-2

God called Jonah to go to Nineveh to preach to the people there. The people of Nineveh were evil, proud, and ruthless. Jonah disagreed with God. He didn't want to do what God wanted him to do, so he ran in the opposite direction. You probably recall where that got him. He ended up getting thrown into the sea and swallowed by a great fish.

He spent three days and three nights in the belly of the fish before he was spit out onto land. Reluctantly, he went to Nineveh and did what God had originally asked him to do. Jonah would have saved himself a lot of trouble had he been obedient to begin with. By running from God, he only made himself more miserable.

You're not always going to agree with God, but there's a reason he's God, and you're you. There will be times when he calls you to do things that you don't want to do. You might think that running is the easy way out, but the truth is that running will only cause trouble and make you miserable. What step is he calling you to take? It's important to remember that there is always a purpose in his plan.

Lord, thank you for your plan. Help me surrender to you, even when you call me to do something I don't want to do. Amen.

OCTOBER 9

And the Lord said, "You pity the plant, for which you did not labor, nor did you make it grow, which came into being in a night and perished in a night."

Jonah 4:10

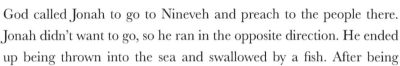

God called Jonah to go to Nineveh and preach to the people there. Jonah didn't want to go, so he ran in the opposite direction. He ended up being thrown into the sea and swallowed by a fish. After being spit out onto land, Jonah went to Nineveh and put little effort into preaching an eight-word sermon. Surprisingly, the people of Nineveh repented, and God decided not to destroy them.

This made Jonah angry. He wanted God to destroy Nineveh, so he left the city to pout. It was extremely hot, so God appointed a plant to provide Jonah with some shade. However, the next day, God appointed a worm to destroy the plant, and the shade disappeared. Jonah began to complain and throw himself a pity party. Jonah was angry enough to die over a plant, yet he didn't care about the people who lived in Nineveh.

Jonah was all for God's grace when it benefited him, but when God extended that same grace to his enemies, he complained, whined, and even became suicidal. What about you? Do you care more about your preferences or God's purposes? Like Jonah, do you care more about your personal comfort than the eternity of others? The proof is in the pudding.

Lord, thank you for your grace. Forgive me for my self-centeredness. Help me care more about your purposes than my preferences. Amen.

OCTOBER 10

God is our refuge and strength, a very present help in trouble.

Psalm 46:1

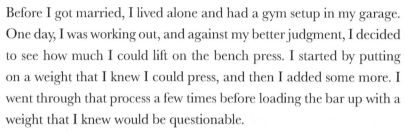

Before I got married, I lived alone and had a gym setup in my garage. One day, I was working out, and against my better judgment, I decided to see how much I could lift on the bench press. I started by putting on a weight that I knew I could press, and then I added some more. I went through that process a few times before loading the bar up with a weight that I knew would be questionable.

I laid down on the bench, lifted the bar off the rack, and brought it down to my chest. I went to push, but it didn't lift an inch. I was pinned to the bench and in serious trouble. Fortunately, I was able to maneuver the bar just enough to wiggle myself out from underneath the weight.

Often, we overestimate our strength and find ourselves in situations that are difficult to maneuver out of in our own power. As a believer, you must acknowledge how weak you really are. It's humbling, but in your own power, you are capable of very little. Thankfully, you have God on your side, and there are no limits to his power. Going forward, instead of relying on your own strength, rely on God, your refuge and strength.

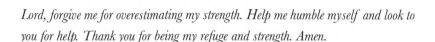

Lord, forgive me for overestimating my strength. Help me humble myself and look to you for help. Thank you for being my refuge and strength. Amen.

OCTOBER 11

And as they were stoning Stephen, he called out, "Lord Jesus, receive my spirit." And falling to his knees he cried out with a loud voice, "Lord, do not hold this sin against them." And when he had said this, he fell asleep.

Acts 7:59-60

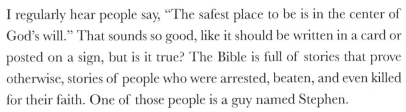

I regularly hear people say, "The safest place to be is in the center of God's will." That sounds so good, like it should be written in a card or posted on a sign, but is it true? The Bible is full of stories that prove otherwise, stories of people who were arrested, beaten, and even killed for their faith. One of those people is a guy named Stephen.

Stephen was certainly in the center of God's will. God was using him to perform great wonders and signs. He was preaching the gospel and furthering the kingdom. Where did that get him? He was dragged outside the city and stoned to death.

The truth is that there is nothing safe about the center of God's will. It is arguably the most dangerous place to be. It is where you should want to be and strive to be, but be warned, it can be challenging. There are people in certain parts of the world who are being persecuted for their faith. The good news is that better things are awaiting those who are in Christ. The Bible says that if you suffer on Earth for Christ, you will be rewarded in Heaven. Are you living in the center of God's will? If not, what's holding you back?

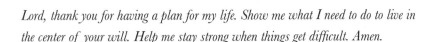

Lord, thank you for having a plan for my life. Show me what I need to do to live in the center of your will. Help me stay strong when things get difficult. Amen.

OCTOBER 12

And he said to her, "Daughter, your faith has made you well; go in peace."

Luke 8:48

In Luke 8, there's a story about a woman who was bleeding for twelve years. She was discouraged and ashamed, but she didn't lose hope. She heard about this guy named Jesus who had been healing others. She worked up the courage to go out and find him, but she wanted to remain anonymous. In the middle of the crowd, she just touched the fringe of his cloak. Jesus asked who touched his robe, and she reluctantly admitted it was her. Jesus said, "Daughter, your faith has made you well; go in peace."

This woman never gave up. She was likely an outcast because of her condition. She likely spent all her money looking for a solution. Despite her efforts, her condition continued to worsen. She made her way through the crowd, looking for Jesus. She felt unworthy to ask Jesus for help, so she tried to touch him without being noticed. As soon as she touched his cloak, she was healed.

There is no situation too far gone for Jesus. You might be discouraged and ashamed, but don't lose hope. Like this woman in Luke 8, do whatever you have to do to get yourself in the presence of Jesus. He will sustain you.

Lord, thank you for sustaining me. Regardless of what life throws my way, give me strength to get into your presence and never lose hope. Amen.

OCTOBER 13

I am not speaking of all of you; I know whom I have chosen. But the Scripture will be fulfilled, 'He who ate my bread has lifted his heel against me.'

John 13:18

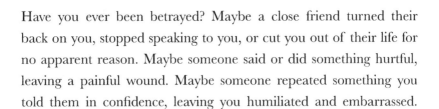

Have you ever been betrayed? Maybe a close friend turned their back on you, stopped speaking to you, or cut you out of their life for no apparent reason. Maybe someone said or did something hurtful, leaving a painful wound. Maybe someone repeated something you told them in confidence, leaving you humiliated and embarrassed. Nothing can hurt you quite as badly as other people.

There have been many times over the years that others have hurt me. People have left the church to go somewhere else without giving an explanation. People have said things about me behind my back. People have opposed me and attempted to sabotage my reputation. When it comes from someone I barely know, it's easy to ignore it and move forward. But when it comes from someone who was a close friend, it's hard to get past.

As you deal with hurt and pain from others, you must remember that even Jesus was betrayed by one of his closest friends. So, if you've done something to upset or offend another person, try to make it right. If not, give it to God and move forward with your life. Don't let others hold you back from doing what you were designed and created to do.

Lord, thank you for loving me in my worst moments. Help me forgive others and show me when I am at fault. Give me the strength to give you my best in the midst of hurt and pain. Amen.

OCTOBER 14

There is neither Jew nor Greek, there is neither slave nor free, there is no male and female, for you are all one in Christ Jesus.

Galatians 3:28

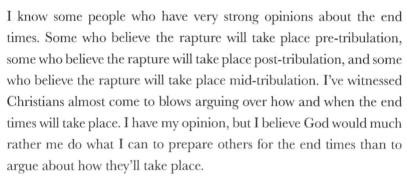

I know some people who have very strong opinions about the end times. Some who believe the rapture will take place pre-tribulation, some who believe the rapture will take place post-tribulation, and some who believe the rapture will take place mid-tribulation. I've witnessed Christians almost come to blows arguing over how and when the end times will take place. I have my opinion, but I believe God would much rather me do what I can to prepare others for the end times than to argue about how they'll take place.

I recently read an article that said there are close to 50,000 Christian denominations. I knew there were a lot, but I would have never guessed it was that many. While I think that denominations are important, I also think that they can divide the people of God. If we're not careful, we can get so caught up disagreeing over little things and miss the bigger picture.

There are so many things that are dividing the people of God, while lost people are dying and going to Hell. The truth is that we are all one in Christ Jesus. We could accomplish so much more if we stopped arguing over the little things and focused on the bigger picture. We could accomplish so much more if we stopped competing and started coming together for a greater purpose.

Lord, thank you for allowing me to be a part of your family. Help me walk in humility, put away my pride, and come together with other believers for a greater purpose. Amen.

OCTOBER 15

Let no corrupting talk come out of your mouths, but only such as is good for building up, as fits the occasion, that it may give grace to those who hear.

Ephesians 4:29

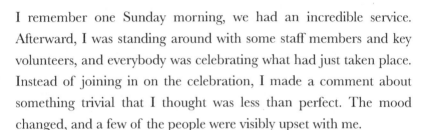

I remember one Sunday morning, we had an incredible service. Afterward, I was standing around with some staff members and key volunteers, and everybody was celebrating what had just taken place. Instead of joining in on the celebration, I made a comment about something trivial that I thought was less than perfect. The mood changed, and a few of the people were visibly upset with me.

Unfortunately, encouragement is not my spiritual gift. I am a perfectionist, and instead of encouraging the good that I see, I tend to critique the bad. This is something I'm working on and have been for years because I badly want to be an encouraging person. By his grace, I am growing and getting better every day.

There are times when constructive criticism is necessary. There is value in providing feedback that will help others grow and better themselves. But encouragement is powerful. It may seem counterintuitive, but people are more likely to change by encouragement than by correction. Would you say that encouragement is your spiritual gift? Or is it an area you struggle in? Are you slow to compliment the good you see in others and quick to correct the bad? If so, will you join me in working toward becoming an encouraging person?

Lord, thank you for placing great people in my life. Help me become an encouraging person and build others up with my words. Amen.

OCTOBER 16

Your word is a lamp to my feet and a light to my path.

Psalm 119:105

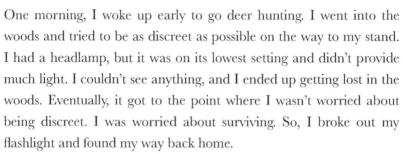

One morning, I woke up early to go deer hunting. I went into the woods and tried to be as discreet as possible on the way to my stand. I had a headlamp, but it was on its lowest setting and didn't provide much light. I couldn't see anything, and I ended up getting lost in the woods. Eventually, it got to the point where I wasn't worried about being discreet. I was worried about surviving. So, I broke out my flashlight and found my way back home.

The psalmist wrote, "Your word is a lamp to my feet and a light to my path." In other words, God's Word enables you to see. His Word illuminates your path. One of the most common spiritual questions that people ask is, "How can I hear God speaking to me?" Maybe they feel like he's speaking to them, but they want to be sure it's him. Or maybe they're going through a crisis and need some direction. Or maybe they've received some life-altering news and just want to hear his voice.

God reveals his will through his Word. I don't care how educated or uneducated you are, if you open the Bible and read, God will lead, guide, and direct you. His Word is a lamp to your feet and a light to your path.

Lord, thank you for your Word. Thank you for giving me direction when I don't know what to do. As I open your Word to read, open my ears to hear your voice. Amen.

OCTOBER 17

For God gave us a spirit not of fear but of power and love and self-control.

2 Timothy 1:7

I was running the soundboard at our church for a funeral. The service had just ended, and the family was in the cemetery for the graveside service. There was a group of women from our church down in the fellowship hall preparing a meal for the family. One of those women came into the sanctuary frantically and told me that there was a snake in the kitchen.

I went downstairs, and there was a giant black snake stretched out across the backsplash of the countertop. I had to go and change my underwear! I'm not afraid of much, but I am terrified of snakes and all these women were looking to me to do something about it. I was the youth pastor at the time, so I called in the senior pastor to help. Fortunately, we captured it and set it free in the woods.

How often do you allow fear to cripple you and keep you from what God has for you? Fear of failure? Fear of rejection? Fear of the unknown? To get to where God wants to take you, you must get past your fear. That doesn't mean that you never experience fear. It means you refuse to allow fear to keep you from moving forward. Remember, God didn't give you a spirit of fear but of power and love and self-control.

Lord, forgive me for the times I've allowed fear to keep me from what you have for me. Give me the courage to face my fears and become who you've created me to be. Amen.

OCTOBER 18

Put on the whole armor of God that you may be able to stand against the schemes of the devil.

Ephesians 6:11

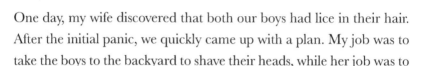

One day, my wife discovered that both our boys had lice in their hair. After the initial panic, we quickly came up with a plan. My job was to take the boys to the backyard to shave their heads, while her job was to go to the store to buy every lice product she could find.

Before shaving their heads, I sent the boys out back while I took a few measures to protect myself. I found some rubber gloves, medical masks, and trash bags. I put them all together and made myself a redneck hazmat suit. I love my boys, but I also love my hair, and there was no way I could risk contracting lice. Fortunately, my contraption did the trick, and I remained lice-free.

You are called to be in the world but not of the world. That's only possible with the full armor of God. The armor of God enables you to stand against the schemes of the devil. It protects you against his attacks. It equips you to fight the battles that you will face each day. It gives you the strength to live a life of integrity in a world full of compromise. Before you begin each day, make sure you suit up in the full armor of God.

Lord, thank you for your armor. Help me begin each day by putting it on. Give me the strength to stand against the schemes of the devil. Amen.

OCTOBER 19

For we do not wrestle against flesh and blood, but against the rulers, against the authorities, against the cosmic powers over this present darkness, against the spiritual forces of evil in the heavenly places.

Ephesians 6:12

———❧❧❧———

Whether you realize it or not, there's a battle taking place. Every morning, when you wake up and put your feet on the ground, you are entering a battle zone. It's not a battle against flesh and blood. It's not a battle against humanity. It's not a battle against other people. It's a spiritual battle. A battle "against the rulers, against the authorities, against the cosmic powers over this present darkness, against the spiritual forces of evil in the heavenly places."

Many are oblivious to this very real battle that is taking place in their midst. They're being obliterated by the enemy without even realizing that they're under attack. Before you can begin to resist the attacks of the enemy, you must recognize the attacks of the enemy.

If you are living for the Lord, there's a target on your back. The enemy is coming after you. He's out to steal, kill, and destroy. He wants nothing more than to disrupt the work that God is doing in your life. He wants nothing more than to distract you from God's call and purpose for your life. This is not a battle you can win on your own. Only God can deliver you from the power of the devil.

———❧❧❧———

Lord, thank you for your goodness. Help me recognize the attacks of the enemy and rely on your power to be victorious. Amen.

OCTOBER 20

Stand therefore, having fastened on the belt of truth, and having put on the breastplate of righteousness.

Ephesians 6:14

In ancient days, one of the first pieces of armor a soldier put on was his belt. The belt wrapped around the waist and protected the lower body. It also provided a place for the soldier to attach his breastplate and store his sword. The belt was crucial as it held everything together, and other pieces of armor were dependent upon it.

The devil is the father of lies. In the very beginning, he lied to Eve and got her to question God's truth. Eventually, she gave in and ate the forbidden fruit. Times have changed, but his tactics remain the same. He wants you to question God's Word and believe his lies. If he can get you to do that, he can get you to sin.

We are instructed to fasten on the belt of truth because, without truth, we have nothing. Unfortunately, we are living in times where the truth is being watered down or avoided when it might be offensive. Many alter God's Word to make it consistent with their lifestyle instead of altering their lifestyle to make it consistent with God's Word. Be sure to begin each day by fastening on the belt of truth. In a world full of compromise, stand firmly in the truth of God's Word.

Lord, thank you for the belt of truth. Help me see the devil's lies for what they are. Give me strength to stand firmly on the truth of your Word. Amen.

OCTOBER 21

Stand therefore, having fastened on the belt of truth, and having put on the breastplate of righteousness.

Ephesians 6:14

In ancient times, soldiers wore a breastplate into battle. The breastplate was usually made of metal, covering the soldier from their neck to their thighs, front and back. The breastplate protected the soldier's most vital organs, such as the lungs and, most notably, the heart. So, if a soldier went into battle without the breastplate, he left himself vulnerable to attacks that could cause serious damage or even death.

The breastplate of righteousness serves several purposes. It keeps you humble, accountable, and protected. It keeps you humble by serving as a reminder of where your righteousness comes from. It comes not from your own doing but from God. It keeps you accountable by serving as a reminder that you are called to a higher standard. Your righteousness comes from God, but as you wear the breastplate, your decisions and actions should become more righteous. Finally, it keeps you protected by serving as a reminder that this is not your final destination. Regardless of what happens on this Earth, you can look forward to an eternity in Heaven.

Be sure to begin each day by putting on the breastplate of righteousness. Without it, you will leave yourself vulnerable to attacks that can cause serious damage.

Lord, thank you for the breastplate of righteousness. Help me wear it each day. Keep me humble, accountable, and protected. Amen.

OCTOBER 22

And, as shoes for your feet, having put on the readiness given by the gospel of peace.

Ephesians 6:15

I remember when I got into middle school, that's when shoes became important to me. One day, I was at the store with my mom when a pair caught my eyes. They were blue and gray and the coolest pair I had ever seen. There was only one problem: they were expensive, and I had no money. I don't recall the specifics, but my dad gave me an opportunity to earn the shoes, and I did. A few months later, I went back to the store to make the purchase. I still remember how confident I felt the next day at school.

The third piece of God's armor is the shoes. The shoes are defensive. Soldiers would wear special shoes into battle that enabled them to stand their ground and maintain a firm footing. The shoes are also offensive as they make it easier to travel. The shoes soldiers wore made it easier for them to move from place to place.

As you put on the shoes, they help you stand your ground. They help you keep a firm footing, even when you're under attack. The shoes also help you live out the Great Commission. When you put on the shoes, it doesn't matter where you go, you're going with a purpose. That purpose is to tell others about Jesus. Be sure to begin each day by putting on the shoes.

Lord, thank you for the shoes. Help me keep a firm footing, even when I'm under attack. Help me go and tell others about you. Amen.

OCTOBER 23

In all circumstances take up the shield of faith, with which you can extinguish all the flaming darts of the evil one.

Ephesians 6:16

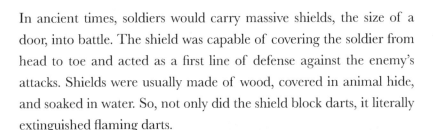

In ancient times, soldiers would carry massive shields, the size of a door, into battle. The shield was capable of covering the soldier from head to toe and acted as a first line of defense against the enemy's attacks. Shields were usually made of wood, covered in animal hide, and soaked in water. So, not only did the shield block darts, it literally extinguished flaming darts.

For the Christian, the shield represents faith. You take up the shield of faith by placing your complete trust and confidence in the Lord. Life is full of unexpected difficulties. You never know when that diagnosis, loss, financial emergency, challenge, or epidemic may come. It can be tempting to place your trust and confidence in the things of this world or to lose hope all together. That's what the enemy wants you to do. He is constantly firing off flaming darts of doubt that can only be extinguished by the shield of faith.

Maybe you're in the middle of a difficult season. Maybe you're doubting God's plan and his goodness. Maybe you're under attack. Maybe the enemy's darts are causing serious damage. Take up the shield of faith by placing your complete trust and confidence in the Lord.

Lord, thank you for the shield of faith. Help me put my complete trust and confidence in you and extinguish the flaming darts of the evil one. Amen.

OCTOBER 24

And take the helmet of salvation, and the sword of the Spirit, which is the word of God.

Ephesians 6:17

This year, my oldest son transitioned from flag to tackle football. Our local recreation department loans equipment to the kids, but we decided to purchase our own. I researched helmets for hours because I wanted to purchase one that would provide maximum protection. After narrowing it down to a couple of brands, we went to a store and ended up purchasing the helmet that fit his head the best. I feel much better watching him play, knowing his head is protected.

Still to this day, soldiers wear helmets into battle. The helmet is arguably the most important piece of armor. You can recover from certain injuries, but a blow to the head can be life-threatening. For the Christian, the helmet represents salvation. You are saved the moment you place your faith and trust in Jesus, but salvation is not limited to a one-time event that took place in the past. Salvation is an eternal state that God's children enjoy in the present.

If you are saved, the enemy no longer has any hold on you, but that won't stop him from trying to convince you otherwise. Today, make sure to equip yourself with the helmet of salvation to protect yourself from the enemy's schemes.

Lord, thank you for the helmet of salvation. Help me equip myself with your armor. Protect me from the enemy's schemes. Amen.

OCTOBER 25

And take the helmet of salvation, and the sword of the Spirit, which is the word of God.

Ephesians 6:17

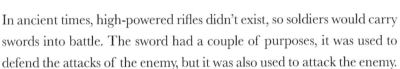

In ancient times, high-powered rifles didn't exist, so soldiers would carry swords into battle. The sword had a couple of purposes, it was used to defend the attacks of the enemy, but it was also used to attack the enemy. The sword was the main offensive weapon in the soldier's arsenal. For the believer, the sword represents the Bible, the Word of God.

The Bible is much more than just some book. The Bible is much more than just words on a page. The Bible is much more than just some great piece of literature. The Bible is living and active. It has the power to make the enemy squirm and ultimately surrender. Imagine a soldier going into battle without a weapon, that's the equivalent of a believer attempting to go through life without God's Word. Just as the sword was essential for the soldier, God's Word is essential for the believer.

Are you regularly reading the Bible? Do you value God's Word? Are you equipping yourself with the sword of the spirit? Or are you attempting to go through life unarmed? There's no better time to pick up your Bible than now. Start today by taking up the sword.

Lord, thank you for the sword of the spirit. Forgive me for the times I have failed to read your Word. Help me do better going forward. Amen.

OCTOBER 26

Praying at all times in the Spirit, with all prayer and supplication. To that end, keep alert with all perseverance, making supplication for all the saints.

Ephesians 6:18

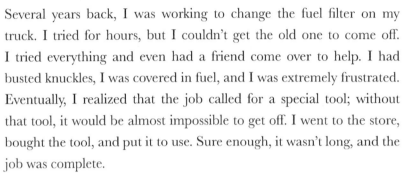

Several years back, I was working to change the fuel filter on my truck. I tried for hours, but I couldn't get the old one to come off. I tried everything and even had a friend come over to help. I had busted knuckles, I was covered in fuel, and I was extremely frustrated. Eventually, I realized that the job called for a special tool; without that tool, it would be almost impossible to get off. I went to the store, bought the tool, and put it to use. Sure enough, it wasn't long, and the job was complete.

The right tool for the job can make a world of difference. After instructing us to take up the armor of God, Paul instructs us to pray at all times. There is no time when prayer is not appropriate. When things are good, pray. When things are bad, pray. When you get overwhelmed, pray. When you get exciting news, pray. When you feel under attack, pray. Prayer is always the right tool for the job.

Suit up in the armor of God, and don't forget to pray. Keep an ongoing dialogue with God throughout the day. Remember, the right tool for the job can make a world of difference.

Lord, thank you for prayer. Thank you for listening to and answering my prayers. Help me pray at all times and keep an ongoing dialogue with you throughout the day. Amen.

OCTOBER 27

Humble yourselves before the Lord, and he will exalt you.

James 4:10

I stopped playing sports after high school but couldn't shake the desire to compete, so I decided to do a triathlon. I was a pretty decent runner, and it didn't take me long to pick up biking, but swimming ended up being my downfall. In my small hometown, there wasn't anywhere to swim in the middle of the winter, so I had to drive to the next town over to train. I didn't go very often because I thought I was a strong swimmer, but I was wrong. On the day of the race, swimming was the first event, and out of hundreds of people, I was the second to last person out of the water. It was embarrassing and humbling. That was my first and last triathlon.

At times, we tend to overestimate our abilities. We tend to think more highly of ourselves than we ought to. The humbling truth is, without God, we are capable of very little. Everything we have, we have because he has blessed us with it. Everything we do, we do because he has given us the ability.

When it comes to being a Christian, humility is a must. You can exalt yourself and be humbled by God or humble yourself and be exalted by God. The choice is yours.

Lord, thank you for what you have blessed me with. Show me where I am prideful and help me humble myself. Amen.

OCTOBER 28

The Lord said to Abraham, "Why did Sarah laugh and say, 'Shall I indeed bear a child, now that I am old?' Is anything too hard for the Lord? At the appointed time I will return to you, about this time next year, and Sarah shall have a son."

Genesis 18:13-14

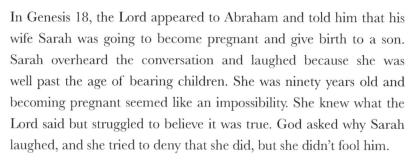

In Genesis 18, the Lord appeared to Abraham and told him that his wife Sarah was going to become pregnant and give birth to a son. Sarah overheard the conversation and laughed because she was well past the age of bearing children. She was ninety years old and becoming pregnant seemed like an impossibility. She knew what the Lord said but struggled to believe it was true. God asked why Sarah laughed, and she tried to deny that she did, but she didn't fool him.

God specializes in using the most unlikely people to do the most extraordinary things. He can use people with a sinful past to reach others that are far from him. He can use that marriage that struggled to help other struggling marriages. He can use that recovering addict to help other addicts recover. He can use that painful experience to alleviate someone else's pain. He can even use a ninety-year-old woman to give birth to a son. God doesn't always play by the rules and sometimes it's difficult to trust him.

Maybe God's telling you that he's going to do something, and like Sarah, you're laughing. You know what he's saying, but it seems impossible. If so, remember that nothing is too hard for the Lord.

Lord, thank you for making the impossible possible. Help me discern your voice and trust you no matter how unlikely something may seem. Amen.

OCTOBER 29

While they were talking and discussing together, Jesus himself drew near and went with them. But their eyes were kept from recognizing him.

Luke 24:15-16

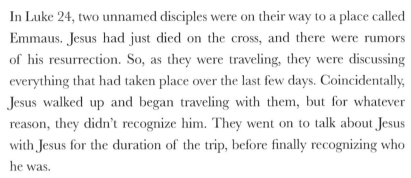

In Luke 24, two unnamed disciples were on their way to a place called Emmaus. Jesus had just died on the cross, and there were rumors of his resurrection. So, as they were traveling, they were discussing everything that had taken place over the last few days. Coincidentally, Jesus walked up and began traveling with them, but for whatever reason, they didn't recognize him. They went on to talk about Jesus with Jesus for the duration of the trip, before finally recognizing who he was.

Like the disciples on the road to Emmaus, how often do you fail to recognize Jesus in your daily life? Maybe there's an unexpected circumstance that takes place, and you run around looking for an answer, failing to recognize that Jesus is walking right beside you. Maybe you receive some unexpected news and go into panic mode, failing to recognize that Jesus is walking right beside you. Maybe tragedy strikes, and you feel hopeless, failing to recognize that Jesus is walking right beside you.

It's easy to become consumed by life and to become focused on the wrong things. Regardless of what you may be going through, slow down and recognize that Jesus is walking right beside you.

Lord, thank you for walking right beside me. Help me recognize you in all circumstances and forgive me for the times that I haven't. Amen.

OCTOBER 30

And he said to him, "What is your name?" And he said, "Jacob." Then he said, "Your name shall no longer be called Jacob, but Israel, for you have striven with God and with men, and have prevailed."

Genesis 32:27-28

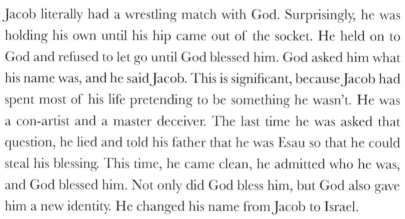

Jacob literally had a wrestling match with God. Surprisingly, he was holding his own until his hip came out of the socket. He held on to God and refused to let go until God blessed him. God asked him what his name was, and he said Jacob. This is significant, because Jacob had spent most of his life pretending to be something he wasn't. He was a con-artist and a master deceiver. The last time he was asked that question, he lied and told his father that he was Esau so that he could steal his blessing. This time, he came clean, he admitted who he was, and God blessed him. Not only did God bless him, but God also gave him a new identity. He changed his name from Jacob to Israel.

Often, we run and hide from our problems. Like Jacob, we attempt to deceive others by pretending to be someone or something that we're not. This technique might get us closer to people, but it only gets us further from God.

Maybe you've been running and hiding from your problems. Maybe you've been deceiving others. Maybe you've been pretending to be something you're not. If so, it's time to come clean. Here's the bottom line: God won't bless who you pretend to be, but he will bless the real you.

Lord, thank you for uniquely making me. Forgive me for the times I've pretended to be something I'm not. Give me the strength to face my problems head-on. Amen.

OCTOBER 31

But seek first the kingdom of God and his righteousness, and all these things will be added to you.

Matthew 6:33

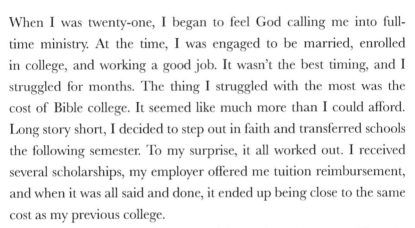

When I was twenty-one, I began to feel God calling me into full-time ministry. At the time, I was engaged to be married, enrolled in college, and working a good job. It wasn't the best timing, and I struggled for months. The thing I struggled with the most was the cost of Bible college. It seemed like much more than I could afford. Long story short, I decided to step out in faith and transferred schools the following semester. To my surprise, it all worked out. I received several scholarships, my employer offered me tuition reimbursement, and when it was all said and done, it ended up being close to the same cost as my previous college.

I could share story after story of God miraculously providing for my family and church. He has proven to me that if he leads me to do something, he will provide the means to make it happen. This doesn't mean that it will happen when or how I want it to happen, but it does mean that it will happen.

Often, we want to know exactly what will happen before we move forward in obedience to the Lord, but it's called a step of faith for a reason. Stop worrying about the details, and start focusing on being obedient.

Lord, thank you for your amazing provisions. Help me hear your voice clearly and move forward in obedience, even when I don't know what the outcome will be. Amen.

NOVEMBER 1

So Moses made a bronze serpent and set it on a pole. And if a serpent bit anyone, he would look at the bronze serpent and live.

Numbers 21:9

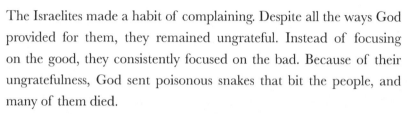

The Israelites made a habit of complaining. Despite all the ways God provided for them, they remained ungrateful. Instead of focusing on the good, they consistently focused on the bad. Because of their ungratefulness, God sent poisonous snakes that bit the people, and many of them died.

Eventually, they recognized that they were wrong for what they did. They asked Moses to pray and ask God to take the snakes away. God didn't take the snakes away, but he did make a way for the people to be saved. God instructed Moses to put a bronze snake up on a pole. When someone was bitten by a snake, if they looked at the bronze snake, they would live.

There's some symbolism here. We live in a fallen, sinful world. God doesn't always take away our problems, but he did make a way for us to be saved. No matter what you go through on this Earth, if you repent and look to Jesus, you will have life. Take some time today to thank God for the gift of salvation. Thank him for his mercy and grace. Thank him for making a way for you to be saved from the bite of sin.

Lord, thank you for your mercy and grace. Thank you for making a way for me to be saved. Thank you for the gift of salvation. Amen.

NOVEMBER 2

This, the first of his signs, Jesus did at Cana in Galilee, and manifested his glory. And his disciples believed in him.

John 2:11

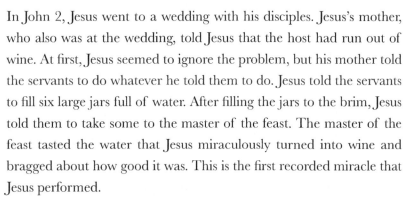

In John 2, Jesus went to a wedding with his disciples. Jesus's mother, who also was at the wedding, told Jesus that the host had run out of wine. At first, Jesus seemed to ignore the problem, but his mother told the servants to do whatever he told them to do. Jesus told the servants to fill six large jars full of water. After filling the jars to the brim, Jesus told them to take some to the master of the feast. The master of the feast tasted the water that Jesus miraculously turned into wine and bragged about how good it was. This is the first recorded miracle that Jesus performed.

As you can imagine, this was likely a humiliating situation for the host of the wedding, but Jesus saved the day. He took what should have been the downfall of the wedding and turned it into the highlight of the wedding.

In that same way, Jesus can take what should be the downfall of your life and he can turn it into the highlight of your life. Regardless of what you may go through on this Earth, remember that he is still God, and he is still good.

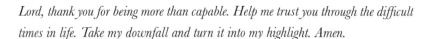

Lord, thank you for being more than capable. Help me trust you through the difficult times in life. Take my downfall and turn it into my highlight. Amen.

NOVEMBER 3

Go therefore and make disciples of all nations, baptizing them in the name of the Father and of the Son and of the Holy Spirit, teaching them to observe all that I have commanded you. And behold, I am with you always, to the end of the age.

Matthew 28:19-20

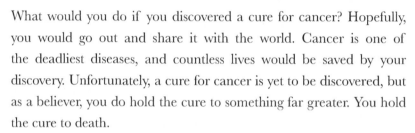

What would you do if you discovered a cure for cancer? Hopefully, you would go out and share it with the world. Cancer is one of the deadliest diseases, and countless lives would be saved by your discovery. Unfortunately, a cure for cancer is yet to be discovered, but as a believer, you do hold the cure to something far greater. You hold the cure to death.

The harsh reality is that billions of people around the world, and many within your community, are on their way to Hell. Jesus is the cure, and you are called to share him with others. It doesn't matter where you're going. It doesn't matter if you're going to work, the grocery store, or the ballfield. Wherever you go, you should go with a purpose. It doesn't matter what you do. It doesn't matter if you're a teacher, mechanic, doctor, or stay-at-home mom. Whatever you do, you should do it with a purpose. That purpose is to fulfill the Great Commission. That purpose is to set an example, to not only tell others about Jesus but to show others what it looks like to follow Jesus.

Wherever you go today, go with a purpose. Whatever you do today, do it with a purpose.

Lord, thank you for allowing me to play a part in fulfilling the Great Commission. Today, help me go and do, with a purpose. Amen.

NOVEMBER 4

For I could wish that I myself were accursed and cut off from Christ for the sake of my brothers, my kinsmen according to the flesh.

Romans 9:3

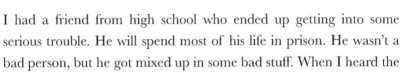

I had a friend from high school who ended up getting into some serious trouble. He will spend most of his life in prison. He wasn't a bad person, but he got mixed up in some bad stuff. When I heard the news for the first time, it really bothered me. I lost sleep thinking about it. I wish I could have done something to help him avoid going down the path that he went. And I pray that he will learn from his mistake, meet Jesus, and turn his life around. As much as I care for my friend, I can't say that I would trade places with him, because I wouldn't.

In Romans 9, Paul was so burdened for the lost. He made it clear that he would give up his salvation if it meant that others would get saved. Think about what that means. Paul was saying that he would spend an eternity in Hell if it meant others could spend an eternity in Heaven. Now, Paul knew that he couldn't give his salvation to someone else, but that's the way he felt in his heart.

Are you burdened for the lost? Burdened to the point that you would give up your own salvation if you could? Do you have that level of compassion for those who don't know Christ?

Lord, break my heart for what breaks yours. Give me a burden for the lost. Help me go out of my way to share you with others. Amen.

NOVEMBER 5

One of the two who heard John speak and followed Jesus was Andrew, Simon Peter's brother. He first found his own brother Simon and said to him, "We have found the Messiah" (which means Christ).

John 1:40-41

My first year in youth ministry, I only took a group of five or six students to summer camp. After each night's service, we spent about an hour talking as a group. At the recommendation of one of the speakers, we decided to make a "God's Most Wanted List." This was a list of people that we were going to commit to praying for, sharing the gospel with, and inviting to church. The list included parents, siblings, and friends. Within a year, many of those on the list got saved and started attending church. The youth group multiplied, and we took a couple dozen students to camp the following year.

In John 1, there's a ripple effect that takes place. Andrew met Jesus and immediately went and found his brother, Simon, to tell him what he had discovered. Both Andrew and Simon followed Jesus and became his disciples.

Before getting into ministry, I attended a church, and one of their core values was, "Found People Find People." The idea is when you are found, when you meet Jesus, your natural instinct should be to go and tell others about him. Why would you keep the greatest thing that has ever happened to you to yourself?

Lord, thank you for finding me. You are the greatest thing that has ever happened to me. Help me go and find others to share the gospel with. Amen.

NOVEMBER 6

For if we live, we live to the Lord, and if we die, we die to the Lord. So then, whether we live or whether we die, we are the Lord's.

Romans 14:8

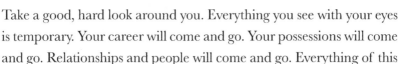

Take a good, hard look around you. Everything you see with your eyes is temporary. Your career will come and go. Your possessions will come and go. Relationships and people will come and go. Everything of this Earth is temporary, but if you are in Christ, your relationship with him is eternal. You live for him now on Earth, and when you die, you will continue to live for him in Heaven. You will always belong to the Lord.

This truth should alter the way that you live. It should nudge you to focus on what is eternal instead of focusing on what is temporary. Everything in your life should revolve around God; you should do everything with him in mind.

How can you love your spouse in a way that is pleasing to the Lord? How can you lead your children in a way that is pleasing to the Lord? How can you do your job or run your business in a way that is pleasing to the Lord? If you are a believer, you no longer live for yourself. The choices you make and the things you do should bring glory and honor to the Lord. Whether you live or die, you are his.

Lord, thank you for saving me and for welcoming me into your family. Help me live my life in a way that will bring glory and honor to you. Amen.

NOVEMBER 7

Therefore, if anyone cleanses himself from what is dishonorable, he will be a vessel for honorable use, set apart as holy, useful to the master of the house, ready for every good work.

2 Timothy 2:21

Do you have a favorite cup? One that you don't leave the house without? One that you pick up every time you need something to drink? There's a cup that is almost always sitting on my desk. Years ago, it was given to me as a gift. It's the perfect color and size. I fill it up throughout the day with ice and water. It keeps my water cold, and it keeps me refreshed. I have 100 other cups sitting in a cabinet, but something about that particular cup makes me want to use it.

In 2 Timothy, Paul explains that in a house there are many vessels. Some vessels are for honorable use, while others are for dishonorable use. Paul goes on to explain that we can become honorable vessels in God's kingdom by cleansing ourselves from what is dishonorable.

You want to make a difference in this world. You want to be used by God, but have you made yourself useful? Have you aligned your ways with God's Word? Have you fought for purity? Have you fled from sin? Have you cleansed yourself from what is dishonorable? If you haven't, what are you waiting for?

Lord, thank you for using imperfect people like me to further your kingdom. Help me cleanse myself from what is dishonorable. Amen.

NOVEMBER 8

For which of you, desiring to build a tower, does not first sit down and count the cost, whether he has enough to complete it?

Luke 14:28

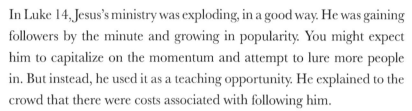

In Luke 14, Jesus's ministry was exploding, in a good way. He was gaining followers by the minute and growing in popularity. You might expect him to capitalize on the momentum and attempt to lure more people in. But instead, he used it as a teaching opportunity. He explained to the crowd that there were costs associated with following him.

Jesus knew many were there just to witness miracles. He knew many were there just because they wanted to receive a blessing. He knew many were there just because he was the talk of the town. He knew many were there for the wrong reasons. He wanted them to understand that he was more than just the latest fad. He wanted them to understand that following him would come at a cost.

Salvation is a free gift from God that is available to all who ask, but it demands everything. When you follow him, you relinquish control of your life to him. He may lead you in a direction you don't want to go in. It may cost you friends, family members, financial security, or even your life. Are you following Jesus for the wrong reasons? Or have you counted the cost and decided to follow him anyway?

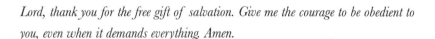

Lord, thank you for the free gift of salvation. Give me the courage to be obedient to you, even when it demands everything. Amen.

NOVEMBER 9

The sluggard does not plow in the autumn; he will seek at harvest and have nothing.

Proverbs 20:4

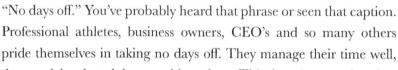

"No days off." You've probably heard that phrase or seen that caption. Professional athletes, business owners, CEO's and so many others pride themselves in taking no days off. They manage their time well, they work hard, and they get things done. This doesn't mean that they never take time off or rest. It simply means that they're intentional in everything they do.

On a scale of 1-10, how disciplined are you? Do you manage your time well or spend an embarrassing amount of time on social media? Do you plan your day and execute the plan? Or do you fly by the seat of your pants? Are you productive, or are you a sluggard? You can probably identify at least a few areas where you can be more disciplined.

Daily discipline is what separates the average from achievers. Managing your time well will enable you to reach your full potential. Maybe there's something you've been meaning to do, but you haven't been disciplined enough to start. Or maybe there's something you have started, but you haven't been disciplined enough to finish. You can't do anything about the time that has already passed, but you can make the most of the time you have left.

Lord, thank you for the time that you have given me. Help me use my time wisely, be productive, and get things done. Amen.

NOVEMBER 10

Shepherd the flock of God that is among you, exercising oversight, not under compulsion, but willingly, as God would have you; not for shameful gain, but eagerly; not domineering over those in your charge, but being examples to the flock.

1 Peter 5:2-3

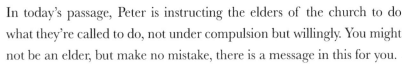

In today's passage, Peter is instructing the elders of the church to do what they're called to do, not under compulsion but willingly. You might not be an elder, but make no mistake, there is a message in this for you.

If I'm not careful, my mindset can become, "I have to write this sermon. I have to go and visit this person. I have to take my kids to practice. I have to read my Bible. I have to tithe." But I don't have to do those things. By God's grace, I get to do those things. I get to preach his Word. I get to go and minister to people when they need it the most. I get to spend time with my kids. I get to read my Bible. I get to give money to the church and play a role in furthering God's kingdom.

God doesn't want you to serve him under compulsion but willingly. He doesn't want you to serve him out of duty but out of desire. Do you have a "have to" or "get to" mindset? If you find that you're serving him under compulsion, take some time and remember why you're doing what you're doing and who you're doing it for.

Lord, thank you for giving me the opportunity to serve you. Help me serve you not under compulsion but willingly. Amen.

NOVEMBER 11

I thank my God in all my remembrance of you.

Philippians 1:3

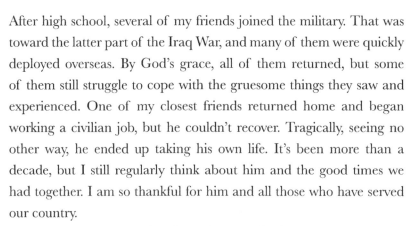

After high school, several of my friends joined the military. That was toward the latter part of the Iraq War, and many of them were quickly deployed overseas. By God's grace, all of them returned, but some of them still struggle to cope with the gruesome things they saw and experienced. One of my closest friends returned home and began working a civilian job, but he couldn't recover. Tragically, seeing no other way, he ended up taking his own life. It's been more than a decade, but I still regularly think about him and the good times we had together. I am so thankful for him and all those who have served our country.

Every day, we enjoy freedoms that we take for granted. The truth is that those freedoms come at a cost. Men and women sacrifice their lives and livelihoods for this country. I'm convinced that serving in the military is one of the most selfless things a person can do.

If you're a veteran, thank you for your selfless contribution to this country. If you're not a veteran, find a veteran today, and thank them for their service. Spend some time thanking God for those who have served and praying for those who are currently serving.

Lord, thank you for veterans. Thank you for the men and women who have and are putting their lives on the line to fight for my freedom. Amen.

NOVEMBER 12

Wealth gained hastily will dwindle, but whoever gathers little by little will increase it.

Proverbs 13:11

When I was younger, I had a buddy that invited me to attend a business meeting that was hosted at someone's house. A well-dressed guy stood up, talked about this life-changing product that he was selling, showed us how much money he was making, and then invited us to be a part of it. It sounded so attractive. Big profits were almost guaranteed. I could make money by selling the product, but I could make even more money by recruiting other people to sell the product.

I signed up in a hurry, excited about this promising opportunity. I figured that it would only be a few weeks before I had enough money to drop out of school and quit my job. Turns out, it was a pyramid scheme, and I never made a cent. Instead, I was stuck with hundreds of dollars worth of product for years before I finally cut my losses and threw it away.

We're easily lured by the promise of instant results. We can't help but look into that product that promises weight loss without exercise or a change in diet. Or that opportunity that promises thousands of dollars a week working from home. Even when it seems too good to be true, we are lured by the promise of instant results. The truth is that lasting results usually come incrementally, not instantly.

Lord, thank you for bringing me this far. Help me stay focused on incremental growth and resist being lured by the promise of instant results. Amen.

NOVEMBER 13

And he withdrew from them about a stone's throw, and knelt down and prayed, saying, "Father, if you are willing, remove this cup from me. Nevertheless, not my will, but yours, be done."

Luke 22:41-42

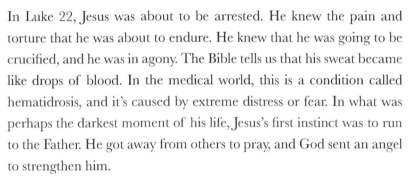

In Luke 22, Jesus was about to be arrested. He knew the pain and torture that he was about to endure. He knew that he was going to be crucified, and he was in agony. The Bible tells us that his sweat became like drops of blood. In the medical world, this is a condition called hematidrosis, and it's caused by extreme distress or fear. In what was perhaps the darkest moment of his life, Jesus's first instinct was to run to the Father. He got away from others to pray, and God sent an angel to strengthen him.

When there's a problem at work, when tragedy strikes, when there's a challenge you're facing, when something bad happens, what's your first instinct? Do you run to people looking for comfort and advice? Or do you run to God in prayer? When something good happens, when a door opens, when a need is met, when a goal is achieved, what's your first instinct? Do you run to people looking for validation and a pat on the back? Or do you run to God to give him thanks?

Jesus gave you the perfect example. As a Christian, your first instinct shouldn't be to run to people but to the Father.

Lord, thank you for always being available. Help me run to you with praise when good things happen. Help me run to you in prayer when bad things happen. Amen.

NOVEMBER 14

Do not be anxious about anything, but in everything by prayer and supplication with thanksgiving let your requests be made known to God.

Philippians 4:6

My first year in ministry was by far the hardest. I had just gotten married, accepted a youth pastor position, and purchased my first house. I felt sure that God was behind it all, but I immediately faced obstacles. At my first church business meeting, I learned that the church was having problems. For starters, the church was looking at a financial shortfall that coincidentally was the exact dollar amount of my salary. There were also many unhappy people, and the attendance was declining rapidly. My gut told me to get out of there. I started applying to other churches, but through prayer, God made it clear that I was exactly where he wanted me to be.

It was during this uncertain season of life and ministry that I really learned to pray. I learned to do my best and to trust God with the rest. And things got worse before they got better. Attendance continued to decline, the finances continued to get worse, and eventually, the senior pastor resigned. I had no plan or desire to become the senior pastor, but that's the door God opened several months later.

Maybe you're in an uncertain season of life and unsure how any good could ever come out of what you're going through. If so, let this encourage you. Do not be anxious about anything, but take everything to God in prayer.

Lord, thank you for hearing my prayers. Give me the strength to make it through the difficult circumstances that I face on this Earth. Amen.

NOVEMBER 15

And the Lord said to Satan, "Have you considered my servant Job, that there is none like him on the earth, a blameless and upright man, who fears God and turns away from evil?"

Job 1:8

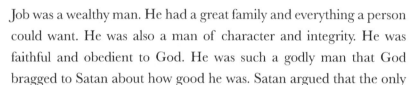

Job was a wealthy man. He had a great family and everything a person could want. He was also a man of character and integrity. He was faithful and obedient to God. He was such a godly man that God bragged to Satan about how good he was. Satan argued that the only reason Job was good was because God blessed him with a life of ease and that if he took away the stuff, Job would turn his back on him.

God gave Satan permission to attack Job. The only thing off-limits was his life. In an instant, almost everything Job had was taken away. He lost his livestock, his servants, and his children. Then Satan attacked his health. Job's body broke out in boils. The pain was so excruciating he wanted to die. Through it all, Job was faithful. And in the end, God blessed him with twice the amount he originally had.

Job did nothing wrong. Quite the opposite, he became a target because he was doing everything right. Be warned, the more you pursue God, the more Satan is going to pursue you. The bigger the difference you make, the bigger the target you become. So, if you feel under attack, that might be a sign that you're doing something right. And if you don't feel under attack, that might be a cause for concern.

Lord, thank you for using me to play a role in furthering your kingdom. Like Job, give me the strength to remain faithful when I am under attack. Amen.

NOVEMBER 16

About midnight Paul and Silas were praying and singing hymns to God, and the prisoners were listening to them.

Acts 16:25

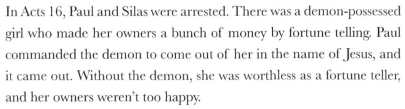

In Acts 16, Paul and Silas were arrested. There was a demon-possessed girl who made her owners a bunch of money by fortune telling. Paul commanded the demon to come out of her in the name of Jesus, and it came out. Without the demon, she was worthless as a fortune teller, and her owners weren't too happy.

They beat the tar out of Paul and Silas and had them thrown into prison. They did nothing wrong, yet they were treated like criminals. As they sat in prison, they were sore, they were hurting, they had every reason to feel sorry for themselves, yet they chose to pray and sing hymns. God ended up sending an earthquake that shook the prison doors open. Instead of running free, Paul and Silas decided to stay and minister to the jailer. As a result, the jailer and his entire family ended up getting saved.

When you find yourself in difficult circumstances, you probably want to figure out how to escape as quickly as possible. You want to endure, move on, and get back to the way things were before. But what if God doesn't want you to escape? What if he wants you to embrace whatever circumstance you find yourself in? Remember, God can use even the worst circumstance for your good and for his glory.

Lord, thank you for working, even when I don't see it. Help me embrace whatever circumstance I find myself in. Amen.

NOVEMBER 17

And we urge you, brothers, admonish the idle, encourage the fainthearted, help the weak, be patient with them all.

1 Thessalonians 5:14

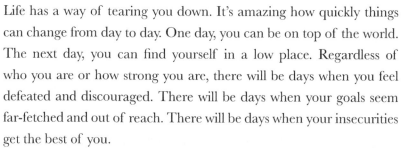

Life has a way of tearing you down. It's amazing how quickly things can change from day to day. One day, you can be on top of the world. The next day, you can find yourself in a low place. Regardless of who you are or how strong you are, there will be days when you feel defeated and discouraged. There will be days when your goals seem far-fetched and out of reach. There will be days when your insecurities get the best of you.

We all have plenty of friends when life is great, but pay attention to those who are by your side through the most difficult times in your life. Pay attention to those who are there for you when you're hurting and discouraged. Pay attention to those who come alongside you and help you when you need it the most. Pay attention to those who lift you up when you are down. Pay attention to those who comfort you when you are alone. Pay attention to those who stick by your side when you have nothing to offer them in return. Those are the ones you need to surround yourself with.

Life has a way of tearing you down. That's why you need friends who have a way of building you up.

Lord, thank you for the friends you've given me. Thank you for those that encourage me and build me up. Help me be that kind of friend to others. Amen.

NOVEMBER 18

Now the serpent was more crafty than any other beast of the field that the Lord God had made. He said to the woman, "Did God actually say, 'You shall not eat of any tree in the garden'?"

Genesis 3:1

God created Adam and Eve, and he placed them in the Garden of Eden. He gave them everything they needed and so much more. There was just one rule: do not eat of the tree of the knowledge of good and evil. Well, it didn't take long for them to do the very thing God told them not to do. Eve had a conversation with the serpent. He convinced her that God was a liar and that he was only trying to keep her from something. So, she ended up eating the forbidden fruit and sharing some with her husband.

Millenniums have passed since Genesis, but the enemy is still using the same ole tactics. He's crafty. He wants to do everything in his power to get you to do the very things God tells you not to do. He wants to make you question God's Word. He wants to convince you that God is a liar. He wants to make you think that God is just trying to keep you from something.

God doesn't want something from you. He wants something for you. He's not trying to keep you from something. He's trying to protect you from something. Don't let the serpent convince you otherwise.

Lord, thank you for wanting what's best for me. Help me stay on high alert and resist the attacks of the enemy. Amen.

NOVEMBER 19

Be not quick in your spirit to become angry, for anger lodges in the heart of fools.

Ecclesiastes 7:9

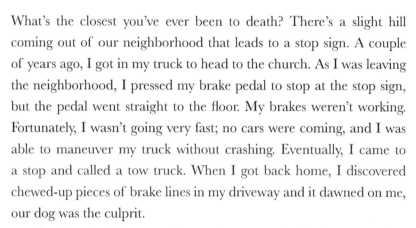

What's the closest you've ever been to death? There's a slight hill coming out of our neighborhood that leads to a stop sign. A couple of years ago, I got in my truck to head to the church. As I was leaving the neighborhood, I pressed my brake pedal to stop at the stop sign, but the pedal went straight to the floor. My brakes weren't working. Fortunately, I wasn't going very fast; no cars were coming, and I was able to maneuver my truck without crashing. Eventually, I came to a stop and called a tow truck. When I got back home, I discovered chewed-up pieces of brake lines in my driveway and it dawned on me, our dog was the culprit.

Our dog, Axel, has tested my patience more in the three years that he's been alive than any other person or thing ever has. He's caused hundreds of dollars worth of damage and even attempted to murder me. Unfortunately, I have responded to his shenanigans in ways that I'm not proud of. I've done and said things that I wish I could take back.

There's a difference between reacting and responding. A reaction is impulsive, while a response is more thought out. When unexpected things happen, you can choose to react in a way that's not pleasing to God, or you can choose to respond in a way that is.

Lord, forgive me for the times I have reacted in a way that is not pleasing to you. Help me respond in ways that are pleasing to you going forward. Amen.

NOVEMBER 20

And when he had finished speaking, he said to Simon, "Put out into the deep and let down your nets for a catch." And Simon answered, "Master, we toiled all night and took nothing! But at your word I will let down the nets."

Luke 5:4-5

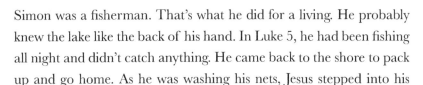

Simon was a fisherman. That's what he did for a living. He probably knew the lake like the back of his hand. In Luke 5, he had been fishing all night and didn't catch anything. He came back to the shore to pack up and go home. As he was washing his nets, Jesus stepped into his boat and asked him to put out a little from the shore. Jesus sat down and taught the people from Simon's boat.

When Jesus finished teaching, he told Simon to go out deeper and let down his nets. Simon was reluctant but willing. He explained that they had fished all night and caught nothing, but then agreed to do what he was asked to do. Simon let down the nets and caught more fish than the boat could hold. On his own, Simon caught nothing, but with Jesus, he caught more than enough.

Maybe there is something you are attempting to do, but you continue to fail. There may be several reasons why you are failing, but what if one of those reasons is because you are attempting to do it on your own? On your own, you are limited, but with Jesus, the possibilities are limitless.

Lord, thank you for intervening in my life. Help me trust you. Show me if there is any area where I am relying on my own power. Amen.

NOVEMBER 21

In all things I have shown you that by working hard in this way we must help the weak and remember the words of the Lord Jesus, how he himself said, 'It is more blessed to give than to receive.'

Acts 20:35

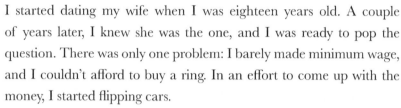

I started dating my wife when I was eighteen years old. A couple of years later, I knew she was the one, and I was ready to pop the question. There was only one problem: I barely made minimum wage, and I couldn't afford to buy a ring. In an effort to come up with the money, I started flipping cars.

I went into business with a friend. We found cheap cars online, fixed them up, and sold them for a profit. Before long, I had enough cash to buy a ring. I went into the jewelry store with cash in my pocket, did some negotiating, and came out with the exact ring I went in to get. After making that purchase, I think my net worth was less than twenty bucks. I was as broke as I could be, but I wouldn't trade that moment for the world.

Consumption is at an all-time high, and coincidentally, happiness is at an all-time low. We have bigger houses, nicer cars, and higher-paying jobs, but less contentment. If you're not careful, you can find yourself in the never-ending trap of pursuing more. You can believe the lie that the next purchase will finally bring lasting contentment, but the truth is that it's more blessed to give than to receive.

Lord, thank you for your many blessings. Help me be generous to others and content with what I have. Amen.

NOVEMBER 22

Then one of them, when he saw that he was healed, turned back, praising God with a loud voice; and he fell on his face at Jesus' feet, giving him thanks. Now he was a Samaritan.

Luke 17:15-16

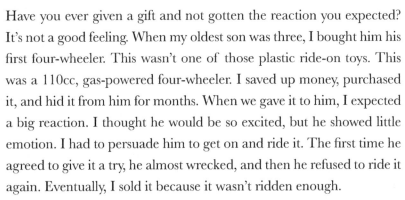

Have you ever given a gift and not gotten the reaction you expected? It's not a good feeling. When my oldest son was three, I bought him his first four-wheeler. This wasn't one of those plastic ride-on toys. This was a 110cc, gas-powered four-wheeler. I saved up money, purchased it, and hid it from him for months. When we gave it to him, I expected a big reaction. I thought he would be so excited, but he showed little emotion. I had to persuade him to get on and ride it. The first time he agreed to give it a try, he almost wrecked, and then he refused to ride it again. Eventually, I sold it because it wasn't ridden enough.

In today's passage of scripture, Jesus heals ten lepers. Leprosy was a terrible disease that required isolation from society. These ten people were not only healed but also allowed to resume their normal lives. Of the ten that were miraculously healed, only one turned back to give Jesus thanks.

God has given you so much, but how often do you fail to give him thanks? Today, will you be like the nine that went on their way or like the one that turned back to give Jesus thanks?

Lord, thank you for everything that you have given me. I am so undeserving, but you continue to bless me. Forgive me for taking your gifts for granted. Amen.

NOVEMBER 23

For what does it profit a man to gain the whole world and forfeit his soul?

Mark 8:36

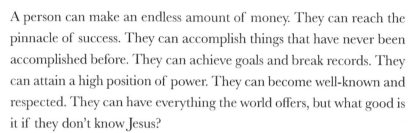

A person can make an endless amount of money. They can reach the pinnacle of success. They can accomplish things that have never been accomplished before. They can achieve goals and break records. They can attain a high position of power. They can become well-known and respected. They can have everything the world offers, but what good is it if they don't know Jesus?

Jesus plus nothing equals everything, and everything minus Jesus equals nothing. You can have nothing, you can be poor, you can be an outcast, but if you have Jesus, you still have everything. One day, regardless of what you didn't have on Earth, you will spend an eternity in Heaven. On the flipside, you can have it all, you can be rich, you can be well-known, but if you don't have Jesus, you still have nothing. One day, regardless of what you did have on Earth, you will spend an eternity in Hell.

There is nothing wrong with having career goals or working to grow your company. There's nothing wrong with saving for that new house or luxury car. There's nothing wrong with working to buy that watch or piece of jewelry. There's nothing wrong with wanting to have nice things, but don't forfeit your soul in the process. Remember, Jesus plus nothing still equals everything, and everything minus Jesus still equals nothing.

Lord, thank you for blessing me with nice things. Help me understand that acquiring stuff means nothing if I forfeit my soul in the process. Amen.

NOVEMBER 24

Each one must give as he has decided in his heart, not reluctantly or under compulsion, for God loves a cheerful giver.

2 Corinthians 9:7

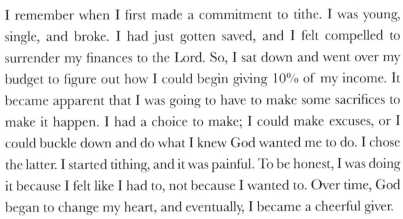

I remember when I first made a commitment to tithe. I was young, single, and broke. I had just gotten saved, and I felt compelled to surrender my finances to the Lord. So, I sat down and went over my budget to figure out how I could begin giving 10% of my income. It became apparent that I was going to have to make some sacrifices to make it happen. I had a choice to make; I could make excuses, or I could buckle down and do what I knew God wanted me to do. I chose the latter. I started tithing, and it was painful. To be honest, I was doing it because I felt like I had to, not because I wanted to. Over time, God began to change my heart, and eventually, I became a cheerful giver.

Today's verse is challenging. You may be doing the right thing, but are you doing it with the right heart? You may serve your church and give your time, but are you doing it with the right heart? You may help people in need and give your resources, but are you doing it with the right heart? You may tithe and give your money, but are you doing it with the right heart?

As a Christian, you should regularly examine your heart and ensure that you're not giving reluctantly or under compulsion. Remember, God loves a cheerful giver.

Lord, thank you for giving me the opportunity to give back to you. Help me examine my heart and become a cheerful giver. Amen.

NOVEMBER 25

The rich rules over the poor, and the borrower is the slave of the lender.

Proverbs 22:7

During our first few years of marriage, my wife and I racked up a decent amount of debt. We had a couple expensive vehicles, a house, and student loans. We quickly realized that debt was holding us back, especially our car payments. Every month, those payments came due, and it was painful. We ended up selling one of our vehicles and paying off the other. The debt reduction enabled us to put money into a savings account each month. Eventually, we invested the money that we had been saving in real estate. Those investments paid off, but they wouldn't have been possible without eliminating some of our debt. We learned that today's verse really is true: the borrower is the slave of the lender.

I certainly don't think that all debt is bad, but it is holding many back. People finance houses, cars, education, furniture, clothing, and the list goes on. Many end up in over their heads. They feel the stress and pressure to make that payment every month. They work longer and harder, often missing what's important, to finance lifestyles that they can't afford.

What about you? Are you in over your head? Is debt holding you back? Have you become a slave to the lender? If so, what steps can you take to become a better steward of your finances?

Lord, thank you for everything you have blessed me with. Show me how to become a better steward of my finances. I don't want to be a slave to anything except you. Amen.

NOVEMBER 26

Give to everyone who begs from you, and from one who takes away your goods do not demand them back.

Luke 6:30

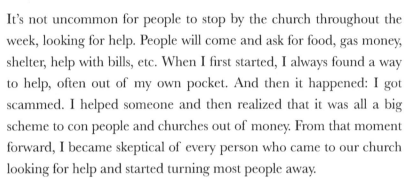

It's not uncommon for people to stop by the church throughout the week, looking for help. People will come and ask for food, gas money, shelter, help with bills, etc. When I first started, I always found a way to help, often out of my own pocket. And then it happened: I got scammed. I helped someone and then realized that it was all a big scheme to con people and churches out of money. From that moment forward, I became skeptical of every person who came to our church looking for help and started turning most people away.

Today's passage of scripture is challenging. We are instructed to give to everyone who begs from us. It doesn't instruct us to screen people and make sure they have a genuine need; it simply instructs us to give. And then, it takes it a step further and instructs us not to demand back what has been taken from us.

This doesn't mean you should be naive and allow people to take advantage of you, but it does mean you should extend the love of Christ to others. It does mean you should give and expect nothing in return. It does mean you should be quick to forgive those who abuse your generosity. And it does mean that you shouldn't allow your compassion to become overshadowed by skepticism.

Lord, thank you for giving me the means to give. Help me give generously to those in need and extend your love to others. Amen.

NOVEMBER 27

And they were selling their possessions and belongings and distributing the proceeds to all, as any had need.

Acts 2:45

Several years back, I decided to get my real estate license to view properties quicker and save money on commission. After getting my license, a lady from our church asked me if I'd sell a property for her, and I agreed to do so. After the property was sold, she turned around and gave a large portion of the money to the church. This came at a time when our church was in the middle of a building project and in need of funds. She gave sacrificially, and it made a difference. I will always remember and be challenged by her generosity.

The early church was unified. They were more than a group of people; they were a family. They were selling their possessions and belongings to help others in need. They understood what it meant to be the church. They were consumed with the mission. They used what they had to further the kingdom of God. And as the church grew, so did its generosity.

Have you forgotten what it means to be the church? Are you consumed with the mission? Are you willing to sell your possessions and belongings to help others in need? Biblical generosity is much more than tithing on your income. It is consistently asking the question: how can I use what I have to further the kingdom of God?

Lord, thank you for the opportunities you give me to help others. Show me how I can use what I have to further your kingdom. Amen.

NOVEMBER 28

But Peter said, "Ananias, why has Satan filled your heart to lie to the Holy Spirit and to keep back for yourself part of the proceeds of the land?"

Acts 5:3

A man named Ananias and his wife Sapphira, both members of the church, sold a piece of property. They kept back some of the funds for themselves while making it appear as if they were giving it all to the work of the church. They probably expected others to praise them and put them on a pedestal for their generosity, but instead, they got caught in the act of embezzlement. The punishment was harsh. Ananias and Sapphira both fell over dead.

The issue wasn't that they kept some of the funds for themselves. After all, it was their money. The issue was that they were making it appear as if they were giving all the money to the church. When they were actually keeping some of the proceeds for themselves.

Are you giving to gain status, to be praised by others, and to be put on a pedestal? Or are you giving from a pure heart? Do you brag and boast to others when you give? Or do you keep it to yourself and give anonymously when possible? In the book of Matthew, Jesus says, "But when you give to the needy, do not let your left hand know what your right hand is doing" (Matthew 6:3).

Lord, forgive me for the times that I've made it appear as if I was doing one thing when I was actually doing another thing. Help me give with a pure heart. Amen.

NOVEMBER 29

My sheep hear my voice, and I know them, and they follow me.

John 10:27

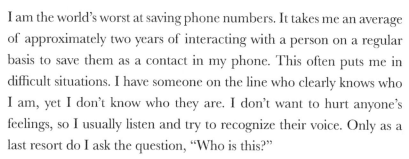

I am the world's worst at saving phone numbers. It takes me an average of approximately two years of interacting with a person on a regular basis to save them as a contact in my phone. This often puts me in difficult situations. I have someone on the line who clearly knows who I am, yet I don't know who they are. I don't want to hurt anyone's feelings, so I usually listen and try to recognize their voice. Only as a last resort do I ask the question, "Who is this?"

Many want to hear from God but struggle to discern his voice. They wonder if it's God that is speaking to them or if it's something else.

In today's verse, Jesus says that his sheep will recognize his voice. This doesn't mean that you're not genuinely saved if you struggle to hear his voice. But it does mean that the more time you spend with him, and the more time you spend communicating with him, the easier it will be for you to recognize his voice. The longer you follow him, the easier it will become to discern what he is saying and when it is him speaking.

Lord, thank you for speaking to me. Help me become so close to you that I instantly recognize your voice. Give me wisdom to discern what you're leading me to do. Amen.

NOVEMBER 30

But Moses said to God, "Who am I that I should go to Pharaoh and bring the children of Israel out of Egypt?"

Exodus 3:11

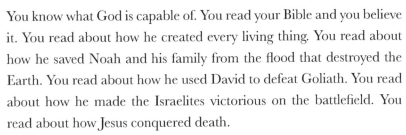

You know what God is capable of. You read your Bible and you believe it. You read about how he created every living thing. You read about how he saved Noah and his family from the flood that destroyed the Earth. You read about how he used David to defeat Goliath. You read about how he made the Israelites victorious on the battlefield. You read about how Jesus conquered death.

You read about how he has used others, but do you believe that he can use you? You know how weak and limited you are. You know how unworthy and messed up you are. You know things about yourself that no one else knows. So many allow insecurity to cripple them and keep them from obeying God. Many allow their weaknesses to blind them from God's strengths.

Moses was arguably one of the greatest leaders of all time, but he initially struggled to believe that God could accomplish his purposes through him. He didn't feel worthy, qualified, or capable. And he was probably right, but he was called by God, and that was all that mattered.

God wants to use you, but you have to believe that he can and move forward in obedience to him. Don't let fear and insecurity keep you from what God has for you.

Lord, thank you for wanting to use someone like me. Help me focus less on my weaknesses and more on your strengths. Give me the courage to be obedient to you. Amen.

DECEMBER 1

What man of you, having a hundred sheep, if he has lost one of them, does not leave the ninety-nine in the open country, and go after the one that is lost, until he finds it?

Luke 15:4

When my wife was about to give birth to our first child, someone jokingly told me that I would have to pay the amount of money my insurance didn't cover before they would let us leave the hospital. There was one problem: I thought they were serious. I went to the bank and took out cash. I don't remember the exact amount of money, but it was a significant amount for us, especially at the time.

To my disappointment, they wouldn't let me pay at the hospital and explained that it would be several months before I received the final bill. And then, on the way home, I realized that I had misplaced the money. We couldn't find it anywhere. We started to panic. We looked everywhere. We searched high and low, and by God's grace, eventually, we found it!

I cared a lot about that money, but it doesn't even begin to compare to how much God cares for you. He will leave the ninety-nine to go search for the one, and he won't stop until he finds it. That resonates with me because I was once the one. Maybe you've blown it. Maybe you're trying to put the pieces of your life back together. Remember, God hasn't given up on you no matter how far you have strayed.

Lord, thank you for the way you care for me. Thank you for the way you pursued me when I wanted nothing to do with you. If I have strayed, help me find my way back home. Amen.

DECEMBER 2

Are not five sparrows sold for two pennies? And not one of them is forgotten before God. Why, even the hairs of your head are all numbered. Fear not; you are of more value than many sparrows.

Luke 12:6-7

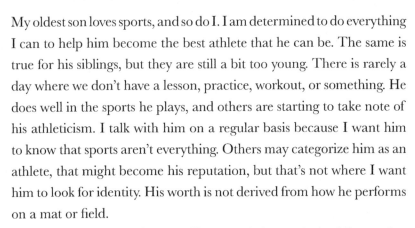

My oldest son loves sports, and so do I. I am determined to do everything I can to help him become the best athlete that he can be. The same is true for his siblings, but they are still a bit too young. There is rarely a day where we don't have a lesson, practice, workout, or something. He does well in the sports he plays, and others are starting to take note of his athleticism. I talk with him on a regular basis because I want him to know that sports aren't everything. Others may categorize him as an athlete, that might become his reputation, but that's not where I want him to look for identity. His worth is not derived from how he performs on a mat or field.

The same is true for you. Your worth is not derived from what you accomplish, how others categorize you, or what you think about yourself. You're worth what someone is willing to pay for you, and Jesus was willing to pay it all. He gave his life for you.

If you continue to let the opinions of other people define you, you are always going to be insecure. It doesn't matter what you accomplish or how far you go. You're always going to feel like you're not good enough and you don't measure up.

Lord, thank you for paying it all for me. Help me stop looking for identity in the things of this world and start looking for it in you. Amen.

DECEMBER 3

Yet you do not know what tomorrow will bring. What is your life? For you are a mist that appears for a little time and then vanishes.

James 4:14

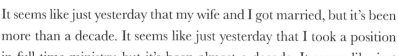

It seems like just yesterday that my wife and I got married, but it's been more than a decade. It seems like just yesterday that I took a position in full-time ministry, but it's been almost a decade. It seems like just yesterday that I became a father, but my oldest is entering the second grade. I'm beginning to learn that time is my most valuable resource.

Time management is one of the most important skills a person can learn, especially with all the distractions we face today. Many waste hours of valuable time browsing social media, watching TV, and procrastinating the things they need to get done. And most are overwhelmed, not because they don't have enough time, but because they don't manage the time they have well.

You can't rewind, freeze, or slow time down, but you can make the most of the time that you're given. For a Christian, this means much more than staying on task and getting things done. Being productive is one thing, and being productive for the kingdom of God is another thing. Do you have your priorities in the right order? Are you using your time in a way that is pleasing to God? Remember, time is your most valuable resource.

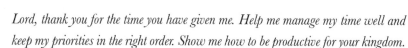

Lord, thank you for the time you have given me. Help me manage my time well and keep my priorities in the right order. Show me how to be productive for your kingdom. Amen.

DECEMBER 4

Though formerly I was a blasphemer, persecutor, and insolent opponent. But I received mercy because I had acted ignorantly in unbelief, and the grace of our Lord overflowed for me with the faith and love that are in Christ Jesus.

1 Timothy 1:13-14

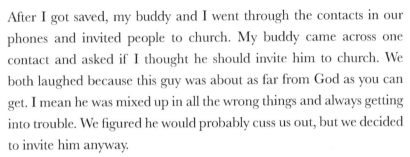

After I got saved, my buddy and I went through the contacts in our phones and invited people to church. My buddy came across one contact and asked if I thought he should invite him to church. We both laughed because this guy was about as far from God as you can get. I mean he was mixed up in all the wrong things and always getting into trouble. We figured he would probably cuss us out, but we decided to invite him anyway.

To our surprise, he immediately responded and agreed to go. And then he said, "I have been wanting to go to church for a long time. I've just been waiting for someone to invite me." What an eye-opening experience that was.

There are people out there, people in your life who are curious and open to hearing about God. There might be someone in your life who wants to go to church, and they're just waiting for someone to invite them. There might be someone in your life who would respond to the gospel, and they're just waiting for someone to share it with them. Will you be that someone? Remember, there's not a person in this world that God can't save.

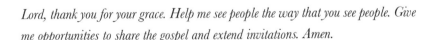

Lord, thank you for your grace. Help me see people the way that you see people. Give me opportunities to share the gospel and extend invitations. Amen.

DECEMBER 5

You are the salt of the earth, but if salt has lost its taste, how shall its saltiness be restored? It is no longer good for anything except to be thrown out and trampled under people's feet.

Matthew 5:13

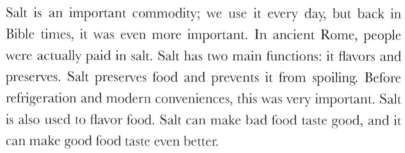

Salt is an important commodity; we use it every day, but back in Bible times, it was even more important. In ancient Rome, people were actually paid in salt. Salt has two main functions: it flavors and preserves. Salt preserves food and prevents it from spoiling. Before refrigeration and modern conveniences, this was very important. Salt is also used to flavor food. Salt can make bad food taste good, and it can make good food taste even better.

In today's verse, Jesus says, "You are the salt of the earth." Look around, the Earth is decaying, not just physically, but spiritually. Every day, people are dying and going to Hell. The longer humanity exists the further humanity gets away from God. Just as salt acts as an agent to flavor and preserve food, you are to act as an agent to flavor and preserve the world.

Jesus goes on to say, "If salt has lost its taste, how shall its saltiness be restored? It is no longer good for anything except to be thrown out and trampled under people's feet." Are you acting as an agent to flavor and persevere the world? Are you the salt of the Earth, or have you lost your saltiness?

Lord, thank you for allowing me to be a part of your plan. Help me be the salt of the Earth and flavor and preserve the world. Amen.

DECEMBER 6

You are the light of the world. A city set on a hill cannot be hidden. Nor do people light a lamp and put it under a basket, but on a stand, and it gives light to all in the house.

Matthew 5:14-15

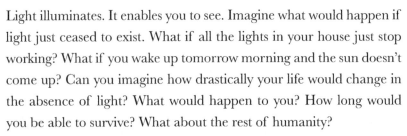

Light illuminates. It enables you to see. Imagine what would happen if light just ceased to exist. What if all the lights in your house just stop working? What if you wake up tomorrow morning and the sun doesn't come up? Can you imagine how drastically your life would change in the absence of light? What would happen to you? How long would you be able to survive? What about the rest of humanity?

Just as physical light is necessary for physical life, spiritual light is necessary for spiritual life. In today's verse, Jesus says, "You are the light of the world." Jesus is telling you to reflect his light to the world. He is the light of the world, and his light should shine through you. It should help others see the world for what it is and point others to him.

How can you let your light shine? By living out your faith on a daily basis. By being the hands and feet of Jesus. By refusing to give in, conform, and look just like everybody. Others should know that you're a Christian, not just because you say that you are, but because of the way that you live. Don't put your light under a basket. Let it shine.

Lord, thank you for being the light of the world. Let your light shine through me and use it to point others to you. Amen.

DECEMBER 7

And without faith it is impossible to please him, for whoever would draw near to God must believe that he exists and that he rewards those who seek him.

Hebrews 11:6

Moses settled down in Midian and started a family. He was comfortable and living a simple life, but then God called him to lead the Israelites out of slavery. He had to step out in faith to do what God wanted him to do. David was just a teenager, not even old enough to become a soldier, but he defeated Goliath. He had to step out in faith to do what God wanted him to do. Gideon had to leave his job threshing wheat to lead an army to defeat the Midianites. He had to step out in faith to do what God wanted him to do. Mary was engaged to be married when an angel told her that she would give birth to Jesus. She had to step out in faith to do what God wanted her to do. Paul was called to preach the gospel after persecuting the church. He had to step out in faith to do what God wanted him to do.

Do you see the pattern? In order to do what God wants you to do, you must step out in faith? Maybe he is leading you to do something, but you continue to make excuses. It may seem too risky, or you may feel like you have too much to lose. Remember, without faith, it is impossible to please God.

Lord, forgive me for not trusting you. Show me what you want me to do and give me the faith to do it. Amen.

DECEMBER 8

When she could hide him no longer, she took for him a basket made of bulrushes and daubed it with bitumen and pitch. She put the child in it and placed it among the reeds by the river bank.

Exodus 2:3

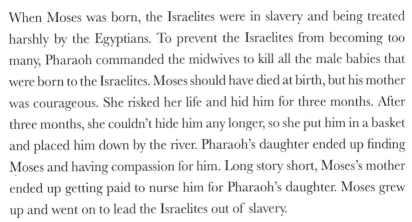

When Moses was born, the Israelites were in slavery and being treated harshly by the Egyptians. To prevent the Israelites from becoming too many, Pharaoh commanded the midwives to kill all the male babies that were born to the Israelites. Moses should have died at birth, but his mother was courageous. She risked her life and hid him for three months. After three months, she couldn't hide him any longer, so she put him in a basket and placed him down by the river. Pharaoh's daughter ended up finding Moses and having compassion for him. Long story short, Moses's mother ended up getting paid to nurse him for Pharaoh's daughter. Moses grew up and went on to lead the Israelites out of slavery.

Moses's mom, Jochebed, was a woman of faith. She did all that she could possibly do and trusted God with the rest. She put her life on the line and hid Moses for three months, but eventually, she had to put it in God's hands. In the end, God took care of her, and he took care of her son.

Faith is not just sitting around and waiting for God to come through in a miraculous way. Faith is doing all that you can possibly do and trusting God with the rest. When you do all that you can, that is when God will show up and do what you can't.

Lord, thank you for always providing. Give me the strength to do everything that I can and give me the faith to trust you with the rest. Amen.

DECEMBER 9

Then Jesus told his disciples, "If anyone would come after me, let him deny himself and take up his cross and follow me."

Matthew 16:24

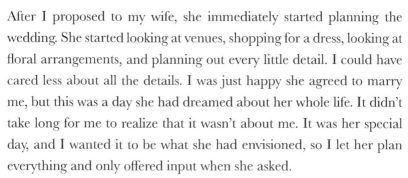

After I proposed to my wife, she immediately started planning the wedding. She started looking at venues, shopping for a dress, looking at floral arrangements, and planning out every little detail. I could have cared less about all the details. I was just happy she agreed to marry me, but this was a day she had dreamed about her whole life. It didn't take long for me to realize that it wasn't about me. It was her special day, and I wanted it to be what she had envisioned, so I let her plan everything and only offered input when she asked.

Unfortunately, Christianity has been consumerized by society. Many view God as a deity who exists to serve them and meet their needs. Many are in it for status and standing. Many are in it because they want to better themselves and reach their goals, and they believe God will help them do it.

The truth is that it's not about you. In order to follow Jesus, you must deny yourself and take up your cross. That means laying your goals, desires, and plans down at the altar and picking up his. That means dying to self daily and surrendering to him. Remember, you exist to serve him. He doesn't exist to serve you.

Lord, thank you for inviting me to follow you. Help me take up my cross daily and follow you. Show me if there is any area of my life that is not fully surrendered to you. Amen.

DECEMBER 10

And there we saw the Nephilim (the sons of Anak, who come from the Nephilim),
and we seemed to ourselves like grasshoppers, and so we seemed to them.

Numbers 13:33

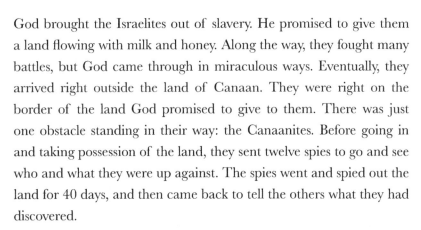

God brought the Israelites out of slavery. He promised to give them
a land flowing with milk and honey. Along the way, they fought many
battles, but God came through in miraculous ways. Eventually, they
arrived right outside the land of Canaan. They were right on the
border of the land God promised to give to them. There was just
one obstacle standing in their way: the Canaanites. Before going in
and taking possession of the land, they sent twelve spies to go and see
who and what they were up against. The spies went and spied out the
land for 40 days, and then came back to tell the others what they had
discovered.

Their report started out good; the land really was special, but
the people that lived in the land were giants. The Israelites became
afraid and decided not to go in and take possession of the land God
promised to give them. They ended up settling for less than God's best
and wasting forty years wandering in the wilderness.

You probably love what's familiar, but if you're not careful, you
can get stuck in your comfort zone. Like the Israelites, you can begin
to wander and settle for less than God's best. Don't allow fear of the
unknown to keep you from what God has for you.

Lord, forgive me for lacking courage. Help me embrace the uncomfortable and step
out in faith. Show me if I am settling for less than your best. Amen.

DECEMBER 11

Since we have these promises, beloved, let us cleanse ourselves from every defilement of body and spirit, bringing holiness to completion in the fear of God.

2 Corinthians 7:1

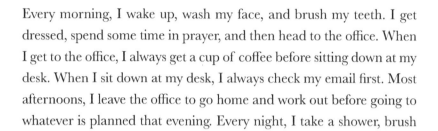

Every morning, I wake up, wash my face, and brush my teeth. I get dressed, spend some time in prayer, and then head to the office. When I get to the office, I always get a cup of coffee before sitting down at my desk. When I sit down at my desk, I always check my email first. Most afternoons, I leave the office to go home and work out before going to whatever is planned that evening. Every night, I take a shower, brush my teeth, and get into bed. I do some reading, watch some TV, and then go to sleep.

Whether you realize it or not, the majority of what you do, think, and say falls into the habit category. This can work to your demise or to your advantage. Your habits determine what you do, and what you do determines who you will become.

Take a moment and evaluate your daily routine. You'll probably realize that you do many things each day without thinking about them. Are your daily habits shaping you into the person God created you to be or keeping you from becoming the person God created you to be? Work to build good habits and eliminate bad habits.

Lord, help me become the person you created me to be. Help me build good habits and eliminate bad habits. Show me where I am falling short. Amen.

DECEMBER 12

Desire without knowledge is not good, and whoever makes haste with his feet misses his way.

Proverbs 19:2

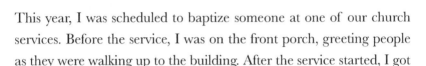

This year, I was scheduled to baptize someone at one of our church services. Before the service, I was on the front porch, greeting people as they were walking up to the building. After the service started, I got caught up talking and forgot about the baptism.

Fortunately, someone reminded me at the last minute. I sprinted into the building, grabbed a T-shirt off the shelf, and ran up the steps to get changed. I got down into the baptismal pool just in the nick of time, but there were a few problems. I grabbed the wrong size shirt. I wear a large, but I grabbed a small one by mistake, so it was skintight and barely covered my belly button. I was also out of breath from running and could barely talk. To top it off, I publicly called the guy who was getting baptized by the wrong name. It was an embarrassing moment, to say the least.

Rushing usually will not produce the results you desire. Instead, getting in a hurry can cause problems and actually delay the results you desire. The Bible tells us, "Whoever makes haste with his feet misses his way." Instead of rushing into things, it's usually best to slow down, spend time in prayer, and plan accordingly.

Lord, forgive me for getting in a hurry. Help me slow down and seek you before making any big decisions. Amen.

DECEMBER 13

A fool gives full vent to his spirit, but a wise man quietly holds it back.

Proverbs 29:11

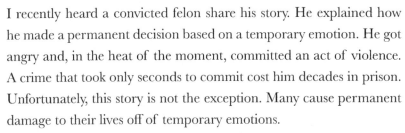

I recently heard a convicted felon share his story. He explained how he made a permanent decision based on a temporary emotion. He got angry and, in the heat of the moment, committed an act of violence. A crime that took only seconds to commit cost him decades in prison. Unfortunately, this story is not the exception. Many cause permanent damage to their lives off of temporary emotions.

I wonder how many relationships have suffered permanent damage because of temporary emotions. I wonder how many opportunities have been lost permanently because of temporary emotions. I wonder how many innocent lives have been permanently affected because of temporary emotions. I wonder how many futures have been permanently destroyed because of temporary emotions.

It's easy to give full vent to your spirit. In other words, it's easy to let your anger get the best of you. You've probably done and said things in the heat of the moment that you regret. When anger sets in, it's usually best to walk away or take a minute to collect yourself. A little bit of self-control can save you from a heap of trouble. Don't make a permanent decision based on a temporary emotion.

Lord, forgive me for losing my temper. Give me self-control and help me handle my anger in a way that is pleasing to you. Show me when I need to ask others for forgiveness. Amen.

DECEMBER 14

Come to me, all who labor and are heavy laden, and I will give you rest.

Matthew 11:28

When robotic vacuum cleaners first started becoming popular, my wife and I received one as a gift. It's designed to go and vacuum the floors until it has just enough battery left to make it back to the charger. Ours must have been defective because it would never make it back to the charger. Instead, it would die, and we would have to go and look for it.

We would find it under the table, bed or couch. Sometimes, it would make it to the room where the charger was; other times, it would die on the opposite end of the house. That thing eventually ended up in the trash, but now that the technology has had several years to advance, we might consider getting another one.

How often do you overestimate how much charge you have left? How often do you find yourself exhausted and burnt out? If you're like most, the answer is frequently. The good news is that you can recharge by spending time in the presence of Jesus. This might mean getting alone, going on a walk, attending church, reading your Bible, spending time in prayer, or all of the above. Jesus invites you to come to him, and if you do, he promises that he will give you rest.

Lord, thank you for giving me rest. Help me slow down, recharge, and spend time in your presence on a regular basis. Amen.

DECEMBER 15

Likewise the Spirit helps us in our weakness. For we do not know what to pray for as we ought, but the Spirit himself intercedes for us with groanings too deep for words.

Romans 8:26

───※○※───

Have you ever struggled to pray? Maybe you committed a sin and you felt too ashamed to face God. Instead of running to him in repentance, you ran from him in rebellion. Maybe you were going through a challenging season and found it difficult to pray, because you partially blamed God for what you were going through. Maybe you just got caught up in the busyness of your schedule and your prayer life took a backseat.

God has shown me time and time again, the times I need to pray the most are usually the times I feel like praying the least. It's easy for me to pray when things are good, falling into place, and moving forward. It becomes more difficult when things take a turn for the worse, but those are the times that I need to pray the most.

Maybe you're in the middle of a season where you are finding it difficult to pray. Maybe you want to pray but don't know where to start. Maybe you open your mouth to pray but the words just don't come out. Good news! Even when you don't know how or what to pray, the Spirit will intercede on your behalf. Remember, the times you need to pray the most are usually the times you feel like it the least.

───※○※───

Lord, thank you for the Holy Spirit. When I don't know what to say or how to pray, thank you for interceding on my behalf. Help me pray, even when I don't feel like it. Amen.

DECEMBER 16

Is anyone among you suffering? Let him pray. Is anyone cheerful? Let him sing praise.

James 5:13

When I first started preaching, there was a guy that passed out in the middle of one of my sermons. I looked to one side of the room, and when I looked back, I saw him slouched over in the pew. People started gathering around him to make sure he was okay. I didn't know what to do, so I just kept preaching. Eventually, everyone's attention was diverted to the commotion that was taking place in the middle of the sanctuary. I stopped preaching until they got him safely out of the room, and then I finished my sermon.

Afterward, I realized that I missed an opportunity to pray. I was so focused on my message and the flow of the service that I missed a great opportunity to pray publicly and collectively with my church for that man's health.

It's always a good time to pray. When you don't know what to do, that's a good time to pray. When you are suffering, that's a good time to pray. When life is great, that's a good time to pray. When something unexpected happens, that's a good time to pray. No matter what you're doing right now, it's a good time to pray.

Lord, thank you for prayer. Thank you for always listening and speaking. No matter what I go through, help me remember that it's always a good time to pray. Amen.

DECEMBER 17

Then David said to the Philistine, "You come to me with a sword and with a spear and with a javelin, but I come to you in the name of the Lord of hosts, the God of the armies of Israel, whom you have defied."

1 Samuel 17:45

The story of David and Goliath is one of the most popular stories in the Bible, and rightfully so. It's an incredible story of faith and courage. David was just a teenager, not yet old enough to go to battle when he witnessed Goliath come out to taunt the Israelite army. All the soldiers were terrified of Goliath, he was a giant who also happened to be a trained killing machine. No one dared to consider stepping on the battlefield with him, but David had a different perspective.

Everyone was focused on the size of Goliath, but David was focused on the size of God. In his own power, David knew that he didn't stand a chance against Goliath, but with God by his side, he knew Goliath didn't stand a chance against him. He stepped onto the battlefield, with no armor, and defeated the giant with just a sling and a stone.

In life, there will be situations, circumstances, and challenges that are bigger than you. There will be times when the odds aren't in your favor. There will be times when it seems like you're fighting a losing battle. There will be times when you find yourself up against a Goliath. When those times come, you can focus on the size of what's in front of you or on the size of God.

Lord, thank you for your power. Help me trust you, even when the odds aren't in my favor. Teach me how to courageously face whatever life throws my way. Amen.

DECEMBER 18

Have I not commanded you? Be strong and courageous. Do not be frightened, and do not be dismayed, for the Lord your God is with you wherever you go.

Joshua 1:9

Moses, the leader of the Israelites, passed away. Now it was time for Joshua to step up to the plate and lead the Israelites into the Promised Land. This was a big task that would come with many challenges. It would require strength and courage. However, God made it clear that he would be with Joshua every step of the way. Joshua had a choice to make. He could allow fear to cripple him, or he could move forward in obedience. Fortunately, he chose the latter, and the Israelites finally took possession of the land God promised to give them.

Today's verse was a command to Joshua, but it's applicable to all of us. There will be times in life when God calls you to do things that will require strength and courage. However, he will be with you every step of the way.

What is God calling you to do right now? Maybe it's a big task that will come with many challenges. Maybe it makes you feel uncomfortable just thinking about it. Maybe you're afraid. You have a choice to make. You can allow fear to cripple you, or you can move forward in obedience. Remember, God doesn't promise it will be easy, but he doesn't promise to be present.

Lord, thank you for always being present. Give me the strength and courage necessary to do what you have called me to do. Amen.

DECEMBER 19

"Repent, for the kingdom of heaven is at hand."

Matthew 3:2

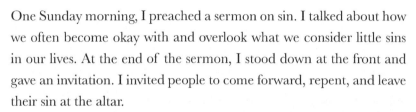

One Sunday morning, I preached a sermon on sin. I talked about how we often become okay with and overlook what we consider little sins in our lives. At the end of the sermon, I stood down at the front and gave an invitation. I invited people to come forward, repent, and leave their sin at the altar.

A woman came forward, she walked up to me and told me about her struggle with smoking. She told me she had been smoking cigarettes for years, that she just repented, and that she wasn't ever going to smoke again. She reached into her purse, handed me a pack of cigarettes, and went and sat back down. It was somewhat awkward for me to be standing in front of the congregation holding a pack of cigarettes, but I commend that woman's obedience to the Lord.

Is there any sin in your life that you need to repent of? Is there any sin that you have become okay with and overlooked? Maybe it's something that has held you captive for years or even decades. Maybe you've tried to stop before and failed. Today is a new day. You can continue on a path that leads to destruction, or you can repent and start fresh.

Lord, forgive me for the times that I fall short. Show me if there is anything in my life that I need to repent of. Amen.

DECEMBER 20

And they went with haste and found Mary and Joseph, and the baby lying in a manger.

Luke 2:16

The shepherds were out working in the field, keeping watch over their flocks when an angel appeared to them. The angel told them that Jesus had been born. The Shepherds went with haste to Bethlehem and found Mary and Joseph, and the baby lying in a manger. They didn't go home and say goodbye to their families, they didn't pack bags, they didn't procrastinate. They went with haste.

Christmas is one of the busiest times of the year. You have gifts to buy, parties to go to, events to plan, and all of this is on top of everything else you already do. There's nothing wrong with any of those things, but they can distract you from what's most important. It's easy to get wrapped up in the busyness of the season and never stop long enough to celebrate the true meaning of Christmas, which is Jesus.

Maybe you're anxious. Maybe you're trying to figure out how you're going to get everything done. Maybe you still have so much to do and so little time to do it. Don't let what's going on around you keep you from celebrating the true meaning of Christmas. Like the shepherds, drop everything and go with haste to spend time in the presence of Jesus.

Lord, thank you for Christmas. Help me slow down, eliminate distractions, and spend time in your presence. Show me if something is distracting me from what's most important. Amen.

DECEMBER 21

And going into the house, they saw the child with Mary his mother, and they fell down and worshiped him. Then, opening their treasures, they offered him gifts, gold and frankincense and myrrh.

Matthew 2:11

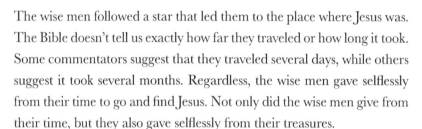

The wise men followed a star that led them to the place where Jesus was. The Bible doesn't tell us exactly how far they traveled or how long it took. Some commentators suggest that they traveled several days, while others suggest it took several months. Regardless, the wise men gave selflessly from their time to go and find Jesus. Not only did the wise men give from their time, but they also gave selflessly from their treasures.

When they finally arrived, they fell down and worshiped Jesus, and then they gave him gifts. They gave him gold, frankincense, and myrrh. These weren't random gifts. These were costly and valuable gifts. Gold is a precious metal, a gift fit for a king. Frankincense was used primarily as an incense and symbolized his priesthood. Myrrh was used to embalm bodies and symbolized that he came to suffer and die for our sin.

Christmas is the season of giving. What better time to give selflessly from your time and treasures than right now? Maybe this means volunteering to serve your church. Maybe this means spending a day serving a local soup kitchen or homeless shelter. Maybe this means providing Christmas gifts or a meal for a family that is less fortunate. Spend some time in prayer and ask God to lay a specific need on your heart.

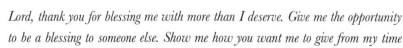

Lord, thank you for blessing me with more than I deserve. Give me the opportunity to be a blessing to someone else. Show me how you want me to give from my time and treasures. Amen.

DECEMBER 22

Then Herod, when he saw that he had been tricked by the wise men, became furious, and he sent and killed all the male children in Bethlehem and in all that region who were two years old or under, according to the time that he had ascertained from the wise men.

Matthew 2:16

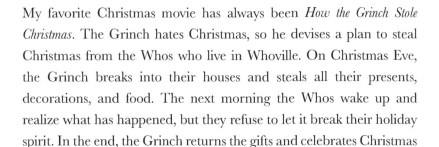

My favorite Christmas movie has always been *How the Grinch Stole Christmas*. The Grinch hates Christmas, so he devises a plan to steal Christmas from the Whos who live in Whoville. On Christmas Eve, the Grinch breaks into their houses and steals all their presents, decorations, and food. The next morning the Whos wake up and realize what has happened, but they refuse to let it break their holiday spirit. In the end, the Grinch returns the gifts and celebrates Christmas with the Whos.

What if I told you there was a real Grinch who tried to steal one of the very first Christmases? His name was King Herod. When King Herod heard others describe Jesus as the king of the Jews, he became jealous. He tried to trick the wise men into telling him where Jesus was, but that plan backfired. He quickly devised a plan B: he would kill all male children under the age of two. After God warned them, Mary and Joseph took Jesus to Egypt and remained there until King Herod died.

King Herod is proof that nothing can stop God's divine plan. God loves us so much he sent his one and only son to die and take our place on the cross. Take some time today to thank God for his sovereignty.

Lord, thank you for your sovereignty. Thank you for allowing nothing to stand in the way of your divine plan. Thank you for sending your son to die in my place. Amen.

DECEMBER 23

And Mary said, "Behold, I am the servant of the Lord; let it be to me according to your word." And the angel departed from her.

Luke 1:38

Mary was just a teenager. She was a virgin who was engaged to be married. One day, an angel appeared to her and told her she was pregnant. Mary asked how she could be pregnant since she was a virgin. The angel explained that the Holy Spirit would be responsible and that she would give birth to Jesus. Not much of an explanation, but Mary responded by saying, "I am the Lord's servant."

A lot was at stake. Mary's reputation was at stake. What would other people think and say about her? Nobody would believe that she was a virgin, and she would likely become the talk of the town. Her relationships were at stake. What would happen to her engagement? Would Joseph stay with her, or would he break it off? What about her family members? Would they stay by her side through the pregnancy or disown her? Her future was at stake. What would happen to her plans? She had her whole life in front of her. Despite everything that was at stake, Mary quickly surrendered to the Lord.

We're not on this Earth to fulfill our dreams but to carry out God's purposes. It's not about our wants but about living out his will. And even when there's a lot at stake, like Mary, you should quickly surrender.

Lord, forgive me for prioritizing my dreams over your purposes. When you call me to do something, help me surrender quickly, regardless of what's at stake. Amen.

DECEMBER 24

And her husband Joseph, being a just man and unwilling to put her to shame, resolved to divorce her quietly.

Matthew 1:19

I have always sympathized with Joseph. He met Mary, fell in love, worked up the courage to propose, and was anxiously waiting to marry the woman of his dreams. He was a man of integrity and refrained from having sex outside of marriage, but one day, he got word that Mary was pregnant. She tried to explain to him that she had not been unfaithful and that the Holy Spirit was responsible for her pregnancy, but who could believe that? Joseph decided to end the relationship. He was deeply hurt, but rather than humiliating her, he opted to divorce her quietly. Before he could go through with it, an angel appeared to him in a dream and explained to him that Mary was telling the truth. Joseph ended up taking Mary to be his wife, and they became the earthly parents of Jesus.

Joseph's story is proof that things aren't always as they seem, and sometimes God calls people to do things they don't understand. His story is also proof that although a person might not understand completely, they can obey fully.

This Christmas, maybe God is leading you to do something that you don't understand. If so, remember, you don't have to understand completely to obey fully.

Lord, thank you for using me. Give me the courage to be obedient, even when I don't understand. Show me what step you want me to take. Amen.

DECEMBER 25

And she gave birth to her firstborn son and wrapped him in swaddling cloths and laid him in a manger, because there was no place for them in the inn.

Luke 2:7

Joseph and Mary arrived in Bethlehem for the census. The long journey was followed by an agonizing labor and delivery. Jesus was born. He came to Earth in the humblest of ways. If anyone deserved a grand entry into this world it was him, but instead, he was born in a stable and laid in a manger. There was no place for him in the inn.

Jesus grew up. He lived a perfect, sinless life. He performed miracles, healed the sick, and gave hope to the hopeless, yet there was still no place for him. He was arrested, tortured, and crucified because he was hated and opposed by many. Fortunately, the story doesn't end there. Three days later, he rose from the grave, once and for all overcoming and defeating death. Sadly, even after his birth, death, and resurrection, many still fail to make a place for him in their lives.

What about you? Have you filled your life with the things of this world? Are you preoccupied with stuff? Is the busyness of the season consuming you and keeping you from making a place for him? Have you drifted from him in a season that is supposed to be all about him? If so, it's time to slow down, reprioritize, and focus on what really matters.

Lord, forgive me for getting distracted. Help me clear everything out of my life to make room for you. Show me when I fall short. Amen.

DECEMBER 26

The Lord is my strength and my shield; in him my heart trusts, and I am helped; my heart exults, and with my song I give thanks to him.

Psalm 28:7

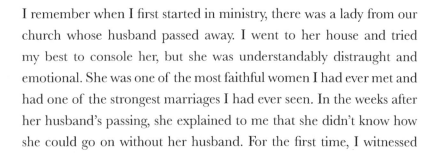

I remember when I first started in ministry, there was a lady from our church whose husband passed away. I went to her house and tried my best to console her, but she was understandably distraught and emotional. She was one of the most faithful women I had ever met and had one of the strongest marriages I had ever seen. In the weeks after her husband's passing, she explained to me that she didn't know how she could go on without her husband. For the first time, I witnessed this woman struggle to keep the faith. I don't share that to put her down, but to say that all of us will go through seasons in life where we don't understand.

The world is a fallen place. It seems as if mass shootings are taking place on a weekly basis. Innocent lives are being taken for no reason. Sin is rampant. Kids are being exposed to drugs, alcohol, and pornography at disturbingly young ages. The economy is unpredictable. Accidents, tragedies, and death are unfortunate parts of life. It's not a matter of if, but a matter of when your faith will be tested.

Maybe your faith is being tested right now. Maybe you're going through a season where you don't understand. If so, remember, the Lord is your strength and your shield.

Lord, thank you for being with me in the most difficult seasons of life. Help me trust you when my faith is being tested. Amen.

DECEMBER 27

I can do all things through him who strengthens me.

Philippians 4:13

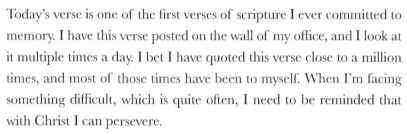

Today's verse is one of the first verses of scripture I ever committed to memory. I have this verse posted on the wall of my office, and I look at it multiple times a day. I bet I have quoted this verse close to a million times, and most of those times have been to myself. When I'm facing something difficult, which is quite often, I need to be reminded that with Christ I can persevere.

When Paul wrote this passage of scripture, he was imprisoned and awaiting trial. Prior to verse 13, he talks about how he has learned to be content in any and every circumstance. He talks about how he has learned to be content when facing plenty and when facing hunger. How has he learned to persevere? What is his secret? Christ, with him all things are possible.

There will be situations when things aren't going your way. There will be times when you find yourself facing difficulties, but that doesn't mean that you can't be content. You have a choice to make: you can place your hope in your circumstance, or you can place your hope in Christ. If you choose to place your hope in him, he will give you the strength not only to survive but to thrive. With him all things are possible.

Lord, thank you for the hope and the strength that you have given me. Help me thrive when I face difficulties. Amen.

DECEMBER 28

Honor the Lord with your wealth and with the firstfruits of all your produce.

Proverbs 3:9

Our church, Cross Roads Baptist Church, was founded in 1871. In the beginning, the church met outdoors, under a brush arbor. Eventually, the founders decided to take a leap of faith and began building the facility that we meet in today. Many of the founders were farmers, and to finance construction, they mortgaged their farms. They put their livelihoods on the line to keep the work of the church moving forward. This facility has served many generations, and we can only speculate how many lives have been changed by the gospel because of the faithfulness and generosity of our founders.

The Bible doesn't instruct us to pay all of our bills, buy a few things we want, and then give the remaining amount to the Lord. The Bible doesn't instruct us to throw a few dollars in the offering plate. The Bible doesn't instruct us to give God what's left. It instructs us to give God what's first.

Is your tithe the first payment you make? Or do you hold it back, make sure you have enough, and then give it after everything else is taken care of? God wants you to surrender your finances to him. That means giving him what's first, not what's left.

Lord, thank you for the opportunity you give me to give back to you. Help me be generous and give you what's first, not what's left. Amen.

DECEMBER 29

One who is faithful in a very little is also faithful in much, and one who is dishonest in a very little is also dishonest in much.

Luke 16:10

A family member once told me, "If you can't manage ten dollars an hour, you won't be able to manage one hundred dollars an hour." It didn't take me long to realize how true that statement is. I know people who make large amounts of money, but they have little to show for it. They are covered up in debt, make careless purchases, and money goes out quicker than it comes in. On the other hand, I know people who make much smaller amounts of money, but they are financially free. They manage their debt, budget well, and save religiously.

It's not how much you have; it's how well you manage what you have. This is not only true when it comes to your finances but every area of your life. If you can't manage what you have now, you won't be able to manage more.

How well are you managing what God has entrusted you with? Are you asking him for more while failing to be trustworthy with what you already have? If so, work to be trustworthy with what he has already blessed you with. Remember, if you can't manage what you have now, you won't be able to manage more.

Lord, thank you for what you have blessed me with. Help me be faithful in very little and manage what you have entrusted me with. Amen.

DECEMBER 30

A tranquil heart gives life to the flesh, but envy makes the bones rot.

Proverbs 14:30

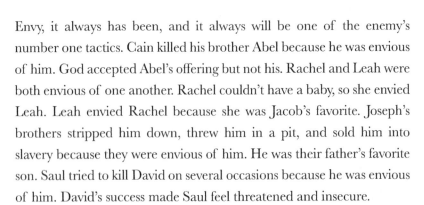

Envy, it always has been, and it always will be one of the enemy's number one tactics. Cain killed his brother Abel because he was envious of him. God accepted Abel's offering but not his. Rachel and Leah were both envious of one another. Rachel couldn't have a baby, so she envied Leah. Leah envied Rachel because she was Jacob's favorite. Joseph's brothers stripped him down, threw him in a pit, and sold him into slavery because they were envious of him. He was their father's favorite son. Saul tried to kill David on several occasions because he was envious of him. David's success made Saul feel threatened and insecure.

Who or what do you envy? Maybe you envy those who have more money than you. Maybe you envy those who are better looking or more physically fit than you. Maybe you envy a relationship. Maybe you envy a business or an organization. Maybe you envy a certain talent or gift that you don't have.

Envy makes the bones rot. It keeps you from getting to where God wants you to go and from doing what God wants you to do. Instead of being envious of what you don't have, work to make the most of what you do have.

Lord, thank you for what you have given me. Forgive me for being envious when you have blessed me with so much. Help me stay focused on what truly matters. Amen

DECEMBER 31

My mouth is filled with your praise, and with your glory all the day.

Psalm 71:8

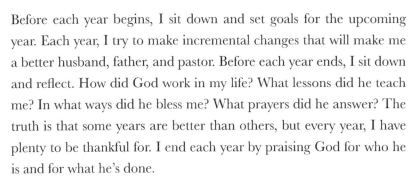

Before each year begins, I sit down and set goals for the upcoming year. Each year, I try to make incremental changes that will make me a better husband, father, and pastor. Before each year ends, I sit down and reflect. How did God work in my life? What lessons did he teach me? In what ways did he bless me? What prayers did he answer? The truth is that some years are better than others, but every year, I have plenty to be thankful for. I end each year by praising God for who he is and for what he's done.

It's the last day of the year. Take some time today to reflect on this past year. How did God work in your life? What lessons did he teach you? In what ways did he bless you? What prayers did he answer? Maybe this was your best year yet. If so, thank and praise him.

Maybe this year didn't go as planned. Maybe you didn't reach any of the goals you set at the beginning of the year. Maybe you faced unexpected challenges. Maybe you made a series of mistakes. Maybe you faced tragedy or loss. Regardless of how bad your year may have been, God is still God, and he is still good. If for nothing else, thank and praise him for allowing you to see another year.

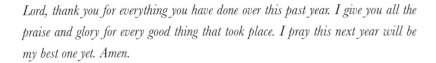

Lord, thank you for everything you have done over this past year. I give you all the praise and glory for every good thing that took place. I pray this next year will be my best one yet. Amen.

Made in the USA
Columbia, SC
20 November 2023

26800627R00202